# ARRIVALS
# AND
# DEPARTURES

BY RICHARD H. ROVERE

*Howe & Hummel:*
*Their True and Scandalous History*

*The General and the President*
(with Arthur M. Schlesinger, Jr.)

*Affairs of State:*
*The Eisenhower Years*

*Senator Joe McCarthy*

*The American Establishment*
*And Other Reports, Opinions, and Speculations*

*The Goldwater Caper*

*Waist Deep in the Big Muddy*

# ARRIVALS
# AND
# DEPARTURES

*A Journalist's Memoirs*

## RICHARD H. ROVERE

MACMILLAN PUBLISHING CO., INC.
*New York*
COLLIER MACMILLAN PUBLISHERS
*London*

Macmillan Publishing Co., Inc.
866 Third Avenue, New York, N.Y. 10022
Collier Macmillan Canada, Ltd.

Library of Congress Cataloging in Publication Data
Rovere, Richard Halworth, 1915–
Arrivals and departures.
Includes index.
1. Rovere, Richard Halworth, 1915–
2. Journalists—United States—Correspondence,
reminiscences, etc.  I. Title.
PN4874.R7A29  1976      070.4'092'4  [B]      76–21865
ISBN 0–02–605400–0

First Printing 1976


Printed in the United States of America

*For*
*Dorothy and Granville Hicks*

# Contents

*A Note and Some Acknowledgments*                        ix

I.   NEW YORK, N.Y.                                        I

II.  SCHOOL DAYS                                          I5
     *1. Failed Anc. Hist. But Saw Total Eclipse of the Sun*
     *2. The Scientifical Genius*
     *3. Postscript*

III. VASSAR, BARD, CENTERVILLE                           4I

IV.  A GOLDBRICKING COMMUNIST                            53

V.   H. W. ROSS                                          6I

VI.  WINTER IN EUROPE                                    7I
     *1. Josephine*
     *2. See Naples and Drop Dead*

VII.    MCCARTHY AND COMPANY      97
       *1. I've Got A Paper Here*
       *2. Tommy the Anarchist*

VIII.    JOHN F. KENNEDY      113

IX.    WALTER LIPPMANN      124

X.    BIOGRAPHIES, PROFILES,      145
     PROBLEMS
       *1. Dr. Bruno Furst*
       *2. John Gunther*
       *3. Henry Blackman Sell*

XI.    LEWIS A/K/A LOUIS HALWORTH      243
     ROVERE, CIRCA 1887–1975
       *1. The Father I Knew*
       *2. The Father I Discovered*

*Index*      267

# A Note and Some Acknowledgments

In a sense, this book has been in the making since 1929, when, at fourteen and away in boarding school, I began writing my parents the letters—excerpted here in "Failed Anc. Hist. But Saw Total Eclipse of the Sun"—explaining away and diverting attention from my deplorable academic performance. Had I been aware of my gifts at the time, I might have prepared for a career as a confidence man or a politician rather than let myself drift into journalism—though there are those who would say that the three trades require much the same sort of talent. But most of what is published here was written in the quarter century between 1951 and 1976, or between the ages of thirty-six and sixty-one. I like to think that if there are different voices to be heard here, altered perspectives to be noted, they are to be accounted for by growth, by sensibilities ripened by experience. But I am hardly in a position to judge.

Through most of these years, it was not part of my plan to write a volume of memoirs. As a political journalist and as a sometime literary critic, I have written mainly in the third person. I am far from being unopinionated and have from time to time expressed my views in print, but for the most part, particularly in middle age, I have been an observer rather than a participant—and a rather passive observer at that. I have lived through several wars, but I have had the good fortune to take part in none, and indeed I have yet to hear a shot fired in anger—though I have recently heard two bombs explode in Manhattan. Once, when

Katharine White, a fiction editor at *The New Yorker* who had read some of the more or less autobiographical pieces that are part of this book, suggested that I might try some more in the same general vein, I replied that my life had been an unadventurous one, that I had done little that seemed worth writing about. "Yes," she said, "but you are the sort of person to whom things happen." Though this, of course, could be said of anyone, I knew what she meant: bad grades happened to me, Charlie Puckette happened to me, Josephine Cianni happened to me, New York and Naples happened to me, the Communist Party happened to me. This is a book about the impact of people, places, and events on its author.

My principal source is my memory, aided by that of members of my family and of friends who have shared some of the same experiences or whom I have sought out for counsel. My diaries, letters, and files have been drawn on heavily; they are my bibliography.

The father I mention passingly in Chapter II is not the man I discuss in Chapter XI. I might have revised sections of the earlier part to square with what I was later to learn, but I chose not to do so.

Some of this material has been published in different form in *The New Yorker*, *The American Scholar*, *Harper's*, and *The New York Review of Books*. I am grateful to those publications for permission to reprint and also for the encouragement their editors gave in the first place.

I will forego naming here any of those mentioned elsewhere in the text. There are some not so named whose advice and assistance I must acknowledge. My editor, Jeannette Hopkins, has done much to give the book its shape and texture and also on occasion to save me from myself. If there are factual errors, they are fewer in number than they would have been without the backup services of *The New Yorker*'s checking department I have worked with over many years. Others who have helped, some in ways they may be unaware of, are Orren Alperstein, Michael J. Arlen, Jacques Barzun, Mary and Clifford Burgess, Lisl Cohn,

Robert J. Donovan, Allen Fay, Jeanne Fredericks, Martin Goch, Lindy Hess, the late Herman Kahn, Edith Loewenstein, Andy Logan, Don Longabucco, Rachel MacKenzie, Paul Malamud, Helen Mills, Irwin Ross, Estelle Rovere, Tony and Carol Russo, Regina Ryan, Margaret Shafer, Lee Starr, Lorraine Steurer, Lora Tredway, Richard Wade, and Virginia Xanthos.

R.H.R.
*Rhinebeck, N.Y.*

# ARRIVALS
# AND
# DEPARTURES

# I

# New York, N.Y.

"You would see things very differently if you lived here in Iowa," a woman wrote me from Des Moines recently. "You would get a clearer perspective on the rest of the country." Displeased readers from other cities and states often write to explain that what they regard as my failures of perception stem from my being a New Yorker and having a New York point of view. To the Des Moines lady I replied as I generally do: that while geography—like race, sex, religion, work, age, and so forth—is undoubtedly a conditioning factor, I have met Iowans in Iowa and Iowans outside Iowa whose outlook on life and on life in America struck me as quite similar to my own and, further, that I don't think that living in Iowa, attractive as it might be, would give me a better understanding of California or Mississippi or New Hampshire than the one I get from New York, aided by a certain amount of travel and an effort at detachment. And at times I point out that much that other people associate with New York, particularly its liberal and radical social movements, had its roots elsewhere in the country. Florida, Pennsylvania, Illinois, and California contributed more than New York to the building of the labor movement. The politics of Minnesota, North and South Dakota, and Wisconsin have often been more radical than those of New York, and perhaps the most seminal thinker among radical American economists was Thorstein Veblen, a pure product of the Middle West. The theories of progressive education that many identify as having sprung up in New York actually sprang up in the head of John Dewey, a backwoodsman from Vermont. And I could go on. But I am sure I have never convinced any of those who believe that New York is unique in the way that it distorts the vision and impairs the sensibilities of its sons and daughters. It seems to comfort many to believe that New York is, if not un-American, somehow extra-American, that it is almost as difficult for a New Yorker as it would be for an Albanian or a Samoan to feel the texture and catch the rhythms of life in the rest of the country. I maintain that this view is rooted in a misunderstanding not only of New York but of the urban experience in general.

As for me, I am very much a New Yorker, but I was not born in the city—not quite.

In March or April of 1915, my mother and father, then living on Washington Heights in Manhattan and financially hard-pressed, decided to move across the Hudson River to share a small apartment with friends in Jersey City, New Jersey, a grimy industrial and shipping center that fronts on New York Harbor and affords an unsurpassed backside view of the Statue of Liberty. A few weeks later, on May 5th, I was born there, and a few weeks 'after that, my parents, dissatisfied with the arrange-ment, recrossed the river and resettled in the neighborhood they had so recently left. For the next thirty years, New York was my home, and indeed it has been the center of my entire life. I become keenly aware of this when I am flying into or out of the city, for there comes a moment when, clouds and smog permit-ting, I can see framed in the window nearest me all the places in which I have lived, studied, or worked for any length of time. Coming in from Washington, D.C., for example, I can look down and see Jersey City and the three boroughs—Manhattan, Brook-lyn, and Staten Island—in which at various times I have lived. East, over Long Island Sound, is, on one side, the Connecticut village in which, for several years, we had a summer cottage and, on the other, the Long Island village (now almost a city) where I was in boarding school for four years. Almost due north, up the Hudson, is Dutchess County, where I spent my undergraduate years and to which, in 1946, my wife and I and the first two of

our three children moved. The third was born there, in Rhinebeck, where our present home is—some eighty-odd miles beyond
the city limits—and where we are generally to be found when we
are not in our apartment in midtown Manhattan.

Though I have seen most of the rest of the country and much
of the rest of the world, I have never spent more than a few
months at a time outside this small area, all of it within a radius
of less than a hundred miles of New York. Since 1948, I have
been a Washington correspondent and have spent what must
amount to several years there, but I have never lived in Washington except as a transient—a guest or a hotel resident. My business
there has always been to report to New York editors and, in the
main, to New York readers, or readers of New York publications.
Therefore, if in New York and its suburbs and exurbs there exists
anything like a discrete culture, something more than the sum
of its American and European components, then I must be one
of its products. I spent eight years in New York public schools
and eight more in private institutions that drew most of their
students from the city and its environs. When I was a boy, my
playing fields were the city streets, parks, vacant lots, and roof-
tops. As a young journalist, I wrote about many aspects of life
in New York—its politics, its commerce, its industry, its crime,
its theatre. So if there is a New York way of looking at life, it
must to some extent be mine—or at least I must know what it
is. If there is a New York idiom, it must be part of my speech,
an aspect of my style. If New York is as provincial as many
people, including many New Yorkers, hold it to be, then I must
qualify as that kind of provincial, for no other province has held
me as long or as closely as New York.

Yet I am not persuaded that any of this follows. I doubt if
there is really anything that bears description as a New York
culture, point of view, *zeitgeist*. There are institutions that flourish
in New York and nowhere else; there are exotic human types that
could have been nurtured in no other soil. But what is indigenous
is not necessarily representative, and I can think of little that is
common to Wall Street and Broadway, to Harlem and Forest

Hills, to Canarsie and Greenwich Village, to Madison Avenue and Mosholu Parkway, to Turtle Bay and Bay Ridge, to Coney Island and Riverdale, to Park Slope and Rego Park, to Brownsville and New Dorp. I know some of these precincts very well; of others, I have only a traveller's knowledge. Some have quite distinct cultures of their own, but they differ from one another as if they were separated by oceans, or by centuries, and they share little more than a geographical locus. "The terrain of New York," E. B. White wrote, "is such that a resident sometimes travels farther, in the end, than a commuter. Irving Berlin's journey from Cherry Street in the Lower East Side to an apartment uptown was through an alley and was only three or four miles in length, but it was like going three times around the world." I have made many such journeys: from Prospect Heights in the interior of Brooklyn to Columbia Heights on the periphery of the borough is less than three miles, but by other measures the difference compares with that between Cairo, Illinois, and Cairo, Egypt. And as for an idiom, a way with words as distinctly regional as an accent, is there one that can be heard on the streets of Greenpoint and Murray Hill, Co-Op City and Cobble Hill, Flushing and Sheepshead Bay, Chinatown and Little Italy? Is there one that is echoed in Radio City and City Hall, in Tin Pan Alley and Carnegie Hall, on the Upper East Side and the Upper West Side, in Boys' High and the Chapin School, in Shea Stadium and the Vivian Beaumont Theatre? Or encountered in the somber columns of *The New York Times* and the raffish ones of the *Daily News*? In *Variety* and *The Journal of Commerce*, *The New Yorker* and *The New Leader*? There are certain modes of expression that stamp the speaker as a New Yorker (the argot of the cabdrivers is perhaps as good an example as any) but nothing that unites all or even most New Yorkers. For as there are eight million New Yorkers, there are dozens, perhaps hundreds of New Yorks. Citizens of each may mingle daily in the subways, in the offices and factories, and they may have common miseries and delights, but what they share is not a particular culture or outlook but the urban condition and the concerns of their various trades, which vary little from place to place. To be a clerk in a New York bank or department store cannot be very different from being a clerk in Philadelphia, or for that matter London. If a policeman's lot is not a happy one in New York, it is probably no more or less so than that of a policeman in Detroit or Rome.

To the world—and for that matter to most New Yorkers— New York is Manhattan, a sliver of an island that is less than a twelfth of the city in area and less than a sixth in population. To the extent that New York is still a capital city for finance, culture, communications, and entertainment, it is Manhattan that contains all or very nearly all the institutions that give the city its position, and nearly all of these are to be found in the southern half of the island, one of the least densely populated parts of the city. Here is the New York of the corporate headquarters, the publishing and broadcasting centers, the theatres, the advertising agencies, the great hotels and restaurants. When Henry James described New York as "the most extravagant of cities," he could only have had in mind this Manhattan, for there was, even in his day, little in Brooklyn, Queens, The Bronx, and Staten Island to symbolize extravagance, and today, except in the more elegant suburbs, there is less. And it is a place in many ways as alien to millions of New Yorkers as it is to so many who have never seen it. Moreover, this Manhattan is itself a number of separate enclaves, and those who spend their working and social lives in one or another of them—a few hundred thousand at the most— know little of the rest. As a journalist, it has been necessary for me to know a bit about milieus other than my own, but there are some about which I know very little, and what knowledge I do have owes nothing to propinquity. Near my office and my apartment in midtown Manhattan are the headquarters of some of the largest banks in the country, but the only banker I have ever known was a Montanan who for a time was the president of the Federal Reserve Bank in Minneapolis. I live and work only a few steps from the theatre district, but although many years ago I reviewed plays and have had some actor and playwright friends, my knowledge of Broadway is really that of a tourist and is surely exceeded by that of theatre enthusiasts who live thousands of miles away and visit New York perhaps once a year for a round of playgoing. Most of the money I earn comes to me by way of the advertising agencies, several of them within easy walking distance, but I know as little about them as I know about nuclear physics—or about the garment industry, the center of which is only a few blocks away.

The New York I know now—or at least know about—I was all but unaware of when I was growing up in it. What I knew were tiny segments of the city, neighborhoods, communities without visible boundaries but almost as self-contained and separated from the great city as walled or moated fortresses. At least for a child, a neighborhood has a life of its own, institutions of its own, even a character distinct from that of those adjacent to it. I know that talk of New York as a great cluster of small "neighborhoods" is the cant of real estate hustlers eager to persuade prospective buyers and tenants that it is really a warm, homey place, that people live in one part of it or another in the kind of comfort and intimacy with one another that is commonly held to be the way people live in small towns in Maine or Kentucky, in Devonshire or Provence. But it is nevertheless true that the reality of New York for most who live there is not that of a great metropolis, a world city, but that of something very like a village —a hateful, hideous village perhaps, one of steel and concrete, joined to others by subways, and tunnels, and bridges, separated from others not by open land but by class, race, religion, and in some cases by language and the trade of workers. Growing up, I knew many neighborhoods, for my parents—first when they were trying to cut expenses, later when they became what is now known as upwardly mobile—moved on an average of once a year. Sometimes the moves were within the same neighborhood, and there was one directly across the street, but often they were from one part of the city to another, and those city neighborhoods bore, as I think back on them now, many resemblances to the rural villages I later came to know, and my life within them was not very different from that of my children in the upstate villages in which they grew up. The city in which these urban villages were embedded was a geographical abstraction, part of a mailing address, a place my parents and I occasionally visited for entertainment or services not locally available. It was also a place we travelled through, by train or car, to get somewhere beyond it— to beaches, to mountains, to the homes of friends and relatives whose lives had taken them elsewhere. Most of the neighborhoods we lived in could, I think, have been part of any good-sized American city with anything like New York's mix of people. There were, of course, sections of which this could not be said: Harlem, Greenwich Village, and Yorkville and the Lower East Side as they used to be. But the parts in which we lived were either lower-middle class or middle-middle, consisting mainly of Protestants, Catholics, and Jews, in roughly equal proportions, and could easily have been relocated in Philadelphia, Chicago, or, for that matter, Bridgeport, Connecticut. In each, for me, the school was at the center, and although it was part of the city system and under the supervision of the Board of Education, the principal, often a neighbor, was sovereign and the teachers his or her minions, and it could have been just about any school anywhere —for this reluctant scholar a disagreeable place where one showed up at nine o'clock each weekday morning and waited for deliverance at three. Like a village, a neighborhood was where one knew and was known by the shopkeepers, where one attended church or Sunday School, which I infrequently did, and Boy Scout meetings, which for two or three years I regularly did. The city did not command my loyalties until I was well into adolescence. In Brooklyn, to which we moved when I was about four, I became a hot partisan of the Brooklyn Dodgers and looked upon the New York Giants, the Dodgers' National League rivals whose home field was Manhattan's Polo Grounds, as being fully as alien, as contemptible as the Chicago White Sox or the Cincinnati Reds. I was a Brooklynite, not a New Yorker, and I was less a Brooklynite than a proud defender of whatever part of the borough I happened to live in, even of a particular street. When I was fourteen and away at school, my mother wrote me about a friend who had outrun a pursuing policeman. "I'm not surprised about Mike Murphy," I wrote back. "A Park Place kid with a busted leg and asthma could never be caught by any Brooklyn flatfoot."

"To be attached to the subdivision, to love the little platoon we belong to," Edmund Burke wrote, "is the first principle (the germ as it were) of public affections. It is the first link in the series by which we proceed toward a love to our country and to mankind." The proposition could well be upended, with hate substituted for love, disaffection for affection. I can look back more fondly than otherwise on most of the subdivisions—neighborhoods, or, as E. B. White called them, "interior cities"—I knew. Though none was elegant or fashionable and some were downright bleak (for drabness and aesthetic poverty, there is little in American architecture that quite matches the New York apartment houses built in the first third of this century) most were, by the usual urban standards, clean, safe, and uncongested. There were then some, but fewer by far than now, that were verminous, dangerous, and overcrowded, but I was fortunate not to have had to live in any of them; if I had, I might well have proceeded from hatred of my immediate surroundings to hatred of the city and of the whole American society, perhaps to a full-blown misanthropy. In any case, my own experience bears out Burke's contention, which, I believe, holds for most people, young and old, in most places most of the time. In an ascending order of awareness and concern, we have the self, the family, the subdivision (in some societies, the tribe), and on through municipalities or regions to the nation and, for the extremely benevolent or the extremely malevolent, humanity. It was not until I got to know something of what lay beyond New York that I began to think of it as my city, my home, a place to accept or reject, love or loathe. Until then, the institutions that I now identify with New York impinged on my life hardly at all. My father worked in a big office in lower Manhattan, but that was his life, not mine, and it meant little to me. Some teacher may have told me that the section was the site of a great many corporate headquarters, but that, too, could have meant little to me, as I imagine it means little to most New Yorkers today. (When, recently, the city fathers and the press became quite agitated by the news that Union Carbide was moving to Danbury, Connecticut, I suspect that not one New Yorker in a hundred had any idea that Union Carbide's headquarters were in the city.)

What did mean something to me was that my father left home each morning and returned each evening, but I do not think it meant more or less than if he had descended each day into a coal mine in western Pennsylvania. (I do recall, though, that his profession—he was an electrical engineer—was one I thought so unglamorous that I lied about it to friends, some of whose fathers were railroad conductors, teamsters, seamen, and the like; when asked, I told them that *my* father was a fireman.) Nor had I, until I was grown up, any sense of living in a cultural capital. My parents made considerable use of local branch libraries, but neither they nor anyone else I knew were regular patrons of the city's theatres, concert halls, or museums; the only connection I had with that part of New York life was an uncle who was a journeyman novelist and poet and something of a figure in Greenwich Village, but although he later had something to do with my becoming a journalist, as a boy I thought of him as an uncle, one I did not particularly like, and I had little interest in what he did or where he lived.

And so it is, I believe, with most New Yorkers even now. The tribal mentality, the mentality of the villager, persists in the urban environment. There are times, especially when adversity strikes, when the subdivisions come together, when the platoons form into legions: there was such a time in the summer and fall of 1975 when the city was going through a great fiscal crisis, and New Yorkers, feeling themselves under siege by Gerald Ford's Washington, united to seek allies throughout the country. (They found enough to force Ford to lift the siege.) But to me the striking thing is not the unity that can now and then be forged but the diversity that makes the city so resistant to generalization, to definition. And it is this resistance, this elusiveness that is the very mark of a great city. Paris, Balzac wrote in *Pere Goriot*, is "a veritable ocean. Take as many soundings as you will, you will never know its depth." Was Whitman really saying anything about New York when he called it a "city of orgies, walks, and joys"? He encapsulated no more than himself: he might have written the same about his other cities—Philadelphia, New Orleans, and Washington; and Sherwood Anderson might have said as much about Winesburg, Ohio. Statistics might confirm James about New York's extravagance, but the people in Michael Gold's *Jews Without Money*, those who manned the industry in which New York was preeminent, knew it as a miserly rather than a profligate place. The skyscrapers that symbolize New York for many, the luxury a few New Yorkers know, the great enterprises that have been launched in the city—these have little to do with the lives of most New Yorkers. The Manhattan skyline cannot as a rule be seen from the interior, the population centers, of Brooklyn, The Bronx, and Queens, and to those who can look out on them, they are distant, lifeless features of the landscape, like the Rocky Mountains as seen from Denver. Great wealth is concentrated in heavily-guarded buildings in a few Manhattan districts: among its visible manifestations are the baubles in Fifth Avenue shop windows and in the sleek limousines now and then to be seen among the taxis, trucks, and buses on midtown streets. The board rooms of the large corporations are not even part of the landscape.

Not all of New York's subdivisions can be plotted on a map or described as even relatively homogeneous. For example, among the regular and irregular tenants of the small hotel in which we have an apartment on West Forty-fourth Street—not the famous Algonquin but a less posh neighbor—are showbiz types; African, Asian, and Latin-American diplomats; cooks and waiters who work in three restaurants on the same block, two Japanese and one Belgian; some employees of nearby department stores; a few writers like myself; and others about whose place of origin and present occupation I can only speculate. The hotel staff has been recruited from Poland, Hungary, Italy, Puerto Rico, and the

American South. In the lobby and in the elevator, one may encounter types out of Damon Runyon, Saul Bellow, Eudora Welty, Juan Luis Borges, E. M. Forster, and Yukio Mishima and hear a cacophony of Yiddish, Spanish, Portuguese, Ibo, Swahili, and several other languages, including several varieties of American English. These are our near neighbors: as best we can, we exchange pleasantries about the weather and the kind of service we do not get from the management, but although destiny has huddled us under one roof, we inhabit very different parts of New York—indeed different worlds. Being a journalist, I know something of the world of the diplomats, but they can know little of mine and less of that of most of their neighbors. The Belgian and Japanese restaurateurs must have little more in common than that they prepare and serve food. The hotel also houses a restaurant featuring Irish cuisine and a cram school for young architects seeking New York licenses. And two doors away is the New York Yacht Club and a few doors beyond that the Harvard Club of New York. Across the street are Touro College (a Hebrew institution), the New York County Bar Association, and the New York Society of Mechanics and Tradesmen, while a short block away are the headquarters of a strange cult, the Reverend Sun Myung Moon's Unification Church of America, whose devotees believe that when Christ returns, He will be a Korean, and the Graduate Center of the City University. Across from that, until it was destroyed by fire in 1975, was The Library, a massage parlor open twenty-four hours a day and offering the services of "eight lovely librarians." Ravenswood in Queens and Parkchester in The Bronx are in many ways as far from Forty-fourth Street as Key West and Seattle.

There is still another aspect to New York's diversity, one that has less to do with space than with time. "The present in New York," John Jay Chapman wrote in 1909, "is so powerful that the past is lost. There is no past. Not a bookshelf, nor a cornice, nor a sign, nor a face, nor a type of mind endures for a generation, and a New York boy who goes away to boarding school returns to a new world at each vacation." There is some hyperbole here. New York's past does survive, though rather as does that of a great and ancient city—Rome, Athens, Jerusalem—in its literature and in its ruins, and the pace of change in New York is not quite so rapid as to be observable between Thanksgiving and Christmas. But it is surely the case that very little endures for a generation, and here I have in mind not only the constant rebuilding of the city, though that of course is part of it, but the impermanence of moods and symbols and the quality of life. The New York—that is, the Manhattan—I knew when I started work in the late 1930s was a buoyant, hopeful place compared with the New York I write about now. It was then, as today, in a severe economic depression, but it was not a place people were fleeing, not a community whose leaders were despairing about the future. There were pockets of crime and violence, particularly industrial violence, but the streets I knew and the subways I rode were safe, and my friends and I did not give a second thought to walking in the parks at any hour of the day or night. That New York has all but vanished. But it was not, as many believe, any truer to the past than the city in which it is now so dangerous and so difficult to live. For the past has known periods very much like the present. It was much as it is today during the Civil War and again toward the end of the century, at the high tide of European immigration. New York is a city of almost countless pasts. Its history resembles that of a much-disputed and fought-over territory in which occupying armies come and go and impose different laws, different religions, even different languages. I first got a sense of this almost thirty years ago when a publisher commissioned me to compile an anthology of writings about New York from its founding by the Dutch through the end of the Second World War. It was to be part of a series of regional anthologies, several of which had been critical successes. The idea was to show the continuity of experience over the centuries, to give a generation of readers a sense of their heritage, their cultural geneology. Seeing how well this had been done for parts of New England and several Southern states and cities, I was confident that the New York volume would be one of the best, for certainly no part of the country has been written about so extensively as New York and none has been favored by finer writers. But what I soon found out was that what could be done for Boston and New Orleans could not be done for New York. In Boston today, that of the Kennedys as well as of the Lowells, the mark of the Puritan theologians, of the Adamses, of Emerson and Thoreau, of the Lodges and the Holmeses may still be found. In New Orleans, the French influence is, though far from dominant, far from obliterated. But what remains of the Dutch in New York? Only a few place and family names and some of the architecture in towns like Rhinebeck. But there is not much Dutch blood in the people with the Dutch names, and the language is never heard except at the United Nations and when Dutch seamen come to town. Who can find anything of the New York they know in the writings of Washington Irving? Not even Walt Whitman could have recognized that New York, and for Henry James, Whitman's New York, though not distant in time from his own, must have been as remote as New Zealand. James and Edith Wharton knew more or less the same city, and there are faint echoes of them in the novels of Louis Auchincloss, but Auchincloss and such contemporaries as Saul Bellow and James Baldwin, Alfred Kazin and Mary McCarthy, each has a New York quite different from anything in the past and very different from many unexplored New Yorks of the mid-twentieth century.

So I put aside the anthology. It simply would not work except as a grab bag. New York has a history, fascinating in many ways, but it is a history of discontinuity. Many writers have captured or portrayed segments of the past and segments of any given present. No one has ever known it in the way that Dickens knew London or as Balzac knew Paris. And if there is anything that can be described as a New York point of view, it is surely acquired, not inherited or inbred. Some of the readers who upbraid me for expressing or representing it regard *The New Yorker* as the embodiment of it. But in its fifty-two years of publication, the magazine has had two editors, the first a Coloradan, the second a Chicagoan. Near my office there are writers and editors from

India, China, England, Canada, Wales, Jamaica, and from Oklahoma, Arkansas, Tennessee, Georgia, Wisconsin, and Missouri. We have very different backgrounds and speak with different accents, but if there is a New York idiom, it is common to all of us. To my mind, *The New Yorker* writer who has done better than any of us in conveying the feel and flavor of many aspects of New York life, particularly its underside, is Joseph Mitchell, a North Carolinian. And so, I think, it goes. New York remains the communications center of the country, and this may be a bad thing. It is a large country and should have many centers; by being a kind of cultural magnet, New York—Manhattan—drains talent from other communities and thus discourages competition. But just as I do not think a New York upbringing is much unlike any other, I do not believe that New York imposes any particular outlook on those who come to it from elsewhere. Indeed, as I have written, I see myself as having come to it from "elsewhere" —from several of those "interior cities," any one of which could have been part of the landscape of any American city with anything like New York's mix of people.

# II

---

## *School Days*

### I. FAILED ANC. HIST.
### BUT SAW TOTAL ECLIPSE OF THE SUN

In my family, I enjoy quite a reputation as a song-and-dance man. This is not to say that anyone thinks I ought to go on the stage. The song-and-dance at which I excel is the rhetorical kind, not the theatrical—the art of Alibi Ike rather than of George M. Cohan. I am, at least in my admiring wife's opinion, a very fancy operator in the field of the cock-and-bull story. So she has me do all her work in this line.

"Do me a favor, will you, dear?" she may say when she has an assignment for me. "Call up Aunt Lucy and give her a song-and-dance about Wednesday night. Tell her we'd love to come but we just can't possibly make it."

"Holy Ned, what can I say to her this time?" I protest. "You put us in a hole by bragging to her about how well the children are—I heard you do that myself. And she knows we're not going anywhere else—I heard admit that, too. And you're always telling her how happy the kids are to stay with Gertrude. You'd think excuses grew on trees, the way you fling them away. If you'd keep quiet about these things, you'd keep us out of trouble. I don't want to go, either, but I can't see how I'm going to kiss her off this time."

I protest too much, of course. The idea is to draw a compliment. I know perfectly well that I can, without greatly extending myself, work out a lalapalooza for Aunt Lucy. After such a recital of the difficulties, my wife may say, "Don't give me the

*15*

song-and-dance. Give it to Aunt Lucy. Just work out something good. You do it so nicely, and I do it so wretchedly. I blush right over the telephone. Now run along and call her before she orders a lot of expensive food for us."

With the job thus forced upon me, I go to work. Riffling through my mental notes, I come on one about Aunt Lucy's fondness for dogs. "With Aunt L., dog with sniffles worth two children with pneumonia, either virus or lobar," it says. A quick crosschecking shows that the dog angle has not been used for eighteen months. This means that it can safely be used again. I clear my throat, call Aunt Lucy, and tell her that we have had distressing indications that our dog may be coming down with a serious canine disease. Lest Aunt Lucy come over to minister to the animal herself, I assure her that we are standing by night and day and that the moment things take a turn for the worse, we will call in a veterinarian whom I know she regards as the Mayo Brothers of canine medicine.

I always have to cope with the corollary problem of why I, rather than my wife, am handling our social arrangements, but it's never a very serious problem. Sometimes a clue may be found in the nature of the alibi. In the case of the dog story, what could be more natural than that my wife should be keeping the vigil at the dog box? For general summertime use, I always have her hay fever. There are times when she can hardly get a word out without sneezing. At other times, I can say, winning myself a small dividend of approval while I sell my bill of goods, that, as a considerate husband, I insisted upon her going to bed immediately after supper, because she looked so tired and drawn. This goes down particularly well with relatives on her side of the family.

In a normal household, there is always plenty of work for a really capable song-and-dance man. I am, for example, in charge of negotiations with all difficult tradespeople. After Christmas and other holidays, I am kept busy composing letters, to be copied and signed by my wife, that say pleasant things about handkerchiefs, compotes, and illustrated editions of *Green Mansions*, a book that is, by my reckoning, the most widely reprinted, re-illustrated, given-away, and unread book of our time. Every so often, there are sudden emergencies, such as those provided by the appearance of Jehovah's Witnesses at the front door or *Rural New-Yorker* salesmen at the back door. On these occasions, my wife calls for me and explains to the visitor that she has a cake in the oven and it's at a critical stage and requires immediate attention. (She has a fair talent for the alibi herself. She hasn't baked a cake since Girl Scout days, and it shows remarkable presence of mind on her part to remember, after all these years, that cakes have critical stages.) In any event, it is always up to me to dispose of solicitors as rapidly and as graciously as possible, and I have grown rather proud of my ability to do so. The art of the verbal song-and-dance is, I know, a base one and would have no place in the good society, but in a world full of injustice, Aunt Lucys, and Jehovah's Witnesses, it helps to make existence a bit more tolerable.

I bring up the matter of my prowess in this line, however, not to boast about it but to introduce some documents that illustrate the early developments of talents such as mine. The documents are letters I wrote to my parents when I was fourteen and fifteen, at which time I was an enrolled but not a practicing student at a boys' preparatory school on Long Island. They came to light recently, in the course of a general housecleaning conducted by my mother. Reading them over with the insight of a mature and seasoned song-and-dance man, I have found that they contain some extraordinary examples of precocious talent in the genre.

A little background will help. At fourteen, an age I reached in the year of the great stock-market collapse, I was sent away to boarding school by my father. He chose a place where he thought I could get a solid grounding in Latin, algebra, ancient history, and some of the other traditional disciplines, and it was his hope that I would eventually qualify myself for a good university. My father shared the boundless faith of his generation in the Higher Learning, but he differed from most of his contemporaries in one significant way. He did not believe that everyone was educable. He was willing to entertain the thought that God might have intended me, even though I was his own flesh and blood, for one of the humbler pursuits in life, and he felt that if he was ever convinced that this was the case, he would, regretfully, abandon his efforts to provide me with access to the wisdom of the ages.

"It wouldn't shame me to have you become a ditchdigger, son," he told me just before I went away to school. "It wouldn't shame me in the least. The world needs ditchdiggers. But if that's to be your future, there's no use in my spending my money having you taught French." He gave me to understand, in a firm but friendly way, that if I did not make what he regarded as suitable progress in my studies, he would withdraw me from private school, send me to public school until the law allowed me to quit, and then see what he could do about finding me a place with some reputable ditchdigging concern.

In general, I was in thorough accord with my father's hope that I would spend four years in boarding school and then four more in college. I expected to enjoy boarding-school life, and, from what I had heard about it, college life sounded as if it would be even more enjoyable. Ditchdigging, on the other hand, was not to my taste. As it happened, though, I failed to make the academic progress my father had hoped for. I didn't come anywhere near it. My first two years were particularly bad. I compiled what I imagine still stands as the lowest all-round record ever made at the institution I attended. There were two schools of thought on the cause of my difficulty. The first, to which the majority of my teachers subscribed, was that my trouble was the result of a simple deficiency of intelligence. My father—largely, I take it, because of my successful song-and-dance work—never wholly aligned himself with this group, but a good part of the time he leaned toward it more than toward the other school, which was militantly led by my mother and me. According to our view, the real trouble lay with my teachers, my textbooks, the state of my health, the fact that the average day was so short, the congenital left-handedness that made it burdensome for me to work in classroom

chairs designed for right-handed students—in short, every imag-
inable cause except a weak brain and an indolent nature. Indeed,
my mother and I even went so far as to evolve the theory that my
poor showing was, in fact, an optical illusion. I was actually, by
this reasoning, so much brighter than my fellow-students that I
was in the position of a distance runner who has got almost a
lap ahead of the others in a race: although he appears to be
bringing up the rear, he is really far out in front.

My father never found himself able to accept this theory. He
complained of lack of evidence. Most of the time, he felt that he
should take the grades the school authorities sent him each
month as a fairly accurate representation of my attainments, and
it was because of this stubborn literal-mindedness on his part that
I was forced into thinking up ways and means of persuading him
that the grades weren't reliable indicia. Once a month, I would
write home an elaborate commentary on my grades. Since these
were posted on the school bulletin board a day or so before they
were sent out to my parents, I was generally able to see to it
that my analyses reached home slightly in advance of the official
reports.

As I now study and classify my various techniques, I see that
one of my commonest devices for averting a ditchdigging career
was the attribution of mathematical error to my instructors. Here
is a sample of that approach, drawn from a letter written in my
sophomore year:

Dearest Folks: You'll notice when you hear from the school that
they gave me a 37 in English and a 24 in Bible. Well, that's wrong.
You see they gave us monthly tests on Monday, and most of the
teachers were in a hurry to make up their marks, so they made them
up before they read the tests. Now you see the tests count for $\frac{1}{3}$ of
the monthly grades. So if you get good marks in the tests and they
don't figure them in, it brings your month's marks way down. They
should never figure up the marks without the tests because they're
bound to be wrong that way. I don't know why they do things like
that out here. It seems very stupid of them, doesn't it. My English
and Bible marks are really going to be pretty good when they count
those tests in. . . .

And another:

> The School is probably sending you a notice that I'm on Probation.
> Well, that's wrong. I'll tell you what happened. When they brought
> my marks before the Scholarship Committee, they read them all 10
> points lower. I called their attention to this fact, and I am soon
> getting off. They said they were sorry when I pointed out this dumb
> bunny thing to them. They probably sent you the wrong marks, too,
> so pay no attention to them. As a matter of fact, I failed in only one
> subject this month, and that was Latin. So my marks came up. . . .

The unquoted portion of this letter throws no light on how it
could happen that persons equipped to educate me could mis-
read a whole series of figures and, still more remarkable, mis-
read them all by exactly ten points. Nevertheless, dodges of this
sort must have proved serviceable, for I used them often. As I
recall it, I banked heavily on the fact that my father had obtained
his own secondary education in Swiss boarding schools, and he
sometimes seemed unclear about the complicated grading system
—one-third for the monthly test, and so forth—used in my school.
I reckoned, therefore, that I was able to count on a bit of paternal
gullibility when dealing with percentages.

Another approach I used was the relativist one. I insisted that
grades had meaning only when compared with other grades:

> Don't be astonished by the Math mark I got as it really doesn't
> mean a thing. You see you have to compare these marks with one
> another. My Math mark was really a very good mark compared with
> the others. He gave us a long test to be done in 45 minutes and hardly
> anyone finished. (I think one did.) He admits that it was too long
> and that my mark is really a lot better. The same thing is true about
> my Latin mark. It looks discouraging, but it really isn't. 53 is quite
> good. Charlie Gremmels got 7.

A variation on the same theme:

> Am now banking everything on the Finals in June. Most masters
> think that is best because if I pull through those decently, I'll get by
> for the year. Am pretty sure to come out okeh that way instead of
> bothering to work for monthly marks, which don't mean much in my
> case.

Why monthly marks should mean much in anyone's case if not in mine, I left to my parents' imagination. I suspect that it boggled my father's imagination and that he asked me to explain this point the next time he saw me, but I have, unfortunately, no recollection of the oral song-and-dance I gave him over that.

Although the teacher's-error and the relativist approaches were both good, I evidently understood that they would lose force if used too often. Sometimes I accepted the accuracy of the school reports and admitted that my grades were poor by any standards. I went on, though, to make the point—a perfectly legitimate one —that I had fallen behind schedule and, like a train delayed at one station, was finding it tough going all along the line:

My marks this month are not good. I admit that. Don't fret, though, as I am making them up and will get the made-up list sent to you. You see, Mother and Dad, I spent so much time last week making up the work of the week before that my last week's marks dropped some. However, I'm working hard on those right now. I just hope I don't miss any of this week's work because I have to work so hard doing last week's things.

As a dutiful son, I wrote home to my parents on an average of once a week, so three letters out of four contained no comment on the reports my parents got. In these interim communiques, my strategy was to call my parents' attention to any little scholastic triumphs I enjoyed, and also to assure them that I was steadily applying myself to my education. Here is a batch of excerpts from these in-between letters:

Well, folks, I'm feeling great and will continue to do so, also getting good marks. Today even the Dean admitted that my Latin was improving.

I'm deep in my work now. It's awfully trying. It's nothing but study, study, study. Tonight there's some musical concert we all have to go to. This guy whoever he is (probably some second-rate radio squawker) will strut his stuff. I wish I didn't have to go and could study Anc. Hist. instead. [The contemptuous reference to the recitalist was a low appeal to my father's prejudices. He loathed radio singers. I must have figured that if I got a low Anc. Hist. grade the next month, he would blame it partly on the squawker.]

I am working and playing very hard. Mr. Isham says he thinks I have a good head for Math. Sure hope he's right, don't you?

They sure do keep us working hard these days. But I seem to be able to hold up under the strain. Just imagine, I got an 82 in a Caesar test. That's very high for Caesar.

We had another English test today, and I think I got a good mark. My English certainly seems to be coming up by leaps and bounds.

At the close of each month, though, I had to deal not in leaps and bounds but in cold, dispiriting percentages, which, regardless of the heights to which they rose in the middle of the month, always seemed to taper down to 40 or 50 by the month's end. Sometimes there just weren't any suitable excuses, and when this was the case, I resorted, often brilliantly, to the ancient technique of the quick switch. I think that in many respects my work was best when my desperation was greatest. The idea was to break the bad news in as casual and unobtrusive a manner as possible and then—a difficult thing for any prose artist—jolt my readers suddenly from morbid affairs to joyous, sunshiny ones. For example:

My month's marks are not quite all they should be, as you will see. I think that by working hard I'll be able to do something about that 47 in English next month. SAY, I HAVE A SURPRIZE I'M GOING TO PULL ON YOU FOLKS NEXT WEEK. I WON'T TELL YOU A THING ABOUT IT NOW, BUT YOU JUST BETTER BE READY FOR SOMETHING BIG.

Flunked Fr. again. Say, this ought to interest Dad. There's a new kid here who is supposed to be a scientifical genius.

As you will observe, I could be doing much better than I am in Bible and Chem. And I think I will do better, too. Sorry to say I failed Anc. Hist. Wait till you hear what I did yesterday. I saw the total eclipse of the sun. I smoked a hunk of glass and looked through it. You certainly learn a lot that way.

Darn it, I failed three subjects. Say, won't you folks be glad to see me next week. Just think, I haven't been home since Feb. I sure will be glad to see you.

My English is below passing, I think. Did I ever tell you that Mr. Ruffner is a great friend of Harold Lloyd's? He said he'd tell me all about him some day. When he does, remind me, and I'll tell you.

I'm working hard on Bible and Fr., which I failed. Well, look for a little package in the mail soon. I'm sending Mother a Mother's Day present. I bought it from a boy here for $0.50. Great bargain. He was a dumb twitch to sell it. You'll like it, I think.

They only gave me a 48 in Math. By the way, Emma the maid does up laundry very nicely and for much less than the laundry. Shall I give her my shirts. It would save money.

I think next month's marks will be higher than this month's marks. I'm taking an eggnog a day. That's what Mother said she wanted me to do.

Pretty low marks coming up in Chem. and Eng., folks. Also Bible and Fr. Ok with you if I bet this week's allowance on the Athletics. I changed my underwear Wednesday.

As I said, in my Aunt Lucy's system of values a sick dog is better than two sick children. In my mother's, fresh underwear and daily eggnogs far outranked high marks in Chem. and Eng. If I didn't have a song-and-dance to give my father, I relied on my pleased mother to give him one. It's no wonder I'm pretty good at this game now; I've been at it for decades.

## 2. THE SCIENTIFICAL GENIUS

### *Wallace*

When I was a schoolboy, my relations with teachers were almost always tense and hostile. I disliked my studies and did very badly in them. There are, I have heard, inept students who bring out the best in teachers, who challenge their skill and move them to sympathy and affection. I seemed to bring out the worst in them. I think my personality had more to do with this than my poor classroom work. Anyway, something about me was deeply offensive to the pedagogic temperament.

Often, it took a teacher no more than a few minutes to conceive a raging dislike for me. I recall an instructor in elementary French who shied a textbook at my head the very first day I attended his class. We had never laid eyes on each other until fifteen or twenty minutes before he assaulted me. I no longer remember what, if anything, provoked him to violence. It is possible that I said something that was either insolent or intolerably stupid. I guess I often did. It is also possible that I said nothing at all. Even my silence, my humility, my acquiescence, could annoy my teachers. The very sight of me, the mere awareness of my existence on earth, could be unendurably irritating to them.

This was the case with my fourth-grade teacher, Miss Purdy. In order to make the acquaintance of her new students on the opening day of school, she had each one rise and give his name and address as she called the roll. Her voice was soft and gentle, her manner sympathetic, until she came to me. Indeed, up to then I had been dreamily entertaining the hope that I was at last about to enjoy a happy association with a teacher. When Miss Purdy's eye fell on me, however, her face suddenly twisted and darkened with revulsion. She hesitated for a few moments while she looked me up and down and thought of a suitable comment on what she saw. "Aha!" she finally said, addressing not me but my new classmates, in a voice that was now coarse and cruel. "I don't have to ask his name. There, boys and girls, is Mr. J. Pierpont Morgan, lounging back in his mahogany-lined office." She held each syllable of the financier's name on her lips as long as she was able to, so that my fellow students could savor the full irony of it. I imagine my posture was a bit relaxed for the occasion, but I know well that she would not have resented anyone else's sprawl as much as she did mine. I can even hear her making some friendly, schoolmarmish quip about too much summer vacation to any other pupil. Friendly quips were never for me. In some unfortunate and mysterious fashion, my entire being rubbed Miss Purdy and all her breed the wrong way. Throughout the fourth grade, she persisted in tormenting me with her idiotic Morgan joke. "And perhaps Mr. J. P. Revere can tell us all about Vasco da Gama this morning," she would say, throwing in a little added insult by mispronouncing my surname.

The aversion I inspired in teachers might under certain circumstances have been turned to good account. It might have stimulated me to industry; it might have made me get high marks, just so I could prove to the world that my persecutors were motivated by prejudice and perhaps by a touch of envy; or it might have bred a monumental rebelliousness in me, a contempt for all authority, that could have become the foundation of a career as the leader of some great movement against all tyranny and oppression.

It did none of these things. Instead, I became, so far as my school life was concerned, a thoroughly browbeaten boy, and I accepted the hostility of my teachers as an inescapable condition of life. In fact, I took the absolutely disastrous view that my teachers were unquestionably right in their estimate of me as a dense and altogether noxious creature who deserved, if anything, worse than he got. These teachers were, after all, men and women who had mastered the parts of speech, the multiplication tables, and a simply staggering number of imports and exports in a staggering number of countries. They could add up columns of figures the very sight of which made me dizzy and sick to the stomach. They could read *As You Like It* with pleasure—so they said, anyway, and I believed everything they said. I felt that if such knowledgeable people told me that I was stupid, they certainly must know what they were talking about. In consequence, my grades sank lower and lower, my face became more noticeably blank, my manner more mulish, and my presence in the classroom more aggravating to whoever presided over it. To be sure, I hated my teachers for their hatred of me, and I missed no chance to abuse them behind their backs, but fundamentally I shared with them the view that I was a worthless and despicable boy, as undeserving of an education as I was incapable of absorbing one. Often, on school days, I wished that I were dead.

This was my attitude, at least, until my second year in preparatory school, when, at fifteen, I fell under the exhilarating, regenerative influence of my friend Wallace Duckworth. Wallace changed my whole outlook on life. It was he who freed me from my terrible awe of teachers; it was he who showed me that they could be brought to book and made fools of as easily as I could be; it was he who showed me that the gap between their knowledge and mine was not unbridgeable. Sometimes I think that I should like to become a famous man, a United States Senator or something of that sort, just to be able to repay my debt to Wallace. I should like to be so important that people would inquire into the early influences of my life and I would be able to tell them about Wallace.

I was freshly reminded of my debt to Wallace not long ago when my mother happened to come across a packet of letters I had written to her and my father during my first two years in a boarding school on Long Island. In one of these, I reported that "There's a new kid in school who's supposed to be a scientifical genius." Wallace was this genius. In a series of intelligence and aptitude tests we all took in the opening week, he achieved some incredible score, a mark that, according to the people who made up the tests, certified him as a genius and absolutely guaranteed that in later life he would join the company of Einstein, Steinmetz, and Edison. Naturally, his teachers were thrilled—but not for long.

Within a matter of weeks, it became clear that although Wallace was unquestionably a genius, or at least an exceptionally bright boy, he was disposed to use his considerable gifts not to equip himself for a career in the service of mankind but for purely antisocial undertakings. Far from making the distinguished scholastic record everyone expected of him, he made an altogether deplorable one. He never did a lick of schoolwork. He had picked up his scientific knowledge somewhere, but evidently not from teachers. I am not sure about this, but I think Wallace's record, as long as he was in school, was even worse than mine. In my mind's eye there is a picture of the sheet of monthly averages thumbtacked to the bulletin board across the hall from the school post office; my name is one from the bottom, the bottom name being Wallace's.

As a matter of fact, one look at Wallace should have been enough to tell the teachers what sort of genius he was. At fourteen, he was somewhat shorter than he should have been and a good deal stouter. His face was round, owlish, and dirty. He had big, dark eyes, and his black hair, which hardly ever got cut, was arranged on his head as the four winds wanted it. He had been outfitted with attractive and fairly expensive clothes, but he changed from one suit to another only when his parents came to call on him and ordered him to get out of what he had on.

The two most expressive things about him were his mouth and the pockets of his jacket. By looking at his mouth, one could tell whether he was plotting evil or had recently accomplished it. If he was bent upon malevolence, his lips were all puckered up, like those of a billiard player about to make a difficult shot. After the deed was done, the pucker was replaced by a delicate, unearthly smile. How a teacher who knew anything about boys could miss the fact that both expressions were masks of Satan I'm sure I don't know. Wallace's pockets were less interesting than his mouth, perhaps, but more spectacular in a way. The side pockets of his jacket bulged out over his pudgy haunches like burro hampers. They were filled with tools—screwdrivers, pliers, files, wrenches, wire cutters, nail sets, and I don't know what else. In addition to all this, one pocket always contained a rolled-up copy of *Popular Mechanics*, while from the top of the other protruded *Scientific American* or some other such magazine. His breast pocket contained, besides a large collection of fountain pens and mechanical pencils, a picket fence of drill bits, gimlets, kitchen knives, and other pointed instruments. When he walked, he clinked and jangled and pealed.

Wallace lived just down the hall from me, and I got to know him one afternoon, a week or so after school started, when I was wrestling with an algebra lesson. I was really trying to get good marks at the time, for my father had threatened me with unpleasant reprisals if my grades did not show early improvement. I could make no sense of the algebra, though, and I thought that the genius, who had not as yet been unmasked, might be generous enough to lend me a hand.

It was a study period, but I found Wallace stretched out on the floor working away at something he was learning to make from *Popular Mechanics.* He received me with courtesy, but after hearing my request he went immediately back to his tinkering. "I could do that algebra, all right," he said, "but I can't be bothered with it. Got to get this dingbat going this afternoon. Anyway, I don't care about algebra. It's too twitchy. Real engineers never do any of that stuff. It's too twitchy for them." I soon learned that "twitch" was an all-purpose word of Wallace's. It turned up, in one form or another, in about every third sentence he spoke. It did duty as a noun, an adjective, a verb, and an adverb.

I was disappointed by his refusal of help but fascinated by what he was doing. I stayed on and watched him as he deftly cut and spliced wires, removed and replaced screws, referring, every so often, to his magazine for further instructions. He worked silently, lips fiendishly puckered, for some time, then looked up at me and said, "Say, you know anything about that organ in the chapel?"

"What about it?" I asked.

"I mean do you know anything about how it works?"

"No," I said. "I don't know anything about that."

"Too bad," Wallace said, reaching for a pair of pliers. "I had a really twitchy idea." He worked his wires and screws for quite a while. After perhaps ten minutes, he looked up again. "Well, anyhow," he said, "maybe you know how to get in the chapel and have a look at the organ?"

"Sure, that's easy," I said. "Just walk in. The chapel's always open. They keep it open so you can go in and pray if you want to, and things like that."

"Oh" was Wallace's only comment.

I didn't at all grasp what he had in mind until church time the following Sunday. At about six o'clock that morning, several hours before the service, he tiptoed into my room and shook me from sleep. "Hey, get dressed," he said. "Let's you and I twitch over to the chapel and have a look at the organ."

Game for any form of amusement, I got up and went along. In the bright, not quite frosty October morning, we scurried over the lawns to the handsome Georgian chapel. It was an hour before the rising bell.

Wallace had brought along a flashlight as well as his usual collection of hardware. We went to the rear of the chancel, where the organ was, and he poked the light underneath the thing and inside it for a few minutes. Then he got out his pliers and screwdrivers and performed some operations that I could neither see nor understand. We were in the chapel for only a few minutes. "There," Wallace said as he came up from under the keyboard. "I guess I got her twitched up just about right. Let's go." Back in my room, we talked softly until the rest of the school began to stir. I asked Wallace what, precisely, he had done to the organ. "You'll see," he said with the faint, far-away smile where the pucker had been. Using my commonplace imagination, I guessed that he had fixed the organ so it would give out peculiar noises or something like that. I didn't realize then that Wallace's tricks were seldom commonplace.

Church began as usual that Sunday morning. The headmaster delivered the invocation and then announced the number and title of the first hymn. He held up his hymnal and gave the genteel, throat-clearing cough that was his customary signal to the organist to get going. The organist came down on the keys but not a peep sounded from the pipes. He tried again. Nothing but a click.

When the headmaster realized that the organ wasn't working, he walked quickly to the rear and consulted in whispers with the organist. Together they made a hurried inspection of the instrument, peering inside it, snapping the electric switch back and forth, and reaching to the base plug to make certain the juice was on. Everything seemed all right, yet the organ wouldn't sound a note.

"Something appears to be wrong with our organ," the headmaster said when he returned to the lectern. "I regret to say that for this morning's service we shall have to—"

At the first word of the announcement, Wallace, who was next to me in one of the rear pews, slid out of his seat and bustled noisily down the middle aisle. It was highly unusual conduct, and every eye was on him. His gaudy magazines flapped from his pockets, his portable workshop clattered and clanked as he strode importantly to the chancel and rose on tiptoe to reach the ear of the astonished headmaster. He spoke in a stage whisper that could be heard everywhere in the chapel. "Worked around organs quite a bit, sir," he said. "Think I can get this one going in a jiffy."

Given the chance, the headmaster would undoubtedly have declined Wallace's kind offer. Wallace didn't give him the chance. He scooted for the organ. For perhaps a minute, he worked on it, hands flying, tools tinkling.

Then, stuffing the tools back into his pockets, he returned to the headmaster. "There you are, sir," he said, smiling up at him. "Think she'll go all right now." The headmaster, with great doubt in his heart, I am sure, nodded to the organist to try again. Wallace stood by, looking rather like the inventor of a new kind of airplane waiting to see his brain child take flight. He faked a look of deep anxiety, which, when a fine, clear swell came from the pipes, was replaced by a faint smile of relief, also faked. On the second or third chord, he bustled back down the aisle, looking very solemn and businesslike and ready for serious worship.

It was a fine performance, particularly brilliant in its timing. If Wallace had had to stay at the organ even a few seconds longer —that is, if he had done a slightly more elaborate job of twitching it in the first place—he would have been ordered back to his pew before he had got done with the repairs. Moreover, someone would probably have guessed that it was he who had put it on the fritz in the first place. But no one did guess it. Not then, anyway. For weeks after that, Wallace's prestige in the school was enormous. Everyone had had from the beginning a sense of honor and pride at having a genius around, but no one up to then had realized how useful a genius could be. Wallace let on after church that Sunday that he was well up on the working not merely of organs but also of heating and plumbing systems, automobiles, radios, washing machines, and just about everything else. He said he could be pleased to help out in any emergency. Everyone thought he was wonderful.

"That was a real good twitch, wasn't it?" he said to me when we were by ourselves. I said that it certainly was.

From that time on, I was proud and happy to be Wallace's cupbearer. I find it hard now to explain exactly what his victory with the organ, and all his later victories over authority, meant to me, but I do know that they meant a very great deal. Partly, I guess, it was just the knowledge that he enjoyed my company. I was an authentic, certified dunce, and he was an acknowledged genius, yet he liked being with me. Better yet was my discovery that this super-brain disliked schoolwork every bit as much as I did. He was bored silly, as I was, by "Il Penseroso" and completely unable to stir up any enthusiasm for *Silas Marner* and all the foolish goings on over Eppie. Finally, and this perhaps was what made me love him most, he had it in his power to humiliate and bring low the very people who had so often humiliated me and brought me low.

As I spent the long fall and winter afternoons with Wallace, being introduced by him to the early novels of H. G. Wells, which he admired extravagantly, and watching him make crystal sets, window-cleaning machines, automatic chair-rockers, and miniature steam turbines from plans in *Popular Mechanics*, I gradually absorbed bits of his liberating philosophy. "If I were you," he used to say, "I wouldn't be scared by those teachers. They don't know anything. They're twitches, those teachers, real twerpy, twitchy twitches." "Twerpy" was an adjective often used by Wallace to modify "twitch." It added several degrees of twitchiness to anything twitchy.

Although Wallace had refused at first to help me with my lessons, he later gave freely of his assistance. I explained to him that my father was greatly distressed about my work and that I really wanted to make him happier. Wallace was moved by this. He would read along in my Latin grammar, study out algebra problems with me, and explain things in language that seemed a lot more lucid than that of my teachers. Before long, I began to understand that half my trouble lay in my fear of my studies, my teachers, and myself. "Don't know why you get so twitched up over this stuff," Wallace would say a trifle impatiently as he helped me get the gist of a speech in *As You Like It*. "There isn't anything hard about this. Fact, it's pretty good right in here. It's just those teachers who twitch it all up. I wish they'd all go soak their heads."

Wallace rode along for quite a while on the strength of his intelligence tests and his organ-fixing, but in time it became obvious that his disappointing classroom performance was not so much the result of failure to adjust to a new environment (as a genius, he received more tolerance in this respect than non-geniuses) as of out-and-out refusal to cooperate with the efforts being made to educate him. Even when he had learned a lesson in the course of helping me with it, he wouldn't give the teachers the satisfaction of thinking he had learned anything in their classes. Then, too, his pranks began to catch up with him. Some of them he made no effort to conceal.

He was easily the greatest teacher-baiter I have ever known. His masterpiece, I think, was one he thought up for our algebra class. "Hey, you twitch," he called to me one day as I was passing his room on my way to the daily ordeal of *x*'s and *y*'s. "I got a good one for old twitch Potter." I went into his room, and he took down from his closet shelf a spool of shiny copper wire. "Now, watch this," he said. He took the free end of the wire and drew it up through the left sleeve of his shirt. Then he brought it across his chest, underneath the shirt, and ran it down the right sleeve. He closed his left fist over the spool and held the free end of the wire between right thumb and forefinger. "Let's get over to that dopey class," he said, and we went.

When the lesson was well started, Wallace leaned back in his seat and began to play in a languorous but ostentatious manner with the wire. It glistened brightly in the strong classroom light, and it took Mr. Potter, the teacher, only a few seconds to notice that Wallace was paying no mind to the blackboard equations but was, instead, completely absorbed in the business of fingering the wire.

"Wallace Duckworth, what's that you're fiddling with?" Mr. Potter said.

"Piece of wire, sir."

"Give it to me this instant."

"Yes, sir," Wallace said, extending his hand.

Mr. Potter had, no doubt, bargained on getting a stray piece of wire that he could unceremoniously pitch into the wastebasket. Wallace handed him about eighteen inches of it. As Mr. Potter took it, Wallace released several inches more.

"I want all that wire, Wallace," Mr. Potter said.

"I'm giving it to you, sir," Wallace answered. He let go of about two feet more. Mr. Potter kept pulling. His rage so far overcame his reason that he couldn't figure out what Wallace was doing. As he pulled, Wallace fed him more and more wire, and the stuff began to coil up on the floor around his feet. Guiding the wire with the fingers of his right hand, Wallace created quite a bit of tension, so that eventually Mr. Potter was pulling hand over hand, like a sailor tightening lines in a high sea. When he thought the tension was great enough, Wallace let two or three feet slip quickly through his hands, and Mr. Potter toppled to the floor, landing in a terrible tangle.

I no longer remember all of Wallace's inventions in detail. Once, I recall, he made, in the chemistry laboratory, some kind of invisible paint—a sort of shellac, I suppose—and covered every blackboard in the school with it. The next day, chalk skidded along the slate and left about as much impression as it would have made on a cake of ice. The dormitory he and I lived in was an old one of frame construction, and when we had fire drills, we had to climb down outside fire escapes. One night, Wallace tied a piece of flypaper securely around each rung of each ladder in the building, then rang the fire alarm. Still another time, he went back to his first love, the organ, and put several pounds of flour in the pipes, so that when the organist turned on the pumps, a cloud of flour filled the chapel. One of his favorite tricks was to take the dust jacket from a novel and wrap it around a textbook. In a Latin class, then, he would appear to be reading "Black April" when he should have been reading about the campaigns in Gaul. After several of his teachers had discovered that he had the right book in the wrong cover (he piously explained that he put the covers on to keep his books clean), he felt free to remove the textbook and really read a novel in class.

Wallace was expelled shortly before the Easter vacation. As the winter had drawn on, life had become duller and duller for him, and to brighten things up he had resorted to pranks of larger conception and of an increasingly antisocial character. He poured five pounds of sugar into the gasoline tank of the basketball coach's car just before the coach was to start out, with two or three of the team's best players in his car, for a game with a school about twenty-five miles away. The engine functioned adequately until the car hit an isolated spot on the highway, miles from any service station. Then it gummed up completely. The coach and the players riding with him came close to frostbite, and the game had to be called off. The adventure cost Wallace's parents a couple of hundred dollars for automobile repairs. Accused of the prank, which clearly bore his trademark, Wallace had freely admitted his guilt. It was explained to his parents that he would be given one more chance in school; another trick of any sort and he would be packed off on the first train.

Later, trying to justify himself to me, he said, "You don't like that coach either, do you? He's the twerpiest twitch here. All teachers are twitchy, but coaches are the worst ones of all."

I don't recall what I said. Wallace had not consulted me about several of his recent escapades, and although I was still loyal to him, I was beginning to have misgivings about some of them.

As I recall it, the affair that led directly to his expulsion was a relatively trifling one, something to do with blown fuses or short circuits. At any rate, Wallace's parents had to come and fetch him home. It was a sad occasion for me, for Wallace had built in me the foundations for a sense of security. My marks were improving, my father was happier, and I no longer cringed at the sight of a teacher. I feared, though, that without Wallace standing behind me and giving me courage, I might slip back into the old ways. I was very near to tears as I helped him pack up his turbines, his tools, and his stacks of magazines. He, however, was quite cheerful. "I suppose Pop will put me in another one of these places, and I'll have to twitch my way out of it all over again," he said.

"Just remember how dumb all those teachers are," he said to me a few moments before he got into his parents' car. "They're so twitchy dumb they can't even tell if anyone else is dumb." It was rather a sweeping generalization, I later learned, but it served me well for a number of years. Whenever I was belabored by a teacher, I remembered my grimy genius friend and his reassurances. I got through school somehow or other. I still cower a bit when I find that someone I've met is a schoolteacher, but things aren't too bad, and I am on reasonably civil terms with a number of teachers, and even a few professors.

### Charlie

The original Wallace Duckworth was a boy named Charles Puckette, known to me as Charlie. The boarding school was Stony Brook, in Stony Brook, Long Island. I went there in 1929 and graduated in 1933. In 1975, some forty-odd years after we met, I decided to renew my acquaintance with Charlie. I remembered that he had lived in Chattanooga, Tennessee, so I began my search there. It turned out that the Puckettes are a large clan in that part of Tennessee. In Chattanooga alone, there were two Charlie (not Charles) Puckettes, Sr. and Jr. I thought I was surely on the right trail when one told me the other could be reached at Combustion Engineering, Inc. But it turned out that neither had heard of my Charlie. Recalling that his father had worked for *The Chattanooga Times*, I phoned that newspaper and learned that the elder Puckette had died more than ten years ago but that Charlie's brother, Stephen, was dean of the University of the South at Sewanee.

I called Dean Puckette, told him I was an old friend of Charlie's and had written about him twenty-five years earlier. He knew about this, he said, and so did most of the rest of the family, but he wasn't sure that Charlie, who hadn't been around Chattanooga at the time, knew. He gave me Charlie's number in a small town in New Hampshire. I finally reached him and asked him if he remembered me or knew of the story. He said he thought he remembered the name but that he had never heard of the story. I said I would send him a copy and asked him if he would be good enough to let me know what, if anything, he remembered as fact and what he thought was fiction.

For several weeks, I heard nothing and was beginning to believe I had made the whole thing up. Then one day he called me at my office. He said he remembered some of the episodes. He was sure, though, that he had never put sugar in anyone's gas tank—"I was brought up with a great respect for property and was not interested in wrecking anything." He didn't recall so much reliance on the word "twitch." As for discombobulating the organ, he said that that had a likely sound, but he doubted ever having put flour in the pipes. He did recall the copper wire business, the flypaper anecdote, and the dust jacket trick. He added a few incidents I had forgotten or had not known about. Once he collected eight or ten alarm clocks, set them to go off at five-minute intervals, and concealed them here and there in the classroom where students who had fallen behind in their work were required to study under supervision for two hours each evening. "I hid them in lamp fixtures, in desk drawers, in bookbags. I did it to bug Mr. Isham." Mr. Isham ("Mr. Potter") was our algebra teacher, and Charlie reminded me that we had called him "The Buzzard." Mr. Isham was in charge of our dormitory, and he had a master switch outside his door to put the lights out at bedtime. Charlie did a bit of rewiring, so that he could keep his own lights on when he wished and so that he could share control of the master switch with Mr. Isham. He had also arranged a network of strings in his room so that he could lie in bed and open and close the window, door, and curtains at his supine convenience. "Quite a sparrow trap," he said. He said I had been right in describing the contents of his pockets, the condition of his clothes, and his general appearance.

He was not expelled from Stony Brook. His leaving was the result of a "mutual agreement between the headmaster and my parents." He went on to the Raymond Riordan School, in Highland, New York. It was a somewhat more permissive place, so he had abandoned his career as a scourge of teachers. From there, he went to Stevens Institute of Technology, in Hoboken, New Jersey. "I flunked out in a hurry. I also flunked out of the Newark College of Engineering." He went into the Merchant Marine in the Second World War. In that, he learned a good deal of engineering—enough to become a licensed practitioner after demobilization. Feeling that he had let his family down by doing so poorly in school, he enrolled in Fairleigh Dickinson University, from which he graduated summa cum laude in 1965, when he was fifty. Unfortunately, his father had died before he could learn of the son's feat.

Charlie worked in New York for several years but tired of it and sought out the quiet of a small town. He is an electronics engineer—just the right thing—and a member of the board of selectmen.

## 3. POSTSCRIPT

In the foregoing accounts of my academic shortcomings, there may be some exaggeration but not, I think, very much. Until I was halfway through college, my performance was almost always deplorable, and even at the end it was far from distinguished. When, in 1958, I was asked to join the editorial board of *The American Scholar*, a publication of Phi Beta Kappa, I felt constrained to point out that I had not only failed to come close to making that or any other honor society but that if they accepted me, they would have in their erudite company a man who had had to repeat first grade and had narrowly missed repeating others. At one point, at public school in Brooklyn, I was removed from my regular class and put in what was euphemistically called the "Opportunity Program"—a program for students unable to meet the normal requirements of the system. After a while, I got out of it and once even made the "Rapid Advance" program, which enabled me to skip a term, but wherever they put me, I seldom rose above the bottom third or fourth of the class. I do not think there were any specific learning difficulties. Reading came easily, and, once I forced myself or was forced to work, I did not find arithmetic or even algebra particularly troublesome. But I did not wish to read what my teachers asked me to, and I hated the labor of memorizing multiplication tables and working out equations. I disliked the very atmosphere of the classroom. I regarded almost every teacher as a natural enemy, and I had the impression, though surely I was wrong, that my teachers saw me in the same light. Some of the same feeling persisted when my own children were in school and I had now and then to deal with their teachers and principals. I have on occasion done some college teaching and have invariably, and irrationally, sided with the students in any student-faculty or student-administration controversy. I suppose it amounts to a form of bigotry, and my efforts to overcome it have never quite succeeded. At the same time, I, like bigots of other sorts, had a sneaking admiration for those I reviled. My teachers, after all, had succeeded where I had failed, and whether I was stupid or merely indolent, I felt some guilt about not knowing what they knew, not doing what they had done. But this intensified my hostility, magnified my sullenness. I had to persuade myself that what they knew was not worth knowing, that they were somehow the worse for all their learning. It was a circular, spiralling illogic, but it was, and to a degree is, mine.

Though I scoffed at what the teachers were trying to teach me, I was not entirely without intellectual interests. Through my mother, I acquired some interest and liking for poetry. It was mostly nineteenth-century and not the best of that—Macaulay, Swinburne, Kipling, and several lesser figures. I enjoyed it all and committed to memory much of the *Lays of Ancient Rome* and *Barrack-Room Ballads*. Though I had little taste for the accepted children's classics, I was a prodigious consumer of such as the Tom Swift series, the Rover Boys, Don Sturdy, and Tarzan. When a popular hero like Charles Lindbergh came along, I applied something of the scholar's zeal to studying his life and exploits. I did not care to memorize logarithms or chemical valences, but I memorized baseball history and statistics without any pain. Also, in writing to my parents as I did, I showed, I believe, some early promise as a polemicist. So I could, when I chose, apply myself. But I seldom chose. I did as little schoolwork as I could, and my grades reflected it. By the time I got to Stony Brook, more than laziness, guilt, and resentment became involved. There were some positive factors—for one, an interest in girls and, for another, a desire to attain some glory as any athlete. I was far from a success with either, but this only made me try harder, and my grades, of course, dipped lower. There was a turning point of sorts when I met Charlie Puckette and another at the beginning of my junior year, in the autumn of 1931. I had returned about two weeks earlier for preseason football practice, and in it I sustained a neck injury that required surgery and several weeks of hospitalization. Bedridden, there was not much I could do, apart from thinking, about either girls or sports, and I had plenty of time for reflection. I came to accept as simple truth that I would never be an All-American anything or even a member of the Stony Brook varsity. Indeed, it came as a dazzling, liberating illumination that football was a game I did not in the least enjoy—a game that in fact I loathed—and that it was only because of some principle of machismo (the word and concept were not much in vogue at the time, but it was close to what I sensed about myself) that I had been seeking to excel in it. And when my mind was not occupied with such thoughts, there was little else to occupy it but reading. I had outgrown Tom Swift et al. and wanted more adult fare. I forget what books I read, but I recall reading a great many news-papers and magazines, and it was an experience that aroused an interest in journalism. When I got back to school, I sought and got a position on the school paper, *The Bulletin*. Being one of its editors was, I told myself, a more significant achievement than being a second-string halfback. It might not seem so to any of the girls I had been trying to impress, but it then seemed so to me.

But the change in my interests, though by my new standards one for the better, did not lead to any improvement in my aca-demic work. My self-esteem may have grown somewhat, for I was enjoying a modest success as a youthful reporter; in effect, all I was doing was putting to new use the time that had formerly gone into avoiding my studies. My first two years at college were as dismal academically as the Stony Brook years. Another change came after my sophomore year when, like so many of my genera-tion, I began to see and feel and think about the economic depres-sion the country—in fact the world—was then in. I became curious about economics and sociology and began to form some sympathy with the Communist Party. I at last had reason for opening books that did more than amuse me. I began shaking off some of my feeling that what I was studying had little or no relevance to my life. Still, I attained no distinction as a student, and the one consolation I could take was that, unlike such writers as Henry Adams and Lincoln Steffens, both of whom felt that after one's education, one had to go through years of "unlearning," the pro-cess would be a simple one for me, there having been so little to "unlearn."

# III

# Vassar, Bard, Centerville

*They* [Vassar students] *wouldn't organize to keep themselves out of a concentration camp.*—Unnamed student quoted in the *Vassar Chronicle*, February 1976

I have known Vassar students since my own undergraduate days at a nearby men's college, and I taught there in the academic year 1975–76, when I came upon the above statement in an issue of the magazine devoted largely to past and present student attitudes toward politics, especially radical politics. I do not know quite how anyone could "organize" to keep out of concentration camps, for by the time they are set up, resistance has been crushed—or at least contained behind barbed wire. But it was not my impression that the students I taught—men and women, all seniors, all English majors—were so docile and spiritless as not to do all they could to avoid confinement. About politics, though, it seemed clearly the case that most of them were apathetic or disillusioned or both. For example, when, after they had been reading Benjamin Franklin and Thomas Jefferson, I solicited their views on the American Revolution, one said he thought it had been "a pointless war into which the people were led by a bunch of politicians who only wanted power for themselves." None of the others went quite that far, but, with Bicentennial celebrations going on all around them, none took the view that 1776 had been a great leap forward in history. They were humane and generally liberal young men and women; they were offended by what they called Jefferson's "racism," but they were unmoved by his and Franklin's eloquence. Nor were they—these children scarred by Vietnam and Watergate—much impressed by those who opposed repression and oppression. They read and liked Norman Mailer's *The Armies of the Night*, but what they mostly admired was Mailer's prose and the degree of detachment he managed to achieve. The concepts and strategies behind the antiwar protests the book described seemed of little concern to them. Once, when I asked if any of them had any serious political commitments, not one gave an affirmative answer.

And this, it seems, was true of most college students in the middle 1970s. The authors of the *Vassar Chronicle*'s articles on students and politics were throwbacks to earlier generations, for they lamented the passing of the kind of activism that was so large a feature of campus life only four years ago, when my seniors were freshmen. "In comparison," one wrote, "Vassar today would seem to be asleep. The rhetoric and the excitement are gone." As one who began a career of student radicalism more than forty years ago, I am somewhat saddened to see it in decline, but I must say that I find today's apathy and skepticism, and even some of the cynicism, vastly preferable to the mindless rage and violence, the intolerance and leftist bigotry of the generation that preceded this one. I was exposed to some of the leaders and I found them ruthless and cruel, embryo Robespierres and Stalins. I was in Chicago during the Democratic National Convention of 1968, when the Democrats nominated Hubert Humphrey and thousands of young people converged on the city to demonstrate against the war in Vietnam and those they held responsible for it, and in Grant Park I heard the leaders inciting the followers to do battle against the police and the National Guard. It was a thoroughly nauseating spectacle. There were thousands who seemed barely past childhood and most of those who huddled on the grass, playing their guitars and smoking marijuana, seemed as vulnerable as the women and children in Vietnam. But fanatics must have their martyrs, and these wanted casualty lists in Chicago.

I suspect that one reason for the apolitical character of those who followed was a revulsion toward the behavior of their older brothers and sisters. For if the young I have been teaching and observing are apathetic, they are at the same time a thoughtful, generous, compassionate lot. Though few are political activists, most have a deep sense of justice and are as sensitive to injustice as any student generation I have known. It is seldom expressed in political terms, and this may be a pity, but I for one find it preferable to the way of those who expressed it in intemperate, inflammatory language, in bombings, in shootouts, in other acts of common felony. Activism in and of itself is not a virtue.

My generation of student radicals, that of the 1930s, was in some ways as doctrinaire and self-righteous as that of the late 1960s. Many became members of the Communist Party or what were then known as fellow-travellers, and it was not until the Soviet alliance with Hitler's Germany in 1939 that some of us began to question the Stalinist tyranny that took the lives of so many dedicated Bolsheviks. But although we accepted the view that our revolutionary ends justified violent means, the revolution, like Moscow, seemed far away; we practiced no violence and would, I think, have been appalled if anyone had asked us to. To be sure, the period was a very different one; we did not have the provocations to rage that our children had when Americans bombed Asian villagers and when Richard Nixon turned the White House into a den of thieves. We opposed the military at least until 1940 or 1941, and we spoke disparagingly of Franklin Roosevelt and the New Deal, but few of us really thought of our government as a malign one. We were a gullible lot intellectually, but few of us were grim, and some of us found a good deal of gaiety in our political movements. The *Chronicle* articles led me to recall the period and the Vassar I then knew. I was a member of the class of 1937 at Bard College, then an upstate branch of Columbia University, and I spent as much time as I could at Vassar, some twenty-five miles away. It is difficult for me now to recall the process by which I, who had previously not thought to question his conservative heritage, became a radical almost overnight, but I am sure that the fact that the Vassar girls I knew (there were then, mercifully for my friends and me, no Vassar boys) were members of the Young Communist League had a lot to do with my speedy conversion. My introduction to activism was in a peace parade—on March 13, 1934, I am reminded by the *Chronicle*—held by some five hundred Vassar students and faculty members on Main Street in Poughkeepsie. This was in the days when the Communists, who a year or so later were agitating for a military alliance with the Soviet Union, were encouraging such demonstrations. Someone asked me to join the march, and I gladly did so, at least as much for the company as for the cause. It was a memorable event in several ways. The president of Vassar, Henry Noble McCracken, risked the wrath of the trustees and of the press by not only endorsing the aims of the parade but by leading the procession himself. It was an unseasonably warm and sunny day, and what began as a rather solemn event turned into a jolly and colorful one. As it happened, a travelling circus was in Poughkeepsie that day, and when its managers learned that the Vassar girls would be parading for peace on the main thoroughfare, they had the company, including an elephant or two, join the march. And so, alongside the marching students and teachers, clowns cavorted, acrobats tumbled, ponies strutted, and caged animals were put on display. Debutantes and professors mingled with bearded ladies, weight lifters, and peep-show performers, and the peanut and popcorn vendors worked the crowds on the sidewalks and the marchers in the street. The circus band's drums and brasses may have drowned out the antiwar chants, but the placards ("DOWN WITH WAR," "SCHOOLS, NOT BATTLE-SHIPS") were visible and probably seen by many who would otherwise have not stopped to watch. I have since seen many protest parades and demonstrations but never one with so festive an air.

Apart from two or three professors and three or four fellow students at Bard, the Vassar girls were the only radicals I knew at the time. I was to meet a good many more just a year after the parade in Poughkeepsie. There was pending in the New York Legislature at the time a bill that, if enacted, would have required all students in New York colleges to take an oath of loyalty to the federal and state Constitutions. The Hearst newspapers, which had proposed the bill in the first place, were featuring front-page editorials calling for speedy passage of the bill, and, by then sufficiently politicized to be against loyalty oaths and anything the Hearst press favored, I was pleased to join students from all over the state who were going to Albany to protest the bill at a Senate hearing. The experience taught me more than one political lesson. Unlike the February day of the peace-and-circus parade, the day of the protest was bitterly cold, and my only means of transportation was my unheated Model A Ford. To keep up my morale and my circulation, I took along a pint bottle of Scotch; bucking the icy winds of the Hudson Valley, I downed a modest amount of the spirits on the way up, leaving enough for adequate protection on the return trip. (I had three or four passengers, and they were similarly fortified.) Arriving in Albany, I stuffed the bottle into my overcoat pocket. But the room in which the hearing was being held was hot and stuffy, and after I had stood in it for a few minutes, I decided to shed the coat, forgetting about the bottle in the pocket. As I squirmed to remove it, the bottle fell out and landed in a spittoon that was set conveniently near the chair of one of the men who had cosponsored the bill. The crash of glass against brass could be heard by everyone, and to make matters worse, the spittoon tilted and began careening on the floor like a top coming to the end of its spin. At first, I thought I had better retrieve the bottle as quietly as possible, but I noticed that most of the people in the room appeared to have no idea where the racket was coming from. Wisdom seemed to dictate that I leave well enough alone. I was very cold on the way back to Bard.

I thought the incident had gone unnoticed until a Vassar friend showed me the next day's *Daily Worker*, the Communist Party newspaper. Apparently one of the *Worker*'s reporters had noticed the dead soldier lying in the lawmaker's cuspidor and decided to use the incident to discredit him. The *Worker*'s story ran on in this vein: "Senator X, the book-burning fascist who wants to gag New York's youth, attended a hearing on his Hitlerite bill yesterday in a state of almost complete intoxication. While 50,000 young revolutionaries demonstrated against his plot against democracy, this debauched Cossack whipped out a pint of Four Roses whiskey, gulped its contents, and flung the empty bottle on the floor."

I was mortified. I had no use for a book-burning fascist, but I did not think it fair that my empty bottle should be used against him. So I sat down and wrote the *Worker* a letter confessing everything and sent a copy to the victim of my mistake. My innocence was still such that I thought the *Worker*, that champion of freedom and of a better social order, would wish to remedy the injustice. The letter, of course, was never printed, though I did get an acknowledgment from the lawmaker and discovered that the affair could not possibly have hurt him, since he came from a Brooklyn district as wet as the bottom of the Gowanus Canal.

No doubt I should then and there have drawn the conclusion that the *Worker* cared no more for truth than the Hearst press, but it was some time before I did. Hating Hearst in those days was a crusade in itself, a mark of one's revolutionary zeal. At that Albany demonstration, there was an attractive young woman, who did not seem to be attached to any of the college groups protesting the loyalty-oath bill. Word got around that she was a reporter for the local Hearst paper, and so, it developed, she was. One of our commissars rushed up to her and grabbed her notes. She chased him up and down the corridors and, with the help of her husband, also a reporter, recovered the notes. Her story the next morning began, "I was the victim of a Communist robbery . . ." Several years later, I met the aggrieved reporter and learned that she had originally been in sympathy with what we had been doing. She had asked for the assignment with a view to treating us as sympathetically as possible. This supposed stooge of Hearst later lost her job for leading a Newspaper Guild strike against her employers. Partly perhaps because of the demonstration, and partly, I am sure, because the Hearst influence was then in decline,* the bill failed of passage.

One of the *Chronicle* articles—"Radical Vassar," by Rachel Greenfield—lists a number of left-wing student organizations that flourished on the Poughkeepsie campus in those days but says nothing about the most radical and influential of them all—the Young Communist League. It was an underground cell, but many student leaders belonged to it, and *The Miscellany News*, the weekly newspaper, was mostly staffed by Communists and, in demure Vassar prose, was a militant exponent of the Communist line. That there was an organized Y.C.L. on the campus was widely known, or at least widely suspected, but the names of the members were kept secret, and there was one occasion when secrecy saved them considerable grief. At the college that year was the daughter of a well-known writer, herself a Vassar graduate and a woman of conservative persuasion. When her daughter, whom I shall call Jane, was a junior, she began a series of articles for a women's magazine with some such title as "Talks with Jane," in which she explained how she had counselled her offspring about such matters as sex, alcohol, religion, education, and the like. While the series was running, Jane, moved perhaps by what she was reading in *The Miscellany News*, or the *Misc*, as it was known, decided that she wanted to become a Communist. She confided this to some Y.C.L. members, and panic soon spread through the cell. As a rule, any convert was welcome but not Jane, who, it was assumed, would have a talk with her mother about her latest craze, and Mama would soon be writing about the Vassar Y.C.L. for millions of American housewives. As Jane kept coming closer and closer to the intrepid Vassar Bolsheviks, they kept pushing her away. They ridiculed her idea of becoming

---

* A Hearst editorial a few days later urged that the Vassar girls who went to Albany—among them "the fairest flowers of the capitalist system" —should be sent to bed with bread and water.

a Communist. How absurd! Communists on the Vassar campus? They were just young women who were interested in social problems, but Communists they certainly were not.

Jane, though, was not to be put off. When she found that no one shared her enthusiasm to join the party of the proletariat, she determined to go it alone. On her next trip to New York, by God, she would visit Communist headquarters and get herself enrolled. Frantically, the Vassar Y.C.L. got in touch with the Thirteenth Street Kremlin and told the leaders there to prepare for a visit from Jane and reveal nothing about the Vassar Y.C.L. Forewarned, they told her nothing about the Vassar comrades but welcomed her to the revolutionary vanguard. Then and there, a second Vassar cell was chartered with Jane as its only member. I do not know whether she withheld this information from her mother or whether her mother found the affair too embarrassing to write about. But for a time there were two clandestine units of the Y.C.L. at Vassar, one unaware of the other's existence.

Though I worked closely with the Vassar Y.C.L., I did not, for reasons explained elsewhere in this book,* join the organization. At Bard there was little for a handful of revolutionists to do except for a bit of agit-prop work through the college paper—*The Bardian*, of which I became editor in my third year—and proselytizing fellow students and faculty. The administration was so tolerant that in my senior year I, known to everyone as a Communist, shared with the best and almost the only athlete in my class the prize for "the student who has done most for the college." (All I can recall doing was raising some money and organizing some campus rallies for Communist causes, especially Loyalist Spain.) In Poughkeepsie, there were nonunion employers to be picketed, stores to be boycotted, voters to be solicited, but, in Annandale-on-Hudson, there were, apart from the Bard community, scarcely a hundred souls, and there were not many more in the surrounding towns. The people in the area were either servants on the big estates or small farmers, peasants more con-

* Chapter IV, "A Goldbricking Communist."

servative than the rich who lived on the banks of the Hudson, a
squirearchy that had, after all, produced the then President and
his wife. My one off-campus political activity was in a town not
half the size of Poughkeepsie but somewhat like it in being the
site of a number of small factories whose owners had fled New
York when unionization threatened some years earlier. Since I
am not sure whether the people I knew there are still living,
I will give them fictitious names and call the place Centerville. I
got to know it because *The Bardian* was printed there. In most
Centerville elections, Republicans and Democrats very nearly
tied, so the people who ran the town decided to save themselves
the time and trouble of political competition—aside from party
labels, they had few differences—by setting up a bipartisan coali-
tion and calling it the Independent Party or something of the sort.
When there was a mayor to be elected, they would settle on one
of their number—a banker, a lawyer, a real-estate broker—and
run him as the Independent candidate. Until 1936, it had, I
gathered, been a relatively smooth and trouble-free system. The
mayor would perform as those who had put him in office expected
him to. In patronage matters, he would divide jobs evenhandedly
between Republicans and Democrats. Favors would be done for
those in favor with the power structure. In 1935, however, they
settled on a man—I shall call him Robinson—who turned out
to be rather different from his predecessors. Robinson owned a
small insurance agency and on most matters his outlook was
probably little different from that of his fellow businessmen. It
turned out, though, that he was unusual in the sense that he
believed in playing the game according to the rules—not the rules
of the masters of Centerville but the rules as found in the Constitution and other such lofty documents. This was first realized in the
autumn of 1936, when the Centerville Communists—all eight or
nine of them—wanted to hold a public meeting to present the
case for Earl Browder, the Communist candidate for President.
The principal speaker was to be Granville Hicks, the eminent
literary critic who then lived not far away. Some private hall had
been rented for the occasion, but when the nature of the meeting

became public knowledge, the American Legion, the Daughters of the American Revolution, and other such groups prevailed on the owners to renege on the agreement. The Communists, with every expectation of being ignored, routinely protested to the mayor, claiming a denial of the freedom of speech and assembly. To their astonishment, Robinson sided with them and said that if the proprietors of the private establishment would not allow a Communist meeting in their facility, he would let them use the Town Hall. He believed in free speech.

And there, indeed, the meeting was held. I was told of this extraordinary development by a man I'll call George Martin, a Communist and an employee of the plant that printed *The Bardian*. He was as baffled by what Robinson had done, or failed to do, as were the local Democratic and Republican leaders, but he sensed an opening to the left and an opportunity for oppressed workers. He was right. He got in touch with a number of labor organizers and told them he thought they could do well in Centerville. They came in and began signing up workers in some of the smaller factories—mostly in the garment industry and related trades— and a good-sized cement factory. A few months later, the unionized cement workers were out on strike. The managers of the factory asked Robinson to order the town police to clear a way through the picket line for strikebreakers they planned to bring in from the outside. Robinson said he would not do so because it was his understanding that the function of the police was to maintain law and order, and it was not part of their job to take sides in an industrial dispute. If that was his view, he was told, help would be sought from the state troopers. Robinson replied that the strike was none of the troopers' business and that if any of them came to Centerville for any such purpose, he would feel duty-bound to have his police escort them out of town. (I do not know whether an effort was made to bring in the troopers, but none of them came. The Democratic Governor of New York then was Herbert Lehman, and I am sure that his administration would not have honored such a request.) When they learned of the stand Robinson had taken, the union leaders in the runaway sweatshops began calling the workers out. In time, half of Centerville was out on strike, and there were frantic efforts to get Mayor Robinson out of office. His best customers began taking their insurance accounts elsewhere. He was relieved of his position on the board of directors of a local bank. The lawyers and others who had been advising him on administrative matters, in which he had had no previous experience, became unavailable.

Martin and I and a few of the labor people called on him to offer what help and support we could. The poor man did not know what had happened to him. He had, he said, nothing against the local businessmen; he was, after all, one of them. He had no use for Communists, but he believed they had a right to meet and speak freely. He didn't know whether or not the cause of the strikers was just, but, since there had been no disorder, he didn't feel the police should interfere. We told him that we thought he was altogether right, that we applauded his courage, and that if he continued on his present course, he would win the support of the grateful Centerville workers. We told him we thought we could get him the backing of the newly-formed American Labor Party, the political arm of the industrial unions in New York. He thanked us for our praise and encouragement but said he was not sure that he wanted anything more to do with politics and that he didn't know enough about the A.L.P. to commit himself. But he did not reject our proposal at that or at the three or four subsequent meetings we had with him.

It seemed to me a fascinating and promising situation, and although the promise was not to be fulfilled, it contributed several things to my political education. In April or May of 1937 it was agreed by those of us who had been in Centerville that, when I graduated from Bard in June, I would go to the A.L.P. in New York, tell the Centerville story, and propose that I be sent back there to establish a new political presence in the town. I got an appointment with Alex Rose, a trade-unionist who was then running the A.L.P. and was soon to become a major power broker in New York and national politics. Had he known of my Communist connections, he, then zealously purging any Communist infiltrators he could find, would no doubt want nothing to do with me, but he plainly did not know. However, he showed little interest in my vision of Centerville as a bastion of working-class strength. Though it functioned only in New York State, the party was primarily interested in national politics. The leaders wanted to help elect Presidents, Congressmen, and Governors, but electing mayors of small upstate towns like Centerville was not considered by the leaders an efficacious use of their money and manpower, and I found them uninterested in my talk of working-class strength. Rose was the first practicing politician I had dealt with, and while I was disappointed in having been unable to sell him on Centerville and Robinson, I was later rather glad that he spared me a period of service in his trade, for which, I was soon to realize, I was by temperament unsuited. But the experience with Robinson taught me that there are in the world a few incorruptible men and that some of them are to be found outside the ranks of the rebels.

I stayed in New York, and Martin moved to Philadelphia early in 1938. I did not revisit Centerville for almost a decade, and when I did, I learned that Robinson had resigned the mayoralty and moved elsewhere some time before his term would have expired. No one seemed to know what had become of him. Centerville was safely back in the hands of its Republican and Democratic bosses, wearing the colors of the Independent Party.

# IV

## A Goldbricking Communist

During the 1950s, when I was writing a good deal about Senator
Joe McCarthy, I often wished that he would call me before his
committee to ask me about my life, many years earlier, as a
Communist. I would have been a willing witness, and I think I
would have been a unique one. As I imagined the course my
testimony might have taken, part of it would have gone something like this:

Q: Are you now or have you ever been a member of the
  Communist Party?

A: I don't know.

Q: What do you mean you don't know?

A: Well, I know that I am not a member now, but as to the
  past, I simply do not know.

Q: Are you aware of the fact that you are testifying under oath?

A: Very much so, and I am giving you the only truthful answer
  I can. I simply do not know whether I was in the past a
  member of the Communist Party. Maybe I was, maybe I
  wasn't.

Q: Are you saying that you have forgotten?

A: No. It's simply that I do not have the information with
  which to answer your question.

I can't figure out where it might have gone from there, but I
know that, if given the chance, I would have said that if anyone
produced authentic evidence of my past membership, I would,
of course, acknowledge it. And I would have added that I was

in any case willing to assume whatever moral responsibility was attached to having been a member of the Party, since, in the years between 1935 and 1939, I thought of myself as loyal to it, supported its policies, worked in its interests, and from early 1938 to the late summer of 1939, served on the editorial staff of *The New Masses*, a publication that consistently, indeed slavishly, followed the Communist line.

I could hardly have blamed my inquisitors for any incredulity over my testimony. How could anyone "not know" whether he had ever belonged to such an organization? I will try to explain. I have a good memory in matters of this nature, and I am not the sort of compulsive joiner who loses track of his affiliations; on the contrary, I am, deep in my bones, antiorganization, and have, if one discounts such things as the Boy Scouts, the Parent-Teachers Association, and the Book-of-the-Month Club, done very little joining.

Here, for the record, is what happened, or didn't happen: in the spring of 1935, I ended an internal debate as to whether I should throw in my lot with the Socialists or the Communists with a decision in favor of the latter. I use the word "debate" rather loosely. I did not marshal the arguments for one course against another to find where the burden of logic lay. The process was far from entirely logical or intellectual. Had I decided on doctrinal grounds—or even according to my basic instincts and temperament—I would almost certainly have joined the Socialists. Though I had had a brief seizure of fundamentalist Presbyterianism at Stony Brook, I am by nature skeptical and undogmatic— or perhaps I should say uninterested in dogma. Though I never described myself as a pacifist and once volunteered for the Abraham Lincoln Brigade to fight in the Spanish Civil War—fortunately, I was rejected—the antiwar position of the Socialists was more in line with my education and my cast of mind than the Communist espousal of violence and militarism. As part of my education, I had absorbed the proposition that the First World War had been a wicked enterprise on both sides, and I was a noninterventionist; this was the Socialist policy, while the Communists were calling for "collective security," which to them meant defense of the Soviet Union. Moreover, I found Eugene V. Debs a more sympathetic historical figure than Karl Marx, and Norman Thomas more interesting and eloquent than Earl Browder, who in retrospect I see as a Bolshevik Gerald Ford.

But in my youthful zeal, I put all these considerations aside for what seemed to me the greater effectiveness of the Communists. They were more tightly organized, they seemed more militant, and they were obviously more numerous. They were more active in the labor movement, and the fact that they incurred more wrath on the part of the reactionaries I took to be evidence that they posed a greater, more immediate threat to the existing order. Though I did not myself respond well to discipline, I had become persuaded that in radical politics it was necessary and that the Communists had it and the Socialists did not. (Like many others at the time, I looked at a brutal authoritarianism and saw discipline.) I was not much moved by the fact that the Communists had the backing of the Soviet Union; I perceived little connection between what was happening in the Soviet Union and what I wished to happen here—not, that is, until the Soviet-Nazi Pact in August 1939, when I finally understood that the first duty of a Communist anywhere was to defend the foreign policy of the Soviet Union and because of that resigned from *The New Masses*. If I cared about any other country in those years, it was Spain. But my real, almost single-minded concern was the United States, and it was an indisputable fact that the Communists here were far more influential than the Socialists—partly, I might have reasoned but did not, because they had so largely succeeded in destroying the Socialist Party that two decades earlier had been so promising.

Finally, communism was more fashionable among my friends. Among the handful of students and professors at Bard who regarded themselves as radicals, nearly all were Communist Party sympathizers. The first girl I was ever seriously interested in, Catherine M., had gone to Smith and promptly joined the Young Communist League. (She was expelled for other than political reasons; she had had a boy in her room, but since the boy was a Communist, she chose to claim that she was the victim of a political purge.) My closest friend throughout adolescence, Tom Leonard, had become a Socialist before going to college and was steadfastly anti-Communist, but he was at Wesleyan and then at Chicago, and we corresponded only intermittently. The friends I met in New York, leaders of the American Student Union and the American Youth Congress, were either members of the Y.C.L. or moving in its direction. Their common view was that the Socialists were reformers, almost imperceptibly to the left of the New Deal; the Communists characterized them as "social fascists," unworthy allies of any truly radical movement. I regret to say that that view became mine.

When I made my decision, there was no Y.C.L. at Bard, though there was one at Vassar, for which my sex disqualified me. A few of us had talked about forming one but had done nothing about it. For my part, I wanted to join the adult rather than the youth organization—I was twenty—so I deferred action until the end of the year, when I was due to go to Silvermine, Connecticut, to take up my duties as press agent for The Theatre in the Woods, which presented opera outdoors. I had spent many summers in Fairfield County, a highly industrialized area and one which was certain, I reasoned, to have thriving Communist units, or "cells." Upon arrival, I made discreet inquiries and in time was put in touch with a woman I shall rename Mrs. Curtis, a handsome and wealthy matron who lived in the highly *un*industrialized town of New Canaan. She talked to me at length, urged me to attend Party meetings, and assured me that I would shortly receive notice of my membership. I do not recall whether or not I filled out any kind of application form, but I am sure I did whatever was necessary. I wanted very much to belong.

For three or four weeks, though I had received no further word about my status from Mrs. Curtis or anyone else, I attended Party meetings. In retrospect, it seems rather odd that I, who might have turned out to be a police agent, was admitted to these more or less clandestine gatherings without any formalities, but

I was. The meetings were held on Tuesday evenings in South Norwalk, either in a room over a store across the street from the railroad tracks or in the tiny apartment of a young couple who lived in a section of town that was a minighetto for workers of East European extraction. The usual attendance was eight or nine. Either we sat around catechizing each other about the minutiae of Communist doctrine or we planned divisions of labor for getting more people to more meetings, for getting signatures on petitions, or for circulating *The Daily Worker* and other items of Party literature. Since I had become a Marxist-Leninist with only a sketchy reading of Marx and an even sketchier one of Lenin,* I could contribute little to the discussions except for the voicing of a few sentiments I knew would be unexceptionable— such as "Capitalism is in its death throes. . . . We must help the Bridgeport strikers. . . . We must redouble our efforts to free Mooney and Billings and the Scottsboro boys. . . . Fascism is an advanced state of capitalism. . . . As Comrade Marx put it, 'religion is the opiate of the people.' . . . The reactionaries will stop at nothing." These shows of orthodoxy were well received; no one accused me of "deviationism."

But I found the meetings almost intolerably dull. It seems to be part of my nature to dislike meetings of any sort, particularly when the main activity is talk. (I had been an enthusiastic Boy Scout and attended troop meetings with pleasure, but there one *did* things—tied knots, practiced first aid, exercised.) Communist meetings were as boring as any I have ever known. I don't know why I had expected anything else. Perhaps I had some grand notion of being in on the planning of high strategy. Whatever I may have had in mind, it was not spending several hours repeating platitudes or going over the logistics of distributing papers and

---

* My mentor was John Strachey, the British author of a popularization of Marx and Lenin—*The Coming Struggle for Power*. I had read the book but wanted a copy of my own. Getting one involved a struggle for power in my own conscience. I noticed an advertisement in which it was being offered for 39 cents in a New York department store. I made a beeline for it, only to find it being picketed. What was more important—my loyalty to trade unions or my revolutionary self-improvement? I crossed the picket line.

tracts. And I was disappointed in the people. Ours was an authen-
tically proletarian group, and I knew enough of the working class
not to expect heroic figures out of the murals of Diego Rivera or
the firebrands encountered in the novels of John Dos Passos. But
the young Communists I had met in New York, many of them
proletarian in origin, made lively companions; they may have
been as doctrinaire as the Connecticut ones, but most of them
had wit and vigor. Those I was meeting with had no such qualities.
They were, so far as I could tell, decent, friendly men and women
who found in Party gatherings something like an avocation, a
form of recreation—what others find in gardening or home
carpentry or bowling or drinking, only more stimulating because
they could pursue it with a sense of virtue and accomplishment.
Their rhetoric was militant—it could hardly have been more so—
but militance seemed not to be a part of their nature; thinking
about them later, I formulated the theory that militant talk and the
sort of action represented by attendance at Party meetings were a
kind of compensating mechanism for people who elsewhere, on
the job or at home, were essentially meek and submissive. I am
sure that overturning the social order was their ideal, but they
were not the sort to overturn anything.

My dislike of talky meetings is almost matched, to the dismay
of my wife and some of our friends, by my dislike of picnics.
Party members, or at least those I then knew, could hardly let a
sunny summer Saturday or Sunday pass without having a picnic.
They were not ordinary picnics in the sense of being planned for
enjoyment alone. Sometimes they were fund-raising picnics, sometimes they were continuations of our meetings, discussions of
Marxism-Leninism over sandwiches and ants. Because I was one
of two or three members of my group who owned a car, one of
my picnic assignments was transport. I am afraid it was the snob
in me that resented this. At about the time of my political conversion, I had bought, for fifty dollars, a four-year-old Ford
roadster—a sort of convertible with a rumble seat—and it was a
source of great pride as well as pleasure for me. I kept it cleaner
and neater than I have kept any car since. But this was a difficult

job after a Communist picnic. I would usually be assigned to pick
up my passengers at a particular intersection between Norwalk and
South Norwalk. On the first occasion, I assumed that they would
be a few members of the group. Those I expected showed up—
but not alone. The comrades had diapered infants and small
children, and the children had friends and dogs, and they swarmed
over my five-passenger Ford as the ants were later to swarm over
them. Most had baskets of food, and the picnicking began in
my car. I suppose that if I had seen the relationship of all this
to the class struggle, I might have overcome my petty bourgeois
instincts. But it seemed to me that a better society could be built
without messing up my car.

Though it was to be some time before I began to have doubts
about the political course I had chosen, I had grave misgivings
about the Party as an organization—at least at the level I was
getting to know. Little that I was being asked to do seemed
relevant to the Party's aims as I understood them. Raising money
for deserving causes was clearly worthwhile, but I didn't see what
this had to do with going over Stalin's or Browder's speeches
clause by clause, which was the kind of activity that consumed by
far the greater part of our time. I had some hope of writing for
Communist publications, but I did not fancy distributing them—
particularly the *Worker*, the shrillness of which always offended me.

I suppose that if I had held on to my job with the theatre and
had been informed that my bid for membership had been accepted, I would, for a time anyway, have endured the meetings
and the picnics and the labors of a newsboy. But in midsummer
I was fired (the theatre was on the verge of closing), and I returned to Brooklyn, where, thinking things over, I resolved not to
press the matter of membership further. Like those who claim
that they can practice their religion without regular church attendance, I felt that I could be a good Communist without going
to meetings every Tuesday night.

Now, it may well be that somewhere—in the Party archives,
wherever they are, or in the files of the F.B.I. or C.I.A.—there is

some document establishing as a fact that in 1935 I was enrolled as a member of the Communist Party. For all I know, Mrs. Curtis is to this day waiting for me to pick up my card.

I went back to Bard for my junior year, loyal but happily unattached. I was editor of the college paper, *The Bardian*, and turned it into an Annandale *Pravda*. I talked no more of setting up a Bard Y.C.L. I worked closely with Communists in the trade unions in Poughkeepsie and Hudson, and did not disabuse them or anyone else as to my Party status. That spring, a few of us organized a campaign to win support for Browder, the candidate for President, and may have won him two or three votes he would not otherwise have had. I spent the better part of two years on *The New Masses* without attending a single Party meeting. I did meet regularly with some Communists from advertising agencies and publishing houses working on publicity for certain Party activities, but these were not Party meetings. I suppose everyone just assumed I was a member. Nobody ever asked me about it, not even Joe McCarthy.

# V

# H. W. Ross

I seem to have mislaid the sheaf of notes I had from Harold Ross
—both the detailed commentaries he attached to the galleys of
*New Yorker* articles and the brief interoffice memoranda (he,
of course, would never have called them that) that were now
and then put on my desk by one of his superannuated messengers.
These messages—at least the ones I got—usually ran to three
or four typed lines on cheap yellow paper. They were mostly
courtesy notes, and they generally went about like this:

Mr. Rovere: I've just read your piece, and I like it fine. Thanks for
doing it. I may as well tell you now that Shawn and I have talked
over your next assignment, and we're both for it, so that makes it
official.

H. W. Ross

My memories of him are not very numerous and are not based
on intimacy. But they are warm, and some of them are still
quite vivid. I do not wish to lose them as I have lost the notes.

I worked for *The New Yorker* in the seven years before Ross's
death in 1951. Unlike James Thurber and a few others who have
written of him, I did not know him as a friend. We were a generation apart. I was twenty-nine when I was asked to join the staff
by William Shawn, his assistant and successor, and Ross was
fifty-two. The only Ross I knew was the editor, and I write of
him now not only to preserve my recollections but with the hope
that they may cast some light that has not been cast before.

I no longer remember my first meeting with him, but I am sure it did not take place until several months after I joined *The New Yorker* in 1944. At that time, I shared with two or three other writers a small, sooty suite on the fifteenth floor at 25 West Forty-third Street—four floors below Ross's. In that period, Ross was a firm believer in decentralization as a means of preventing office politics, office gossip, and office amours. He scattered writers here and there in the building—two, three, or four to a floor— so that they would not have much to do with one another. The only people I knew or recognized were Shawn, Shawn's secretary, and the other writers in my suite. If I had ever seen a photograph of Ross, it hadn't stuck in my mind, and I didn't know what he looked like. I imagine I was first introduced to him in a corridor or elevator by Shawn or Joel Sayre, another fifteenth-floor writer. Apart from brief and generally silent encounters in corridors and elevators (it was, and still is, considered bad form at *The New Yorker* to do more than nod or mumble a greeting in these places), I do not suppose that I saw Ross more than a dozen times in all. Our only meeting on what could even remotely be considered a social occasion was at the twenty-fifth anniversary party of *The New Yorker* at the Ritz—the last great party held in that noble hotel before it was demolished. I chatted briefly with him and with his friends Mayor and Mrs. William O'Dwyer, and all that remains with me is a picture of Ross looking balefully over the ballroom, consulting his watch, and saying that it was one hell of an hour for his young daughter to be at the Ritz Hotel.

About half our other meetings took place when Shawn was out of the office and Ross took over the "editing" of my pieces. This meant that he assembled all the notes on meaning, syntax, punctuation, and so forth of the editors—himself included—and went over them with me, a process that sometimes lasted a couple of hours. There were writers who found such meetings—with Ross or any other editor—an ordeal. I enjoyed them. Before coming to *The New Yorker*, I had done a lot of editing and rewrite work myself, and I had acquired, I guess, a taste for the minutiae of syntax and style. Also, when I worked with Ross, I was entertained by what I learned of his own interests and experiences and of the importance he attached to them. Once, in an article on the New York District Attorney's office, I wrote, rather thoughtlessly, about an express elevator that made its first "scheduled" stop at the seventh floor or some floor above the second. This annoyed Ross very much.

"I'm a specialist on elevators," he said. "You probably weren't born when I first started studying them, and, by God, this is the first time I ever heard of an elevator 'schedule.' It sounds pretty damned ridiculous. What do you mean, Rovere—they've got an elevator timetable down there on Centre Street—you catch the, for God's sake, 8:19 elevator or something like that? I just don't believe it. I'll put one of the checkers on it."

If he had only stopped talking, I would quickly have conceded that I had chosen a misleading word and was glad he had pointed this out. But I couldn't bring myself to interrupt the flow, for I liked it. I liked those times in his office very much and wish there had been more of them. Of the office itself I remember very little, except that its principal decoration was an immense commercial poster—I believe a tea advertisement—of a decorous, recumbent, Chinese nude, life-size or larger, tacked to the wall above his desk.

I found Ross a great and, in many ways, an inspiring editor. I know he had large faults. He was a fussbudget. His interest in ideas didn't match his interest in small, and often silly, facts. Much of the time he saw neither the forest nor the trees but only a bit of the undergrowth. Still, his passion for accuracy was admirable, and his passion for precision of expression was tonic, especially in a day when our leading literary critics were making light of precision and clarity and arguing that awkward, choked-up writers like Dreiser and Faulkner showed how mistaken it was to put mere correctness high on the scale of literary values. My own instincts may have been petty, but in general I agreed with Ross. I liked his endless and, as I saw it and still see it, gallant fight against the slovenly, the flabby, and the needlessly ambiguous.

I do not mean to say that there was no merit in the view of the critics hostile to Ross's approach or to that of *The New Yorker* today. Many writers incomparably greater than those *The New Yorker* regularly publishes could not have been printed in the magazine without extensive and probably emasculating revision. Ross would never have put up with Dickens, Tolstoi, or Balzac. Or at least one assumes that he wouldn't have. Yet he was by no means inflexible, and some of his and *The New Yorker*'s views on writers and editors have been misunderstood. The late Gustave Lobrano once told me of a discussion of the system he had had with Ross when he, Lobrano, had just joined the staff as a fiction editor.

"Let's take an extreme case, Lobrano," Ross had said. "Take a writer who comes in here with a story we like but that has one sentence that is upside down. I mean upside down, so that to read it you'd have to turn the magazine around. We're against that, and we'd tell him so. We'd tell him there's a firm house rule on the subject—absolutely no upside-down sentences. Now, suppose the writer begins to shout at us and say he'll take his piece to some fifty-cent magazine published in Chicago or someplace. [*The New Yorker* then sold for fifteen cents and now sells for sixty. I know of no magazine that in 1976 sells for less than fifty cents.] We are then, Lobrano, in a position in which we must decide whether we think more of the rule than of the story. If we want the story very much, we may have to humor the writer and print the sentence upside down. That's the rule, Lobrano."*

*The New Yorker* has never, so far as I know, printed an upside-down sentence, and I do know of cases in which a refusal to submit to revision has led to rejection. On the other hand, I know of far more cases in which writers determined that their way was the better one have prevailed against the editors.

In *The Years with Ross*, Thurber turns over and over the ques-

---

* Shawn is of the opinion that the exact opposite was Ross's attitude. But Edward Newhouse, who has written some of the finest short stories the magazine has published, was present, and, while he does not recall the incident, he finds it in keeping with his memory of Ross, of whom he said, "He thought all writers were idiots and had to be humored in order to keep them producing, particularly when it came to so unimportant a matter as typography."

tion of whether Ross made *The New Yorker* or *The New Yorker* made Ross. He never does settle it. As a latecomer, I am in no position to bear witness. By the time I knew Ross, he was already a creature of myth, and everything he did or didn't do contributed to the myth. His most commonplace decisions were set down as the marks of a genius. Everything he said was regarded as proof of his wizardry. For example, a good many people have told me that Ross showed a miraculous editorial instinct when he decided to have a Washington correspondent who maintained his home elsewhere. It was true that when I first started the "Letter from Washington" he often told people that in his judgment Washington could best be covered by someone who didn't live there. But this doesn't make it a sound judgment, and it does not even mean that Ross was very serious when he said it. It was mainly, I think, a judgment that suited his convenience and mine, and one that he found amusing. In 1948, when I was asked to try reporting from Washington, I had recently settled my family in Dutchess County, almost one hundred miles north of New York City. At the time of the move I expected that the bulk of my writing would be non-political. I had been intensely political in my early twenties, and most of my journalism before I went on *The New Yorker* had been political in one sense or another. In my first four years on the magazine, I had found it a great pleasure to be writing about other things—lawyers, criminals, food faddists, memory experts —and even a bit of fiction. I was pleased by Shawn's suggestion (the idea originated, I believe, with him rather than with Ross) that I try a regular Washington column, but I did not anticipate that it would be the only thing I would do for the magazine, or even that it would be my major job. Also, I wasn't certain it would last. Nor was Ross. "We'll give it a try, Rovere," he said. "Nobody's yet persuaded me that there's anything for us down there. But there may be. They tell me it's becoming an international city now. That might make a difference. Anyway we'll see."

In time, Ross began telling people that he had laid down the law and told me that if I ever moved to Washington, I'd no longer be the magazine's Washington correspondent. He even worked up a theory that the only way to cover Washington was by staying there a few days at a time and then clearing out; Lippmann, the Alsops, and the rest were going about it entirely the wrong way. The theory was, I think, an afterthought and an essentially playful one—yet people have often told me that only a genius like Ross could have conceived it. It is nonsense.

Two or three encounters with Ross stand out in my mind. One took place after I had been on the magazine about a year and had decided that it wasn't the place for me—or, at any rate, that I wasn't the writer for it. I had accepted, in the form of advances, a good deal more money than I had earned, and I was much oppressed, like so many other writers before and after that time, by the thought of my debt to the magazine. Thinking about it gave me severe writer's cramp. I thought I'd better clear out before I ran up a debt I could never hope to repay. I confided my anxieties to Shawn, and he gravely proposed that we talk the whole matter over at lunch the next day. We went to the Hotel Algonquin, and after we had been there for a few minutes Ross came shambling into the dining room. I was sure this had been prearranged, but Ross pretended surprise and a certain gruff pleasure at seeing us together there. "Hello, Shawn," he said. "Hello, Rovere. All right if I sit down here?" He began to question me in an offhand way about the article I was supposed to be doing. Whom had I seen? How was the writing going? He acted as if he had heard not a word of my difficulties and was just making talk. I answered his questions and some that Shawn asked—none of which bore on the problem of whether I was to quit the magazine or stay with it. But by the time the lunch was over (I ate heartily while Ross, as I recall, had a soft-boiled egg and Shawn had cornflakes—dishes which cost, I was scandalized to learn, as much as I paid for steak) it seemed to be the common assumption of the three of us that there were no problems worth talking about. Possibly I figured that if they could pay Algonquin prices for eggs and cornflakes I need not fret too much about owing them money. Anyway, I stopped fretting and began to produce articles, thereby reducing, and in time discharging, my debt.

The article Ross had questioned me about had led me to have several talks with another magazine editor, whom I shall call Foley. We got along fairly well, and Foley evidently conceived some interest in me. I learned of this one day, not long after the Algonquin lunch, when Ross phoned me from his office. Our only phone conversation went about like this:

"Hello, Rovere. Ross. Sorry to bother you, but the damnedest thing just happened. I got a call from that fool Foley. I don't understand it. Once a year, just about this time, he calls me on the telephone. I can depend on it. Hardly need a calendar. I know a year's gone by when I hear from him. He wanted to know about you."

"What about me?"

"Well, he wanted me to tell him about you. I couldn't think of a thing to say. Jesus, how would I know what to say about you? What'll I tell him?"

"I've no idea," I said. "Do you know what he's got in mind?"

"I figure he must be thinking about offering you a job. Would you like a job over there?"

"I don't think so," I said, perhaps a bit nervously. "I like it here."

"Well, it's none of my business. It's just that I've got to tell Foley something about you. Then, by God, he won't bother me for another year. I don't know why he always calls me. What shall I say?"

"I still don't know," I said. Then I had a thought that struck me as being in keeping with the spirit of this conversation. "Why don't you," I said, "tell him I'm a Communist? I think that will put a stop to the whole thing."

"Jesus, a Communist. A Communist! That's it. I'll tell him you read what's his name, Marx, all the time. You're all for the Russians. He won't need to know anymore. He may not even call me next year. That's just fine. Thanks a lot, Rovere."

Ross was often said to be a Republican. I don't know what he was. His thoughts on politics always seemed to me casual and improvised. He had an interest in the working of politics that was technical and dispassionate, rather like his interest in the life of eels—or, perhaps, his interest in how parking tickets were fixed. His knowledge was quite broad, though, and he frequently raised shrewd points about my articles.

He did not wish to be committed to any partisan viewpoint in the magazine, and I did not wish to be committed. When, however, Senator Joe McCarthy came along, a couple of years after I had started the "Letter from Washington," I told him that I thought it would be impossible and quite irresponsible to suspend judgment on this mountebank. McCarthyism, I argued, was not a political issue but a moral one. Though the term made him uneasy, he agreed, and I was free to commit the magazine—to the degree that I could commit it by anything I wrote—against McCarthy. *The New Yorker* lost a few subscribers on this account but not, so far as I know, any advertisers.*

In one of the first "Letters from Washington," I wrote at length on a report on racial segregation in the District of Columbia. The report said there was a lot of segregation and that it ought to

---

* In assembling materials for this book, I came upon some of the Ross memoranda I thought I had lost. Since the paraphrase I used can stand for most of them, I have not included the texts. There is one, however, I do wish to get on the record. Although my experience in dealing with McCarthy and McCarthyism in the magazine under Ross was as reported above, others have claimed that he didn't want the issue discussed in *The New Yorker*. According to Conor Cruise O'Brien, for example, "The editorial policy of *The New Yorker* was to say as little as possible about McCarthyism and let truth and falsehood do their grappling somewhere else, out of earshot of the advertisers." And Thurber wrote that Ross "didn't encourage, he even discouraged, pieces on McCarthyism." Ross sent the note below to me after an article in which I described McCarthy's technique as employing a variant of Hitler's "big lie" which I called the "multiple untruth"—a mixture of many outright lies with occasional half-truths and occasional truths. After reading this, Ross wrote me as follows:

April 14, 1951

Mr. Rovere:
The latest Washington Letter seems to me just wonderful. I hope it will be useful, but as you indicate, the untruths probably won't be overtaken.

H. W. Ross

be ended. My piece was clearly sympathetic to this point of view. I enlisted the magazine on the side of the victims.

At the usual time, Shawn and I met to go over the piece. Shawn had Ross's notes on his desk, but they had been placed where I could not easily see them. When we came to the section that dealt with the report, Shawn grew visibly agitated. He said he thought I ought to know that Mr. Ross, splendid man that he was, had certain blind spots. On the Negro question, for example, he did not share the enlightened view. It was quite strange, he said, that so generous and humane a person should have this failing. But there it was. One had to face it.

I had had intimations of this and was not greatly disturbed. I admired Ross hugely as an editor. I liked him very much. I thought that *The New Yorker* was an ornament of American civilization. It has seldom bothered me to observe that some of our ornaments are tarnished. Shawn had no need to apologize to me for a touch of prejudice in Ross, and I said so. "Does he object to anything specific?" I asked. Well, no, Shawn said, nothing specific, really, but he does have some pretty harsh comments on the whole piece. I asked if I might see them. Almost trembling, Shawn handed me Ross's notes and pointed to the offending passage. I remember it as vividly as anything Ross ever wrote or said, and I know I am not more than a few words off in this paraphrase:

This section is silly and pernicious. Rovere plainly doesn't know what he's talking about. Believe me, these race questions are complicated. I know—I've lived with them. [He had worked, briefly, as a reporter in New Orleans but what he probably meant, I was later told, when he said he had "lived" with the race question was that he had lived for some time in San Francisco and knew all about the Chinese there.] This is damned foolish stuff, and altogether too much of it is getting into the magazine. I don't know about the rest of you, but I'm saying right now that if the Oak Room [of the Algonquin] goes black, I'm clearing out. I suppose we've got to print this, but I hereby file a protest. I don't see why this magazine has to draw every Abraham Lincoln in New York.

What struck me at once, of course, was that Ross had said, "I suppose we've got to print this." I asked Shawn whether he proposed that I withdraw the section. He said he proposed no such thing. He asked if I myself wished to withdraw it. I said I did not. The piece ran as written.

My admiration for Ross was at that moment almost limitless. The man clearly despised what I had written for his magazine. He thought it was nonsense. To a degree, he regarded me as an enemy of his values. Yet the article was factually accurate, reasonably well written, and a serious piece of reporting by a man he had asked to cover Washington, and that, for Ross, was that. I told Shawn that this seemed to me absolutely splendid. Shawn seemed relieved.

A bit later, I left Shawn's office, and there in the hall was Ross, pacing restlessly and obviously awaiting my emergence. He cornered me. "I hope you're not angry, Rovere," he said. "I guess I blew up. Jesus, I've got nothing against Negroes. To tell you the truth, the only people who worry me are all the Abraham Lincolns here. We've got too many for one magazine. Sometimes I feel as if I'm printing nothing but the Emancipation Proclamation over and over again. I get sick of it. That Dorothy Parker is the worst. She writes this stuff all the time, and then she keeps coming to me and saying, 'Ross, why don't you have a Negro over to your house for dinner?' I told her once that no shine ever asked me to his house for dinner, and I hadn't noticed too God-damned many of them at her place. I guess your piece was all right, Rovere. Just hit me at a bad moment. I hope you don't mind my talking this way."

I said it was quite all right. About a week or ten days later, after the article had been published, I ran into him again, and he made approximately the same embarrassed speech. I probably said something about everyone having his own point of view. If I had thought of it, I might have said that I thought he was something of an emancipator himself. But I didn't think of it. Besides, it wasn't the sort of thing one said to Ross.

# VI

## *Winter in Europe*

### I. JOSEPHINE

Josephine Cianni, as I remember her now, stood about five feet and could not have weighed more than ninety pounds. In 1953 she was twenty, but her angular little body had never developed into even the first stages of adolescence. Her face, though, was waxy and striated, like that of a middle-aged dwarf. I recall that when I saw her for the first time I had the thought that she might have stepped out of a photograph depicting the ravages of war; she was Goyaesque. One had no choice but to call her ugly. Her voice was ugly, too—rasping and metallic. But she bore her ugliness lightly, as if she were quite unaware of it. Probably she was. Once her ugliness had been accepted, one could be charmed by her smile and her natural gaiety. She came from a village near Salerno, and she and her father and an elder sister had migrated, illegally, to France at the end of the war. I did not learn this part of her story until after her death. In fact, it comes to me now that I did not know her last name until I read it on the obituary page of *Nice-Matin*.

My brief acquaintance with Josephine,* now the source of so many painful memories, as well as quite a few sweet ones, began early in October of 1953. My wife and I and our three children had just taken a small villa about halfway between Cannes and

---

* Her name, actually, was Giuseppina. Perhaps because there are several Josephines in our family, we felt more comfortable with the Anglicized version.

71

the village to the west of it, La Bocca. It was a house of absurd architecture—"Florida Boom" was our name for it—and its six rooms were small and dark. Anywhere else, it would have been a place of unbearable gloom and quite unacceptable pretenses. But it suited us well, for it stood in the center of a rectangular piece of land, perhaps an acre in size, that gave on the sea at one end and on the Route de Fréjus, the main highway into Cannes, on the other. The land was beautifully planted, the beach was magnificent, the house was a house, and it afforded a fine view of the Esterel. We planned to spend a few months there, and my wife, Eleanor, and I wanted someone to help with the housework and the care of the children—Ann and Betsy, ten and six, and Mark, eight.

Josephine was brought to us one day by another Italian—a young woman we knew as Onelia, who was the maid of a neighbor. Our first impulse on seeing Josephine was to say that we would not so much as consider hiring her. The prospect of having a maid scarcely any larger than our ten-year-old daughter and far less robust was more than either Eleanor or I could endure. We are the sort who always feel a certain guilt about having any domestic help, and we knew that our guilt would be insupportable if we took on this asthenic creature to clean the house, cart in groceries, and dump heavy scuttles of coal on the little furnace that heated the place. "I couldn't bear it," Eleanor said. "I'd be doing it all myself."

Neither Josephine nor Onelia spoke a word of English; Josephine, in fact, spoke hardly any French. I explained, in French, our misgivings to Onelia, who said that we were deceived by appearances and that Josephine was really a husky girl, who had done heavy work in factories and would be able to do anything we asked of her. Onelia spoke a few words of Italian to Josephine, and Josephine, flashing a smile at us, bounded from the chair in which she had been sitting uneasily. She began picking up every large object in sight—chairs, tables, floor lamps —to show us her strength. She rolled back a sleeve and formed biceps for me to feel. The muscle was unquestionably there.

While this display was going on, Onelia talked of Josephine's poverty and of her great need for the job. I could only reply that Josephine must be stronger than she looked, and that of course we would be happy to have her.

And so we were. Josephine was more than a good and conscientious servant. She was an unfailing delight. She was cheerful and responsive and sensible about everything. She had a native dignity and poise; she was never servile or insolent. We had no fault to find with anything she did for us. As for language, we got along well enough by drawing resourcefully on her small knowledge of French and our small knowledge of Italian, and by making signs with our hands.

The children loved her, and she handled them wonderfully well, though not in a manner that would have won the approval of authorities on child care. She joked and romped with them; she also bellowed at them, cursed them, and, when she felt like it, swatted them. When they angered her, she screamed at them —not as an unnerved adult might scream but as one child screams at another. I always supposed she was hurling Campanian street oaths and obscenities at them. But they never took offense, and neither did she. Josephine believed in direct action. When she wanted Mark to sit down for a meal or get ready for bed, she would not command him to come to her but would take out after him and chase him through the house until she could bring him low with a flying tackle. He loved it, and so did the others. The children were eager to please her. They loved Josephine, and she, we thought and still think, loved them. She often stayed to play with them when she was free to leave, though this may have sprung less from her fondness for them or for us than from her dislike of her own life and lodgings, both of which I imagined to be bleak.

I do not believe that Josephine came into our house only to rob us. I assume she came primarily because she needed a job. She may, of course, have regarded the opportunity to steal as one of the benefits—one of the perquisites, as it were—of any job. This was in Cannes, after all—a city that reeks of inequality

and injustice. Cannes cries out for levelling, and what more direct
way of levelling is there than stealing?

But I simply have no idea what Josephine thought, and I do
not trust my efforts toward sympathy and understanding. I happen not to share the view that no man is an island; I think that
every man is an island in the only sense that matters. How could
I, a middle-class American of formidable insularity, well fed,
satisfied almost to the point of smugness (no doubt I should strike
out the "almost") with the course my life has taken—how could
I conceivably presume to know anything of what this child from
a countryside that Christ Himself is said to have found im-
penetrable, this wasted and pathetic disaster of war who came
to find herself in Babylon, felt or thought, or felt she thought, or
thought she felt, assuming that thought or feeling had anything
to do with it? I have a hard enough time deciding what I myself
think and feel. About Josephine, I know only what events in
fact took place and what I made of some of them.

About two weeks after she came to us, I had to make a trip
to Germany. I was to stay in Bad Godesberg for several days.
On the Monday morning of my departure, Eleanor and I went
in to Cannes, to the American Express office, where I was to
pick up my plane tickets and some money. While we were there,
one of the cashiers asked us to look at some travellers' checks
that had been brought in the preceding Saturday afternoon. The
signatures—Eleanor's on one for fifty dollars, mine on one for ten
dollars—were plainly forged. No one but Josephine could have
got at our checkbooks, and she exactly fitted the cashier's description of the girl who had brought them in and collected some
twenty-one thousand francs. She had presented herself as an employee of ours and had said that the countersigned checks were
wages, and with some misgiving, as the cashier told me, he had
cashed them.

We might have agonized over what to do about this if John
Wason, the office manager, had not settled the matter right away.
He said that in a case like this it was company policy to press
charges immediately. Having our assurance that the checks had

not been signed by us or had been given, unsigned, by us to Josephine, he would file a complaint in the company's name. However, he thought it most unlikely that anything would ever come of it. Josephine, he supposed, had left Cannes as soon as she got the money. He was sure none of us would ever see her again.

I had scarcely any time to talk the news over with Eleanor, for I had left only a few minutes in which to catch the Air France bus for the Nice airport. Eleanor returned to our ridiculous house shortly before noon. She found at the door two plainclothesmen from the Cannes Sûreté, ready to arrest Josephine, who would arrive, if she arrived at all, at one o'clock. (Her hours were from one until seven or eight in the evening.) The "flics" were certain that their quest was futile. Only a fool, they said, would return to her employer after such an adventure in forgery.

Josephine, then, was a fool. Exactly at one, she arrived. She came down the gravelled walk as gay and smiling as ever, and rasped out a "*Bonjour*" to Eleanor, who met her at the door, thoroughly dejected. Eleanor told her there were two men in the living room who wished to talk with her. Josephine showed neither surprise nor fear. She went straight to the living room and, in a few minutes, left with the men from the Sûreté. As far as Eleanor could tell, she was still jaunty.

By evening, I had arrived in Bad Godesberg, and I phoned Cannes and learned these details. Telephoning each evening, I learned more as the week went on, and I heard the last part of the story directly from Eleanor at the end of the week, when I rejoined my family.

Tuesday morning, Eleanor was summoned to the Sûreté, where she found Josephine, Wason, and several police officials. The police began questioning Josephine in Eleanor's presence, and she, with what appeared to be complete self-possession, offered two astonishing defenses. One story was that we had given her the checks and asked her to settle grocers' and butchers' bills with them; we had neglected to countersign them, so she did it to save us the bother. The other story was that she had regularly been cashing checks for me at black-market rates. So persistent had I been, according to her, in availing myself of her brokerage services that the very evening before—that is, the evening after her arrest in my house—I had shown up at her lodgings and implored her to cash some more checks. I had made this visit, she added, accompanied by a woman other than Eleanor. She described my companion—blond and very tall. My wife is brunette and of average height.

Josephine's manner with the police was, Eleanor said, bland, plausible, and altogether pleasant. The police were immediately fetched. They especially liked the black-market story, and encouraged her to fill in more details. (To obtain details about the blond, they took her out of Eleanor's presence. They did not wish to have Josephine provide my wife with grounds for divorce.) They asked none of the questions that seemed painfully obvious to Eleanor and the American Express man: Where did Josephine get the capital to run a *bureau de change*? And why, if she had been cashing my checks at a rate higher than the legal one, had she now taken a heavy loss by redeeming two of them at the legal rate, through American Express?

I suppose that Josephine presented the Sûreté with a portrait of an American that was already fixed in their minds. (Anti-Americanism was high in France in 1953.) Moreover, Cannes was full of tall, blond mistresses, and of men—American or otherwise—low enough to let a poor waif go to jail rather than confess their own waywardness. But better still, Josephine presented them with a story that seemed to have a plot. I have a feeling that policemen the world over are partial to the most fanciful views of crimes. Give them a really farfetched and exotic, erotic explanation of an event and their skepticism begins to dissolve. I first caught on to this back in the Depression, when I earned a living of sorts writing for "true crime" and "true detective" magazines. Once, wishing to know whom to be thankful to, I asked an editor what sort of people read that kind of stuff. "Cops," he said. "Who else? Without cops, you'd be on relief."

The Sûreté men were clucking over Josephine's revelations when Wason interrupted to say that I could not have been at Josephine's the previous evening, with or without a blond, because I had left early that day for Germany, on a trip arranged by his office. He asked Eleanor to confirm the details. She said she had seen me off on the airport bus and that I had phoned her that evening from Bad Godesberg.

The Sûreté men listened indulgently. The head officer said that while he was touched by my wife's confidence in me and had no reason to doubt that it was well founded, surely she would understand that it was the duty of the police to take nothing on faith. Would Madame not agree that seeing me off on a bus to the airport was scarcely proof that I had actually boarded a plane and left the country? And while it was entirely possible that I had telephoned from Germany, the call could just as well have come from any bar or hotel in Cannes or Nice or Monte Carlo. It was infuriating, Eleanor said, to see Gallic logic and common sense come into play that late in the day.

Next, there was an interlude that we might today think of as comic if it had not been so quickly followed by disaster. Wason suggested that Josephine's story could quite easily be tested. I had flown on Air France flight so-and-so. That could be checked. And Air France could easily find out whether I had deplaned in Germany. Also, there would be an exit-visa record at the Passport Control office in the airport. The Sûreté agreed to investigate, and a detective was assigned to check immediately with Air France. (It was not until some weeks later that we learned that all this time another flic had been busily telephoning hotels up and down the Riviera, from Saint-Raphael, to the west, to San Remo, in Italy, to learn whether anyone answering to my description had registered with a blond the night before.) As for the call to Air France, the Sûreté must have known from experience what the outcome would be. Air France said that a ticket had been issued in my name and that a passenger holding the ticket had boarded the plane in Nice; however, the airline would not take the responsibility of saying that the user of the ticket and the man the Sûreté sought were one and the same person. Air France doesn't fingerprint its passengers.

The detective came back to the inquiry room and gravely reported what he had learned, or failed to learn. He was then instructed to check with Passport Control. A short while later, he returned to say that the Nice airport had no record of my *sortie*. Of course, this might be explained by some procedural lag, but at the moment it appeared that I had not boarded the plane at Nice.

This seemed to settle it for the police. Josephine's story had met the test. The case would have to go to trial, if American Express persisted, but it looked to the Sûreté like a feeble one. Josephine and Eleanor were dismissed, pending a further call. Then Wason (he told us the story later) was taken aside and asked if American Express would withdraw the complaint. To go any further with this matter, the police said, would be simply to contribute to the destruction of a family. What had already come out was bad enough. And that was only a beginning. The police hinted that they knew a good deal about me, and that none of what they knew was good. (As it turned out, the Sûreté had borrowed from the telegraph office copies of all the wires I had sent from Cannes. The purpose of most of these had been to make appointments with various people I wished to meet. But the flics, with their love of intrigue, had read these communications as coded messages arranging assignations.*) Their general idea seemed to be that it would be a poor bargain in human terms if American Express recovered sixty dollars at the cost of a broken home. Wason explained to the police, as he had explained to us, that he had no choice in the matter.

---

* They were particularly suspicious of wires inquiring about the availability for lunch or dinner of Mlle. Janette Flannaire in Paris. Janet Flanner, *The New Yorker*'s Paris correspondent, was a good friend, but she belonged to my mother's generation, not mine, and our frequent times together were purely social and professional.

It is possible only to conjecture what happened after that. At some point, evidently, Passport Control at Nice notified the Cannes Sûreté that my *sortie* card had turned up and that it was necessary to presume that I had reached Germany. This must have been disillusioning to the police; they had sold themselves on the idea that I was really at Eden Roc with my blond, living riotously on money I had practically extorted from poor little Josephine. But, disillusioned or not, they must have got in touch with Josephine to advise her that because her story no longer seemed to hold together, they wished to see her in the morning.

I suppose that pathos follows the classic rule of tragedy and that its measure is the distance between what might have been and what is. Chaucer says that there must be a "dite of prosperite" before the ending in "wrecchydnesse." Did Josephine feel she was prospering when the police believed her absurd tale? Who could know, or even make an intelligent guess? I suspect it was luck, rather than art, that made her such a success with the police. She had had no practice at that sort of thing. She had never been arrested before—had no police record at all. This knowledge gave us our sense of what might have been. Since the offense was her first, nothing really terrible could have happened to her. The court would probably have been lenient with her as a first offender; she could have made some arrangement to pay back the sixty dollars, and for the rest she would probably have been given a suspended sentence. Possibly she would have been sent back to Italy—not too dreadful a fate by 1953.

If only the police had not made a big police deal out of the whole affair, Josephine could have been taken aside and had it explained that the sixty dollars wasn't a great amount—she could earn the sum in about a month—and that she was a very foolish girl to attempt to brazen it out. But what might have been was not. The police must have told Josephine she was in deep trouble. That evening, someone in her building smelled a noxious odor outside her door, entered, and found Josephine Cianni with her head in the oven.

She was taken to the hospital and put in an oxygen tent. She did not die until the next evening, but she never regained consciousness.

I returned from Bad Godesberg not knowing this, and hoping to help clear things up. Eleanor and I had decided, in our phone talks, that we should offer to take Josephine back. We were transient in France, and if we were simply to carry our checks around in our pockets, there would be nothing of value for her to steal. What Eleanor had to tell me when she met me at the airport was that unless we hurried, we would be late for Josephine's funeral. We hurried.

I hope that I shall never again have to go to a pauper's obsequies in France. Seven people attended. Besides ourselves, there were Josephine's father and sister; a girl who had tended a machine with Josephine in a factory; Onelia, who had talked the church into giving her a Christian burial, probably advancing the theory that her death was not suicide but an accident; and our landlady, Mme. Jaugey. Eleanor had not told the children of Josephine's death, and had arranged for them to be elsewhere that afternoon. Mme. Jaugey had not known Josephine, but had found it convenient to go along because it was All Souls', the Catholic day of remembrance, when it is customary to tend and decorate graves. We rode with her, in her '52 Vedette.

We were introduced by Onelia to Josephine's father and sister, but neither we nor they did more than acknowledge the introductions. Perhaps they thought us responsible for Josephine's death. They gave no sign of thinking anything. (That morning's *Nice-Matin* had said that Josephine left a note proclaiming her innocence. The note was not quoted, and when I later tried to learn about it from the police, I was rebuffed. I suspect there was no note and the story that one had been left was merely a face-saving invention of the police.) Eleanor had been told by someone that the father had a long record as a petty criminal, and that Josephine was probably acting under his instructions. We never particularly wanted to learn the truth of this.

The seven of us sat in the front of the church while an unshaven, expressionless young priest raced through the shortest possible service. Josephine's coffin was tossed onto a pickup truck. We had sent some flowers, and so had her factory friend. These hung from spikes at the sides of the truck. There was a great throng in the cemetery, which was on a hill overlooking the sea and was surrounded by gorgeous thickets of mimosa. We had nothing to do with the throng. We proceeded to the paupers' section—an open ditch in which the cheap coffins were put down end to end. Josephine was hurriedly lowered into the ditch while the unshaven priest hastily mumbled a short prayer, after which an aged pensioner, almost ready for the ditch himself, began to shovel.

We returned to our preposterous villa as soon as Mme. Jaugey had arranged some flowers around her family tombs, which were expensive and chic.

## 2. SEE NAPLES AND DROP DEAD

*Vedi Napoli e poi muori.*
See Naples and die—Italian proverb
*See Naples and Die*—Title of a 1929 play by Elmer Rice

Whenever there is talk in our house of what to do about New Year's Eve, my mind goes back to 1953 and the New Year's Eve we spent in Naples, Italy—or, to be more precise, in Appartamento 336 of the Grand Albergo de Londres on the Piazza Municipio in that city. This was not quite what we had planned. We had been living for a few months in the South of France, and we had arranged a week's trip to Italy while the children were on holiday. The five of us, joined by my mother, had gone by boat from Cannes to Naples, via Genoa and Palermo, and although we expected to spend three or four days sightseeing in and around Naples—Pompeii, Vesuvius, Amalfi, the regular guidebook rounds —we had thought we would do the whole thing up brown by celebrating the arrival of 1954 on Capri. "Spend New Year's Eve at the Quisisana," a knowledgeable friend in Cannes had said. "It'll be something you'll never forget." We reserved rooms at the Quisisana. We never saw the place. We never saw Capri, owing to certain misfortunes that befell us in Naples. Indeed, in a manner of speaking, we never saw Naples, either. What we mostly saw was the gloomy interior of Appartamento 336. Still, the time we had was memorable. Not many New Year's Eves stand out in my mind the way December 31, 1953, does.

Our troubles were largely—in fact, entirely—financial. I wish I had a record of how much money we took on our trip, but I haven't. I had been travelling around Europe a good deal, juggling currencies like a Zurich *bankdirektor*. The funds for our Naples trip were partly in dollars, partly in French and Swiss francs, partly in lire I had left over from a visit to Rome the month before, partly in assorted other currencies. In any case, I know that what I took should have been enough to cover expenses—and then some. I have the heart and mind of an accountant—I love making audits, balancing assets and liabilities, adding things up, making advance estimates—and I cheerily applied myself to the problem at hand. Having recently been in Italy, I knew pretty well what things cost. For this trip, I planned generously, not to say lavishly. In a way, it was to be our farewell to Europe, for we were due to return home in January. Also, it was the only real excursion our children were to have during their stay abroad. "Let's make this a real caper," I said, and that was what I figured on as I got things ready. I remember that when I had everything worked out, and all the money in hand, I decided to take along a hundred-dollar traveller's check besides. I questioned my own judgment on this, for I could conceive of no emergency I had not already reckoned on. But I already had the check, the last of an earlier series, and I decided in favor of taking it when I recalled that the *cambios* in Italy were selling French francs at a favorable rate. Might as well improve our lot by cashing it there, I told myself.

I was catastrophically wrong. My error, as I was shortly to learn, was in thinking of Naples as another Italian city. It didn't take me long to learn that Naples is a conspiracy. I was not, of course, ignorant of its reputation. I have a modest knowledge of history, and it served to remind me, even as I was planning our trip, that many of the techniques of larceny and highbinding that one encounters in our own great civilization were developed and refined over the centuries by gifted Neapolitans. I expected to be preyed upon, and my budget estimate included sums set aside for both defense and tribute. But I was guilty of an excess of pride and national spirit. Though I knew that I had not seen everything, I thought that a man who had spent most of his life in New York, who had met up with fleecers and flummoxers westward to the blue Pacific and eastward to Paris and Berlin, would not encounter too much that was unfamiliar to him in Naples, a city that had, as I understood it, already seen its best days.

How foolish I was, how mistaken my self-confidence had been, I knew on New Year's Eve, as I sat despondently in Appartamento 336, my ears assailed by a din comparable in volume to the siege of Stalingrad, my mind vainly attempting to concentrate on the horrible thing before me—a writing table littered with frayed and filthy lira notes and addled scratching on the Londres stationery. As I awaited, tremblingly, the momentous year that was drawing to a close, I was engaged in some of the most frantic and irregular bookkeeping in the entire history of accountancy. The ugly truth was that the Neapolitans had worked me like creamery butter. I was suffering acute financial embarrassment. So skillfully and so remorselessly had they parted this fool from his money that there was serious doubt as to whether I, together with those nearest and dearest to me, would be free to board the Andrea Doria on the morning of January 2nd and return to France, where, I reflected fondly, thievery was an artless, primitive thing.

I was dealing, of course, with imponderables. Who can know how often he is to be cheated? Was the banditry I had thus far experienced to continue at its present rate? Would the holiday weekend bring, perhaps, a spirit of mercy, of live-and-let-live, to the Neapolitans, or would resolutions be made of increased flimflamming efficiency? How was I to know? True, I could work out certain rough calculations as to what our hotel bill would be. *"Quant'è?"* I had asked in my phrase-book Italian when we registered, and I had been given a basic figure that was somewhere on the good side of exorbitant. A notice posted in the room informed us of the extra charges—service, taxes, heating, and so forth. But innkeepers are resourceful men, and I realized that any estimate I made would be rough indeed. Surely, the amount we would be expected to turn over to the Londres would be greater than the sum of the parts. My respect for the management was considerable.

What made my situation truly desperate was the fact that I faced it on New Year's Eve. At almost any other time, there would have been some way out. I might, for example, have persuaded the local office of American Express to honor a personal check. Or I might have gone to the American Consulate and thrown myself on the mercy of my government. Or I might have wired my office in New York and tested the loyalty of my employers with a request for a cash advance by cable. But it was New Year's Eve, a Thursday. The American Express, the Consulate, and my office in New York would all be closed until Monday morning, by which time we were due back in Cannes. In Naples, I knew only one man, a former Hollywood scenarist who had become a successful Italian book publisher. However, I had met him only once in my life, and I did not think I could summon the nerve to arrange a second meeting for the purpose of borrowing money.

I had got into this fix after spending less than three days in Naples. We had arrived, flush in more ways than one, on the evening of December 28th. We all liked the idea of visiting Naples and had our plans carefully laid. On the boat, we had picked up a lusciously illustrated brochure entitled "Four Days in Napoli." Since four days was exactly what we had—less one night on Capri—we studied it attentively. It recommended a scheme for seeing the wonders of the city and the region in four separate swings, and we agreed to adopt it, with certain minor modifications. A copy of it was on the hotel desk as I totted up figures on New Year's Eve. It quoted Shelley, as nearly as I can remember:

> Naples, thou Heart of men, which ever pantest
> Naked, beneath the lidless eye of heaven!

The first Neapolitan we met was the first to fleece us. The second was a confederate. (This is a tautology of sorts, since all Neapolitans are confederates.) The first was a dockside baggage handler. He took our bags from the ship and moved them to customs. When I met up with him there, I reached in my pocket and fished out about five hundred lire—eighty cents or so. I knew this was meagre payment for handling the baggage of six people, but it was, as I tried to explain and as I am quite certain he understood, all I had at the moment. I had distributed a king's ransom in tips before leaving the boat, and was awaiting a chance to buy more lire at the pier exchange. I knew we would meet again after customs, and I tried to convey the notion that I would reward him more suitably then. *"Piu-dopo,"* I said, feeling very much of a dopo as I said it but being reasonably certain that he, too, spoke basic Berlitz. After inspection, however, and after my visit to the exchange, the man was nowhere in sight. Other passengers were moving along nicely and getting into taxis or cars, but the Roveres were stuck, almost alone, in the great shed. Just as I was about to take some sort of direct action—carry the bags myself or find another porter—I was approached by a brisk young man, who addressed me by name and in confident English. He said he was a travel agent and had been notified of our arrival and of our probable need for guidance. I thought this an unlikely story, but I was glad to see him anyway. I told him of our problem, and he said he would see what could be done. He went off, and reappeared in a suspiciously short time. Our porter, he said, was sulking. How so? Because, he said, I had given him only twenty-five lire. Before I could nail this lie, he had begun to explain that my error was not only pardonable but easily understandable. As an American, he said, I must have thought of twenty-five lire as the equivalent of twenty-five cents—"I think you call it one quarter"—and this, unfortunately, was not the case. I wanted to point out that this was a double insult, but I didn't bother; I simply listened as he went on to say that we could assuage the porter's hurt feelings with a thousand lire. The sum did not seem unreasonable—it was about what I'd have given him anyway—so I forked it over. The speed with which the porter returned suggested that he had been lurking behind a nearby pillar the whole time. He put the baggage on his dolly and wheeled it out to the taxi stand. The rest of the family boarded the conveyance we were taking to the Londres, and I stood by while the bags were being loaded in the trunk. As I prepared to get in, after the job was done, I found the porter barring my access. By this time, I had a heavy wad of thousand-lira notes and a few smaller ones to fill out the dollar value. Happy to be on our way at last, I did not begrudge the porter all the bills of smaller denominations. I was still in a fool's paradise. "Get that sort of thing on any waterfront," I told Eleanor as I settled down beside her.

It was no ordinary cab that we took to the Londres. Our friend the travel agent had told us that on thinking our problem over, in advance of our arrival, it had occurred to him that we might suffer discomfort if we had to ride from dockside to the hotel in an ordinary Naples taxi. He had therefore ordered a limousine. It would cost a trifle extra, of course, and we could dismiss it if we wished, but it seemed to him that we would be better off in a limousine. It seemed so to me, too. I had no idea how long a ride it would be to our hotel, and the Naples taxis were not very roomy. We were six and with all our impedimenta, we would have had to take two cabs, as we had often done before. The limousine hire, the agent said, would be two thousand lire—a little under three-and-a-half dollars. Fair enough, I said. The travel agent, who seemed to enjoy our company, sat up front with the driver. The echo of the slamming door had scarcely died away before I heard him saying, "And this is your hotel, *prima-classe*, one of our finest."

"Already!" I said. Ah, yes, we had chosen well, the Londres

was centrally located. Central or not, it was handy for fishermen; it was, in fact, just across the square from the pier, and we could have walked the distance in three minutes.

We climbed out of the car we had so recently climbed into. I paid the driver the two thousand lire and gave him a thousand note for a tip. I had to do this, since I had nothing but thousands left. I made a mental note to get some change at the first opportunity. The driver went off, the hotel porters took our bags, and I found myself in the lobby with the travel agent. He wanted, he said, to devote himself exclusively to us during our stay in Naples. I explained that we were an adventurous lot and would try to get along on our own. I suggested that he give me his card, so that we could get in touch with him if our adventurousness flagged. He gave me his card. I gave him three thousand lire and thanked him.

Appartamento 336, when I reached it, was swarming with people—porters, maids, bellhops, and some well-dressed men I took to be executives of the Londres corporation. From president down to the lowest menial, each got his thousand lire. "For God's sake," I said to my wife, "remind me to get some change in the morning. These dollar-and-a-half tips could ruin a man." I spoke, unknowingly, with the voice of a prophet. We all went to bed.

After breakfast, which we took in the hotel dining room, I went to the cashier and asked if he would kindly break a few of my thousand-lira notes up into hundreds and five hundreds. Of course, he said, but would we mind waiting until a bit later in the morning? He had not yet had time to send a courier to the bank, and he had no change on hand. Our time in Naples was short enough anyway, and we decided not to wait. "You can get change anywhere," Eleanor said. "Let's take a cab to the Museo Nazionale and start out from there." This seemed reasonable but wasn't. The metered taxi fare came to two hundred and forty lire. Here's my chance, I thought as I yielded up one more thousand-lira note and stood awaiting my change. The driver observed my happy, expectant look, and it obviously pained him to disappoint me. He took his wallet from his hip pocket and opened it for my inspection. Empty. I decided that I had been bilked for the last time. I was not going to tip seven hundred and sixty lire for a two-hundred-and-forty-lire ride. We had stopped just outside a small shop, and I pointed to it. *"Uno secondo,"* I said, as commandingly as I could. I went into the shop and asked the clerk to change a thousand-lira note. I do not know whether any signals passed between clerk and driver, but I did observe the clerk looking through the door and seeing the taxi, with my family standing beside it, and I have no doubt that he sized up the situation for what it was. He opened his cash drawer, picked out a few notes and coins, and shrugged. He couldn't make it. The driver got his three-hundred-percent tip.

Naples, for us, was a city in which the cost of everything had to be computed to the nearest—or, rather, the farthest—thousand lire. Now and then, we got change by making small, pointless purchases, but we ran through it in no time and, more often than not, found ourselves with nothing but what we took to calling G notes. Of course, we were never stuck with the same ones very long. I can scarcely begin to describe the boldness and variety of the techniques used to relieve us of them. There was, for example, the matter of the double fare to Pompeii. On the morning of our second day in Naples, we set out for the famous ruins. We went in a rickety sightseeing bus that left from the Piazza Municipio. The round trip for six was eighty-four-hundred lire—or nine thousand, since the driver could not make change. I paid up cheerfully. "This will be no ordinary bus ride," I told my wife. "It is not space we are to traverse but time. Fifteen dollars is not much for a trip back across the millennia." In anticipation of my approaching rendezvous with Bulwer-Lytton, I put all care aside and prepared to enjoy the trip. In a few minutes, we were outside Naples and, to our surprise, witnessing a change of drivers. The new man came aboard and started down the aisle to collect fares. The first passenger he approached— there were perhaps a dozen people in the bus besides us—pointed out that we had all paid our fares in Naples. I could not follow all the talk that ensued, but I gathered that the new driver's point was that the laborer is worthy of his hire, and that so far no one had paid him anything. Our choice now was between going on to Pompeii, at double fare, and walking back to Naples. We and our fellow-passengers chose Pompeii.

Even the children of Naples had a go at us. Still adhering slavishly to the advice of "Four Days in Napoli," we set out, after our morning visit to Pompeii, to walk the length of the Via Caracciolo. As we gloried in the sights along this splendid boulevard, our advance was halted by massed artillery fire. Some fifty feet ahead of us was a band of Neapolitan urchins firing some sort of guided missiles that shot along the sidewalk at ankle elevation. Unfamiliar with this type of ordnance and, in any case, uncertain of the enemy's intent, I ordered my advance units—Ann, Mark, Betsy—to pull back and join the rest in a defensive position afforded by a parked truck. Barely had my command been obeyed when a youth of fourteen or so—the others, I judged, were a good deal younger than that—emerged from a doorway, strode briskly up to the guerrilla lines, and arranged a cease-fire. "It's all right now," he called back to us. We came out from behind the truck, our former assailants stepped aside to give us safe passage, and the youth fell in alongside us, keeping pace long enough for me to rummage in my pockets for a few lire. I could not find a few lire, but I could find a thousand, which he got.

It was in our home away from home, the Londres, that the heaviest assaults on our stake were made. I have spent more of my life than I like to think about in hotels, and the sly, grasping ways of room clerks, bellhops, busboys, and maids are as familiar to me as the ways of butchers, bakers, and the rest are to Eleanor. But nothing in my long, rich experience had prepared me for the staff of the Londres. To this day, I am at a loss to understand how the entire working force of that hotel managed to assemble outside our rooms every time we left them. It was a miracle of communication and mobilization. Not once did we attempt a break from Appartamento 336 without finding our course of egress lined with maids, porters, waiters, valets, and various other sub-Boniface types. They did not "line" the corridor exactly but, rather, were deployed in it in such a way that if I averted my gaze from a charwoman whose eyes told me that she needed money for six undernourished *bambini*, it fell upon the insolent countenance of a bellhop that clearly advised me that if I wanted to hang on to the possessions I had left behind in the appartamento, I would pay off—and fast. I could no more have run that broken field untouched than I could have plunged through the Fordham line when it was manned by the Seven Blocks of Granite. My calculations show that our exits from our quarters and our descent from third floor to lobby cost on an average seventeen-hundred-and-sixty lire each. The staff was somewhat less successful at rallying for our return trips, and I do not seem to have any computations on the cost of reentering our rooms. But I know that just as we never left the Londres without paying, so we never returned without being the poorer for it.

It was a small transaction I had with the man at the Londres travel desk that revealed the Neapolitan genius at its most effulgent. My mother was planning to leave us on the morning of December 31st and spend a few days in Rome. She had been advised that the trip was most beautiful by bus, and she planned to make it that way. Arrangements had been made in Cannes, and she was already ticketed when we arrived in Naples. But there had been some uncertainty in the Cannes office of American Express about the exact time of the bus's departure, and we decided to clear this up when we got to Naples. The evening before my mother was to leave, I went down to the travel desk—paying the usual bribes to get there—and asked the agent on duty if he would be good enough to fill in on her ticket the time the bus was scheduled to leave. From the blank, incredulous look he gave me, one might have thought I had requested a brief discourse on Hegelian dialectical method. The information I sought, he said, was very difficult to come by, and surely I could not be so unreasonable as to expect him to supply it at that late hour of the day. This was, as I recall, about six o'clock. Flabbergasted, I said that I had assumed he could just consult a timetable and tell me when Bus 169, or whatever it was, left Naples. I was now favored with a look of infinite condescension and pity. It would be nice if things were that simple, the agent said, but, alas, they were not. To learn the hour of the bus's departure would require, for one thing, patience; for another, hard work; and, for still another, the exercise of influence. It was now my turn to look incredulous, as this double-tongue told me in fruit peddler's English how lucky it was for me that he knew some people of substance in Naples. It was barely possible, he said, that if he exploited these associations of his he might have the good fortune to be able to serve me as I wished to be served. It all sounded as though I were negotiating the purchase of Cabinet secrets. He said he thought—at least he hoped—he would be able to offer me some encouragement by midnight. As his last word on the subject, he pointed out that to undertake my project he would have to make extensive use of the telephone.

I got the point; in fact, I was way ahead of him. As he was talking, I had been toying with the possibility of sneaking around behind him and snatching from beneath his counter the stack of timetables I knew was there. But there was a kind of Old World weariness in me, too, and I gave him a few hundred lire—I was in change at the moment—and implored him to do his best. I snake-hipped my way upstairs, then paid my family's way back downstairs, to dinner. As we were about to enter the hotel restaurant, the agent called me aside and told me that, contrary to all his expectations and by an almost unimaginable stroke of good fortune, he had been able, at this early hour, to find out when the bus left. Well, when, I said. He smiled and began riffling some papers on his counter. I could see that it was a case of either twisting the brute's arm or ponying up. I chose the coward's way.

We saw my mother off for Rome in the morning. New Year's Eve was upon us, and I had to decide quickly whether we could afford Capri. I decided we could not. Indeed, I didn't see how we could afford to do anything more in Naples. Mount Vesuvius was on the schedule for that day, and Mark and Ann, who had been on a volcano kick for months, were looking forward to it more than to anything else. I had to tell them the volcano was out. "Hush," I said as they began to whine and beef about seeing museums and castles and statues of repulsive old cornballs but never, never, oh, no, never any craters. "You don't know when you're well off. There's a vice lord from New York named Lucky Luciano who's moved in on this Vesuvius thing. They say that if you don't pay him nine zillion lire, you're as likely as not to go for a ride in the boiling lava. Maybe it's better this way." "You're so right," Ann said. I explained our plight, and announced that we were giving up sightseeing and going on short rations until we boarded the Andrea Doria. "We can afford three light meals a day," I said, "but that's all."

We passed the day glumly. We took a brief walk after breakfast and another after lunch, but it was too cold for this form of sightseeing, and we could afford no other. It was along about sundown when I was seized with the realization that we might very well not have enough money to pay our hotel bill and get out of Naples on the morning of January 2nd. Until then, I had taken it for granted that our economies would see us through, but suddenly I sensed that, even with the spare traveller's check, this was by no means certain. The thing that gave rise to this and struck icy terror into my heart was the sight of a more fortunate resident of the Londres making his getaway. I was at the cashier's desk for some reason—probably to plead for change— and I caught sight of the departing guest going over his bill. A glance was enough to tell me that this was a document of a length and complexity never dreamed of even by the Bureau of Internal Revenue. Immediately upon my return to Appartamento 336, I began my feverish audits. I asked Eleanor and the children to go through all pockets and pocketbooks in search of currency in any denomination from any country. While this was being done, I began my efforts to strike an estimate of our probable expenses for the thirty-six hours we were still to spend in Naples. "Think," I said. "Think hard. We must count the number of porters we are going to need before we board ship. Our transportation requirements must be cut to the bone, and we must figure their cost. We must rack our brains to think of the things they are going to put on the hotel bill. Believe me, these people have racked their brains. There'll be things we've never before heard of. I would not be surprised to find a percentage for wear and tear on the rugs. Probably a fare for every elevator ride. I saw that other man's bill. It was the size of a census taker's chart. The one word I caught was '*sciroppi*.' He was charged for many thousand lire's worth. In God's name, fetch the dictionary and see what it is. *Sciroppi* could make all the difference between our leaving on Monday and languishing here until the Embassy makes representations in Rome. How many lire for five Swiss francs? . . . '*Sciroppi*' means 'syrup'? Who ever heard of syrups on a hotel bill? Oh, we're .in for a kitty-hopping all right, all right."

It is a weakness of my nature that I get into these feverish states whenever my plans threaten to go awry. Our plight, after all, was not as desperate as I made it out to be. At the worst, we would have had to stay over only a day or so—until we could get money from New York or Cannes. It was not as if we had been cast loose in a desert or adrift at sea. But such calming thoughts never come to mind until after a crisis is past. And even if I had been differently constituted, I would have found it difficult to entertain calming thoughts at that particular time. For as New Year's Eve settled over Naples, and as I moved deeper and deeper into the realms of pure speculation, a clatter from outside began to assail my ears and further derange my powers of reason. It was a strange, wild noise—not a hubbub, or what we used to call a Dutch concert. It was not the sound of gaiety or revelling; in fact, human voices only occasionally punctuated it. It was rather as if inanimate objects—furniture, machinery, pipes, and the like—were dropping, throwing, kicking, and generally assaulting one another. At any rate, it had the effect of increasing my anxieties and disordering my calculations.

At about half past ten, after the children had gone to bed, I decided that there was no point in any more bookkeeping. I suggested to Eleanor that we should not let New Year's Eve pass wholly uncelebrated. "It's in the lap of the gods," I said. "Let's go to the bar and order one glass of inexpensive wine. At least we can watch other people enjoying themselves." From the noise outside, growing in volume all the time now, I assumed that at last we would be treated to some of the more ingratiating Neapolitan characteristics. Although, as I have said, the human voice was not much heard in the din, we took it for granted that the spirit behind it was one of joy and festivity, and I guess we both expected to find the lobby and bar of this prima-classe hotel full of people having a better time than we were. The lobby was empty, utterly deserted. The bar was patronized by exactly two people— sailors from our own Sixth Fleet, attached to the NATO headquarters in Naples. They sat at a table drinking Italian beer and were as much the picture of dejection as we were. We ordered some wine and, after a time, engaged them in a spiritless conversation, which elicited such information as that one came from Troy, New York, the other from Harrisburg, Pennsylvania; that the first was a mechanic, the other a cook; that the Troy man was expecting an early transfer and the Harrisburg man wasn't. We went along on that level until Eleanor asked how it was that they had chosen to spend the evening in as dull a fashion as this. "They must be having a good time somewhere," she said. "Just listen to all that noise outside."

The Troy man shuddered. "We know," he said. "That's why we're here. We came in when all that started, and we don't leave until morning. It wouldn't be safe to."

"How is that?" I asked.

The inquiry stimulated the only true animation we had encountered up to that point. "I'll tell you how it is," the Troy mechanic said. "I'll tell you all about it. I've spent four years here, and I think I know. You see, these people here are poor. Nice people, wonderful people, but poor. I guess you can see that for yourselves. Now, what they do is this: they put aside little bits of money all through the year. Fifty lire here, a hundred there —everyone in the family chips in. They save and they scrimp and they do without things, so they'll have a little something by the end of the year. Well, then they go out to the store and they buy themselves"—here he looked at my wife and chose his words with delicacy—"they buy themselves a commode. A beautiful commode, shiny, with roses painted on it. They have real pretty commodes here; you just look in the stores and see. They get one packed up nicely, and they take it home very carefully, maybe a day or two before the end of the year. You get the picture now—the year's savings are tied up in that commode, and they're very happy about it. They look at it and say *bellissimo*, and think to themselves how lucky they are to have it by New Year's Eve. Then"—and now our narrator became rather agitated, his voice loud and unsteady—"then New Year's Eve comes, and they fling open the windows, and they pitch the Goddamned commode out into the street. That's what they do—they smash that beautiful thing into a million pieces. So you see—that's what's going on out there now. All the commodes in Naples are flying around."

Shaken by the mariner's tale, we finished our wine, said our farewells, and left. In the bar, a dreary but apparently well-insulated place, we had heard only faintly the crashing of commodes outside. In the deserted lobby and in our rooms, the roar now—it was, I should judge, about eleven-fifteen—was deafening. It had waked the children, and it made sleep impossible for us. We threw open the shutters to see what we could of the destruction outside. Our rooms were not very advantageously located for this, but we could see perhaps a half-dozen places where the arrival of 1954 was being celebrated by the hurling of objects to the pavement below. I could not tell whether any new commodes were part of the fallout, but doubtless they were. From what we saw and heard, the sailor knew his Naples well. We stood gaping at the lunatic scene until about three in the morning, when the racket began to subside. Then we retired for a few hours of fitful sleep.

We lived frugally on New Year's Day and had a long, untroubled sleep that night. The next morning, full of apprehension, I paid our way downstairs for the last time, went to the cashier's counter for the last time, and called for our bill. It came—the same massive form I had seen the other guest studying. I quickly looked at the total, and discovered that it fell about five dollars short of my total holdings. That being the case, I asked no questions. About four of the five dollars went in getting us and our luggage safely aboard the Andrea Doria. In the stateroom, I sat down and studied the bill. We had been taken for five hundred lire's worth of syrup.

# VII

## McCarthy and Company

### I. I'VE GOT A PAPER HERE

I first met Senator Joseph R. McCarthy in May 1949, about a year before he went to Wheeling, West Virginia, and held aloft the piece of paper that made him famous. (He said it was a list of Communists in the State Department. It turned out to be a letter from Secretary of State, James F. Byrnes, Representative to Adolph Sabath of Illinois, and had no list of Communists or of anything else in it.) I was in Washington, and I dropped in at a Senate hearing at which testimony was being taken on the alleged mistreatment by Americans of some German S.S. men, members of an outfit called the Blowtorch Battalion, who had been accused of massacring a hundred and fifty United States troops and a hundred Belgian civilians at a crossroads named Malmédy, in December 1944. I had been in the hearing room only a few minutes when McCarthy became involved in an altercation with Senator Raymond E. Baldwin of Connecticut, a fellow Republican who has since become a judge on the Supreme Court of Errors in Hartford.

It was an angry exchange. McCarthy took the view that the Americans had in fact been guilty of brutal conduct. In this first brush with the Army, he claimed that it was coddling not Communists but sadists and crooked lawyers. He said that he had documentary proof of this but that Baldwin, intent for some unexplained reason on protecting the accused men, wouldn't pay any attention to it. Baldwin insisted he wasn't trying to protect anyone. After a while, McCarthy rose from his seat, stuffed a lot of papers into his briefcase, and left the room, saying he would no longer be a party to a shameful farce, a "deliberate and clever attempt to whitewash the American military."

Curious about the dispute and at that time ignorant of its background, I followed McCarthy into the corridor and asked him if he would be kind enough to tell me what he was in such a stew about. He said he would be glad to, and suggested that I go with him to his office. "It's time the American people knew about this," he said. "These documents will speak for themselves." He hefted up the bulging briefcase to give me some idea of the sheer bulk of them. "When you've looked at a few of my documents, you'll agree with me that this is one of the most outrageous things the country has ever known." I said that if this was the case, I'd certainly feel privileged to be allowed to inspect them. "You'll see them, all right," he said. "I'm not holding anything back. I'm through with this investigation, and I'm taking my case to the public."

He struck me as being a bit overwrought, but on the whole he seemed an earnest and plausible young Senator. Though he used extravagant language, his tone was restrained, his manner almost gentle. As we walked along through the wide, echoing corridors of the Senate Office Building, he kept talking of the magnitude of his revelations, and although I had wanted—for a starter, at least— just a brief résumé of his side of the story, he succeeded in whetting my appetite for the contents of the briefcase.

We reached his office at last and sat down at his desk. He emptied the briefcase and piled the papers up in front of him. "Let's see, now," he said as he thumbed his way down toward the middle of the pile. "I know just the thing I want you to see first. I've got one thing here that's a real eye-opener. Oh, yes, here we are now." He pulled out several pages of photostat paper and handed them to me. "I think the facts will mean more to you than anything I could say. Once you've looked this over, you'll see that Baldwin has been playing a pretty sinister role in trying to whitewash the administration."

I read rapidly through what he gave me. Then I read it a second time, more carefully. When I'd finished the second reading, I was certain that the Senator had selected the wrong document. I no longer recall just what was in it, but it was a letter from one Army officer or government official to another, and although it had, as I recall, some bearing on the Malmédy affair, it didn't seem to me to prove anything about anything. I told McCarthy that as far as I could see, it was a pretty routine piece of correspondence.

"You're certainly right about that," he said. "Don't get me wrong, now. I didn't mean you'd find the whole story there. Standing alone, it doesn't mean much—I know that just as well as you do. But it's a link in a chain. It's one piece in a jigsaw puzzle. When you've seen some of the other documents, you'll know what I mean."

This was reassuring. In fact, I felt a bit ashamed of myself for expecting to master a complex situation in a few minutes. I began to read the next document McCarthy handed me. "Now, when you put these two together," he said, "you get a picture." The second document was mainly a listing of names. None of them meant anything to me. I tried to think what connection they might have with the letter I'd just read or with Senator Baldwin. I tried to "put them together," as McCarthy had advised, and "get a picture." No picture came. I confessed this to the Senator.

"Exactly," he said. "That's exactly my point. Those names mean nothing to you. They didn't mean anything to me, either, when I began to look into this conspiracy. But they're going to mean something to you before long, I can guarantee you that. I wanted you to have a look at them, because when you've seen some of the other things I've got here, you'll see how this jigsaw puzzle fits together. Now just bear those names in mind."

I tried to bear the names in mind and found it was impossible. Nothing unsticks faster than names you can't associate with real people. But although it was, I thought, curious that the Senator hadn't shown me the documents explaining the significance of the names before showing me the names themselves, I continued to be impressed by his manner. And the papers themselves were impressive—not by virtue of their contents but by virtue of their existence. Photostats and carbon copies and well-kept newspaper clippings have, I think, an authority of their own for most people; we assume that no one would go to the bother of assembling them if they didn't prove something.

As McCarthy sat at his desk sorting out the papers, putting some in a stack to his right and some in a stack to his left and consigning others to a filing cabinet behind him, he seemed knowledgeable and efficient. "I'm just trying to put this picture together for you," he kept saying. Two or three times in the course of our interview, which must have lasted about an hour and a half, he called in a secretary and asked her to fetch him some document that wasn't among those he had taken to the hearing. I wondered as I watched him what had become of the promise to provide a blinding illumination with a single document, but for quite a while I assumed it was my fault, not his, that I wasn't grasping the details very well.

McCarthy kept handing papers across the desk to me. "Here are a few more links in the chain," he would say as he handed me more correspondence, more lists, and a good many pictures of the Germans who had accused the Americans of brutality, of the accused Americans, of Malmédy farmhouses, and of Army barracks in Occupied Germany. None of them seemed to advance his argument by very much—by anything at all, in fact—but then he was no longer claiming very much for them.

"You don't get to the bottom of these things in a few minutes," he said. "Especially when so many powerful people are trying to hide the truth. Believe me, it wasn't easy for me to put this story together."

At one point he handed me a rather thick document. "I don't want you to leave without seeing this," he said. "Here we have the facts in the Army's own records. This is a transcript of the first hearing on this affair. This is what Baldwin and the administration are trying to cover up. Remember, now, this is from the records the Army itself kept."

I read here and there in the record the Army itself kept, and told McCarthy that, perhaps because of my ignorance, I was unable to see any holes in the Army's case.

"Of course you don't," he said. "Naturally, they're going to make out the best case they can for themselves. You wouldn't expect them to spill the beans in their own records, would you? The whole thing is a pack of lies."

I was beginning to get a bit impatient, though I tried not to show it. I said that as I understood the situation, he, McCarthy, was persuaded that the Malmédy massacre was a fiction of our own military authorities, that Germans had been tortured into confessing acts that had never been committed, and that a Republican Senator, a man with a considerable reputation for probity, was trying to protect the torturers. I was about to go on to say that thus far nothing he had shown me established the truth of all this. But McCarthy interrupted me.

"That's right," he said, in a manner that suggested appreciation of my insight and my gift of summation. "You're beginning to get the picture now. I think the next thing I'll do is show you some of the affidavits we've gathered on this case."

He handed over a stack of affidavits. They were the sworn statements of the S.S. men held as war criminals, and they alleged the most hideous mistreatment by the Americans. It was because these statements were being published in newspapers throughout Germany and, the government had been advised, were being believed by large numbers of Germans that the Senate Armed Services Committee had decided to conduct its own hearings, assigning the job to a subcommittee led by Senator Baldwin and including, besides Baldwin, Senator Kefauver of Tennessee, and Senator Lester Hunt of Wyoming. Although McCarthy had given the impression of resigning from this group, the fact, as I later learned, was that he couldn't resign, because he hadn't been a member to begin with. He had merely exercised the privilege of sitting with the committee during the hearings, at which, from most newspaper accounts, he had done most of the talking. He was able to do this, incidentally, only after he had won a long fight to get from Senator Baldwin the right, which isn't normally regarded as part of the privilege, to cross-examine all the witnesses. Senator Baldwin later said it was McCarthy's bullyragging of him in the Malmédy affair that finally led him to give up politics.

After scanning some of the affidavits, I said that while it was entirely conceivable that a Nazi under sentence of death or imprisonment could be telling the truth about his own past behavior, it was at least equally conceivable that he would falsify. I wondered, I said, what McCarthy had in the way of evidence that it was not the convicted Nazis but the Americans who were lying.

"You've put your finger on it," he said. "Those are precisely the facts that Baldwin and the administration don't want me to bring out. That's why I walked out of that hearing. They're concealing all the evidence. I've shown you some of the pieces in this jigsaw puzzle, and believe me, when I take this story before the American people, the truth will be forced to come out."

I asked McCarthy if he had anything else he wanted to show me. "Well, I've got the affidavits of the Army people here," he said. "But I guess you can imagine what's in them. Lies from start to finish. Naturally, they're trying to protect themselves. I've got them here if you want to see what's in them."

I said I thought I'd skip them. I thanked the Senator for his courtesy and left.

## 2. TOMMY THE ANARCHIST

In 1959, four years after his political collapse and two years after his death, I finished a short book on Senator Joe McCarthy. It was not a formal biography or anything like a full account of his career in Washington: it was a character study of sorts, and I felt no obligation to compile a record for historians. There were, however, certain events I wished to describe, either because I found them interesting in themselves or relevant to my purposes. One story I wished to tell because it was both interesting and relevant was that of a former newspaperman named Thomas McIntyre, who was known to me and to a few others in Washington to have played an important but almost unknown part in bringing McCarthy low. In 1954 and 1955, I had often heard him tell bits and pieces of his story, but in those days, I had no plan to write a book about McCarthy, so I made no notes. Nor, I found, had other reporters who had listened to him at the bar in the National Press Club. When I undertook the book, though, I wanted to get his story and get it straight, but when I tried to run him down, I could find no trace of him. This didn't surprise me. He had spent much of his life as a drifter—with, he gave us to understand, several interludes on Skid Row—and it was quite in character for him to have left no forwarding address when he headed out of Washington. After a while, I gave up and finished the book with no mention of him except in the acknowledgments. One thing I knew for certain was that I owed a large part of whatever understanding and knowledge of McCarthy that I had to Tommy McIntyre.

Tommy died, at sixty-seven, in Detroit, his adopted city, in 1971, but—fortunately for me and, I like to think, posterity— I managed to get in touch with him in 1965, six years after the publication of my *Senator Joe McCarthy*. What spurred me to this effort was the appearance of a wretched and meretricious book titled *Days of Shame*, by Charles E. Potter, a former Republican Senator from Michigan. Potter, too, played a part in putting an end to McCarthy's power, but, as will be shown, he did so only because of Tommy's plotting and cajoling. Potter's small place in history derives from the fact that he cast the vote that led to McCarthy's condemnation by his peers, but without Tommy, his press secretary, he would never have done so. What enraged me about this book was that it pretended, as its title shows, to a pious anti-McCarthyism, but failed to include a single mention of

Tommy, but for whom Potter would not even get this foot-note.

But I am getting ahead of my story. First a few words about Tommy. As a newspaperman who had flourished in the twenties and thirties, he was pure Central Casting. He was a cocky, garrulous little Irishman with a large gift for wisecracking and drinking. He had what Ralph Nelson, who wrote his obituary in *The Detroit Free Press* described as a "lived-in face"—it was delicate, deeply lined, intelligent, ravaged, and angry. He was a native of Brookline, Massachusetts, and I imagine that he was self-educated. No one seems to know what brought him to Detroit—he settled there in 1923—but he had great affection for that city and, I am told, served it very well; as a crime reporter during Prohibition, he was said to have had excellent contacts with the Purple Gang and with the Police Department, betraying no secrets of either. "Easily the best in the field in this city and probably in any city," a former colleague told me recently. He had several periods of unemployment due to booze ("the curse of my race") and also to a congenital dislike of bosses and regular office hours. "I give myself orders, and I don't like clocks." He could discuss American flophouses with the authority of a Michelin Guide. But his talents were valued, and his employers were indulgent. He worked for both the Detroit *Times* and the *News*; in 1942, he went to Washington to put in a stint on the *Star*. Somewhere along the line, he developed a flair for political management and public relations, and worked in the successful campaigns of former Governor George Romney, County Prosecutor Samuel Olson, and several judges of the Wayne County Circuit Court. A fellow Detroiter, Charles ("Engine Charlie") Wilson, Eisenhower's Secretary of Defense, sent him to South Korea to do some P.R. work for the American military there. Later, after helping to do in McCarthy, he managed the mayoral campaign of Jerome Cavanaugh (a liberal idol until he withdrew from politics after his wife, in widely publicized divorce proceedings, charged him with mental and physical abuse) and later wished he hadn't.

When I first met Tommy in 1953, he was very much on the

wagon—it was always Cokes and 7-Ups for him at the bar—and he appeared to have no trouble staying dry. He was a natty dresser and fastidious about his person—he looked ravaged but not dissipated. His conversational style was clipped, brisk; he almost talked cable-ese. And he was all business.

He came to Washington as a dragon-slayer, but this, of course, was not what he had been hired for. He had been hired not to conduct a crusade but to have a go at a serious problem for the Michigan Republicans and their rich friends in the automobile industry. (Tommy was no Republican. When asked where his own political loyalties lay, he would squint at the questioner and, in a hushed, confidential voice, say "I'm an anarchist.") The problem had to do with Senator Potter, who had been elected with Eisenhower in 1952. Like the President, Potter was a war hero. He had lost both legs in Germany shortly after the Battle of the Bulge. Like Eisenhower, too, Potter had a hard time focusing on politics. As Tommy used to say, the Senator had a kind of "permanent charley horse between the ears." He had served without distinction in the House, which was the way he served in his term in the Senate. Early in his first and last term, he found himself in deep trouble. For one thing, he had hired as a press secretary a rabid McCarthyite named Robert Jones. The fact that Jones was a McCarthyite did not in itself bother Potter, who may not himself have been pro-McCarthy—hardly anyone in the Senate ever was—but certainly wasn't anti-McCarthy. (McCarthy had campaigned vigorously for him in his 1952 race against Blair Moody, whom he accused of being a pawn of "Moscow-trained" Walter Reuther, the president of the United Automobile Workers.) He had, though, struck up a friendship with Margaret Chase Smith, of Maine, whom McCarthy wanted to drive from the Senate. The Senator from Maine one day complained to the Senator from Michigan that the McCarthyites were running his employee Jones against her in the Republican primary. They had a large bundle of Texas oil money for this enterprise, and Mrs. Smith was afraid. Potter asked Jones about his plan to run in the Maine primary, and Jones said he had no such plan. But Potter, having caught his press secretary in this act of disloyalty, fired him. Now Potter found himself in trouble with his Michigan boss, Arthur Summerfield, a Chevrolet dealer from Flint who, as chairman of the Republican National Committee, had run the 1952 campaign for Eisenhower and became Eisenhower's Postmaster-General. To Summerfield, McCarthy was a statesman, Potter an errand boy. He didn't want the errand boy to fire a friend of the statesman. On the other hand, the Motown barons, many of whom had been heavy contributors to Potter's campaign, didn't want to get mixed up in a plot to get rid of Mrs. Smith. They weren't fighting McCarthy either—bad for sales—but they did have their ties with the Eastern Establishment and, thus, with Senator Smith, who, incidentally, had no trouble defeating Jones in the primary.

Potter was getting it from all sides, and someone in Michigan figured out that only Tommy McIntyre could get him out of the mess. This task held little attraction for Tommy, who was half cynic, half romantic. Saving a cipher could appeal to neither side of his nature. Nevertheless, he jumped at the offer, for he saw in it an opportunity to perform a large service for the nation. He had been brooding about McCarthy, and there had descended upon him a large sense of mission. He had become seized with a vision of himself as a St. Patrick. He would drive out the snake. He and he alone, of all one hundred and eighty million Americans, was the man for the job. At the bar, he would tell us why he thought this was so. There was, to begin with, his general political savvy. And though he was no Republican, he had, thanks to services rendered, very good connections with the Republicans. Moreover, he would say, he was singularly well equipped to deal with the bum upon whose destruction he was bent. "Takes one to know one." He was Irish—more Irish than McCarthy, who was half German. Though he came from the East, he was now, like McCarthy, a son of the upper Middle West. He had, he said, known a hundred McCarthys in his day, and this one was an open book to him—there but for the grace of, etc. Finally, there wasn't anything McCarthy could do to frighten or hurt Tommy. "I'm alone in this world. No wife, no kids, only me." He might lose his job with Potter, but he'd lost better jobs before. Finding another might be rough, but so what? He could always settle down on Skid Row. It held no terrors for him. He was, indeed, drawn to it. There, he later wrote, "is the greatest concentration of honest folk in any community." But he didn't plan to go before McCarthy went. He was in Washington to do a job and fulfill a compact with himself. He would stay off the sauce at least until he got this destroyer off the country's back.

Tommy agreed to work for Potter on one condition, which was that in all matters concerning McCarthy, the Senator would follow, not lead, his assistant. Whether this was clearly understood and agreed to by Potter, who before and later expressed considerable admiration for McCarthy, I do not know: when, years after the fact, I talked with Tommy about it, he was rather incoherent, to put it mildly, and I formed the impression that the condition was in his mind rather than in any written or oral agreement and that he, sizing up Potter for the dummy he was, thought he could enforce it, which, by and large, he did.

It was the hearings before the subcommittee of the Committee on Government Operations—the Army-McCarthy hearings—that undermined McCarthy's power and unstrung the Senator himself —and it was Tommy more than anyone else who caused these hearings to be held, at least when they did and the way they did. To be sure, by the spring of 1954, the Department of the Army had come to feel that there had to be a showdown of some kind, and the chances are that if McCarthy and Roy Cohn had kept bugging the Pentagon long enough, the generals would have had to strike back. But it is a matter of record that Potter was the first member of McCarthy's committee to inquire into the allegations of improper behavior on the part of McCarthy and his staff, and it is a matter of my personal knowledge—checked in 1965 with Tommy and double-checked with others—that Potter was prodded into this by Tommy. It took, as it happened, quite a bit of prodding. What Potter wanted was to get McCarthy to compromise a bit and let the trouble blow over. In his account of this, he writes that he went to McCarthy and said, "Joe, you've got to

make sense on this. . . . Get rid of [Roy] Cohn. The Army will
sacrifice Adams [John Adams, the Army's chief counsel and the
man who endured the worst of McCarthy's and Cohn's bully-
ragging] and the whole thing will be forgotten in a week." (How
this search for the easy way out squares with his pose as a
political hero, the Senator did not, of course, explain.) But Tommy
didn't want it forgotten—in a week or ever—and he worked tirelessly to see that it wasn't. He worked on Potter, he worked on
Senators and their staffs, he worked on the press. It was to reach
as many reporters as possible that he came to the Press Club
night after night and consumed gallons of soft drinks. He seemed
to work on the assumption that every journalist had the power
of a Lyndon Johnson and on the further assumption that every
ally is a potential defector. In my case, there was not much chance
that I would ever take McCarthy's side, but that didn't stop
Tommy from lecturing me on McCarthy's wickedness. Fortunately, Tommy was eloquent when angry, which was most of
the time, so it was never boring.

It is a fact far beyond dispute that without Tommy, there would
never have been an anti-McCarthy majority on the subcommittee.
The situation was this: the membership consisted of four Republicans and three Democrats. The Republicans were McCarthy
(chairman), Karl Mundt, Everett Dirksen, and Potter. The Democrats were John McClellan, Henry Jackson, and Stuart Symington,
all anti-McCarthy in varying ways and degrees. Being the principal
subject of the investigation, McCarthy graciously yielded his chair-
manship to Mundt, which was like yielding to himself. Henry
Dworshak, an Idaho potato, sat, which was what he did and all
he did, in McCarthy's seat. Mundt, Dirksen, and Dworshak doubtless loathed McCarthy, but their fear was greater than their loath-
ing and was expressed in sickening praise. Even under Tommy's
inspired and frantic tutelage, Potter, a born mouse, was mousy.
He now and then showed some disapproval of Cohn's badgering
of the Army, an institution he venerated, but he did not once
arouse McCarthy's hostility, and, despite his ridiculous book, his

attitude may be gauged from the eulogy he delivered on the Senate floor shortly after McCarthy's death and long after his liberation from Tommy. "Even the severest critic of Senator McCarthy would say that he—more than any other person—did one very valuable thing: he awakened the American people to the dangers of communism. . . . As a result of that awakening . . . the country is much more aware of the sinister aspirations of international communism. Mr. President, Joseph McCarthy is missed from the United States Senate."

Potter was never, clearly, the crusader he later affected to be. Nevertheless, Tommy saw to it that, when the ayes and nays were taken, Potter, to his astonishment, found himself, on June 17, 1954, saying nay to McCarthy and tipping the subcommittee balance against him—four to three. Without consulting his boss, Tommy had, several days before the end of the hearings, written a statement in Potter's name and arranged to get it to the press at the appropriate time. Just as the Republican members were making their waffling statements on where it had all ended, Tommy raised a finger and had a Press Gallery aide begin distribution of what the press called the Potter "recommendation." These included perjury prosecutions and the dismissal of Cohn, Schine, and the rest of the committee staff as well as the Army personnel who had sought to appease McCarthy. Tommy had Potter saying, "I believe a criminal case against some of the principals might be developed if the case were taken to a grand-jury room where the testimony would have to be repeated without others being present." "The statement by Senator Potter," according to *The New York Times* the following morning, "clearly overshadowed all the final cross-examination and testimony, the partisan wrangling, and the flowery speech-making because he can cast the decisive vote on any reports resulting from the long hearing." And that is how it went. Poor Potter had no idea of what was going on. A bit after Tommy's release was in the reporters' hands, the Senator was asked to appear before a battery of television cameras and did some waffling on his own. When asked why he hadn't mentioned his "recommendations" on camera, he said, according to *The Baltimore Sun*, that he "did not have a copy."

And here is Potter's 1965 version of the response to the statement he did not have a "copy" of and in fact had never seen:

By now the copies of my statement had been distributed to the committee and the press. I noticed that Joe McCarthy glanced at it casually and started to put it aside, then picked it up and read it. His face changed quickly to a mask of anger, and without looking at me he passed it over to Everett Dirksen. Within a few seconds Dirksen was whispering in my ear.

"Charlie, I think you should withdraw this statement." I shook my head.

"Charlie, this is a time for unity, for sweeping up the mess. I implore you to withdraw it."

"There was perjury by the basketful, and you know it, Everett," I said quietly. "The evidence is in, and now is the time to make my position known."

He stood there for a moment but must have sensed that I wasn't about to change my mind.

This is fiction of a low literary and moral order. "He never knew what happened until it happened," Tommy later said. And he is quoted as saying that "If [Potter] had known about it, he'd have got cold feet and wanted to sleep on it." Tommy could mix metaphors with the best of them.

And that, historians, is how it happened. I would not maintain that Tommy alone brought McCarthy down. The destruction of the Maximum Demagogue was too big a job for any one man. But Tommy had as much to do with it as anyone, and he certainly speeded the process. Without him, there would have been a whitewash, or, as it is put nowadays, a cover-up.

In 1965, when Potter's book appeared, I reviewed it for *The New York Review of Books* and told much of the story as I knew it and as Tommy, when I finally tracked him down, and others recalled it. My memory proved substantially accurate, but I was not able to rely on Tommy alone to verify it. He was by then intermittently deranged. In letters and in phone calls, he told of a crazy-quilt life in which he had gone from Potter to Cuba to work for Fidel Castro, to Detroit to work for Mayor Cavanaugh and to Peking to lend a hand to Mao Tse-tung. He claimed to have made Cavanaugh and to have seen his protégé blow it. He was then, he said, providing "the only journalistic opposition to Cavanaugh" in two columns, "Ad Lib" and "To Tell the Truth"— in a Detroit suburban weekly, the *West Side News*.

When my article appeared, he took offense because I had written that he, like McCarthy, was "shanty Irish." He seemed to think that this implied a lack of culture and wrote to the *Review* that "I was cultured and brought to limited maturity in a suburb of Boston known for the opulence of its principal population. The McIntyres were not of that stripe, but like the Kennedys who took up residence there before moving to Westchester, we had our share of amusement observing the mannerisms of the more seg- regated shanty Irish outside our enclave." He concluded the letter with "To Dick Rovere I owe at least the thanks for disclosing my not unimportant role in closing the book on the most fiendish human being in my long list of confrontations with bestiality, up to that time, below the rank of United States Senator."

I lost track of Tommy again and would not have known of his death if I had not chanced to see an article by Patrick Owens in *Newsday*, a Long Island suburban newspaper. Owens wrote that "for a couple of years in the late 1960s, I lived in an apartment a block down the street from the Royal Palm Hotel, a faded caravansery which McIntyre cohabited [not quite literally, I as- sume] with transient lady wrestlers, truss salesmen, and floozies." He went on: "Tommy, who was then in his early 60s, had a circulatory problem which required him to take long walks two or three times a day. We met by chance one evening and I, having read Rovere's celebration of the man, offered up my bouquet of appreciation. Tommy didn't want to hear it."

Intrigued by this, I got in touch with Owens and undertook some new research. Owens, a burly type, frequently accompanied Tommy on his therapeutic walks so that he could ward off mug- gers. "Tommy was getting mugged every few weeks," Owens said.

"He was a setup, small and frail and at the same time belligerent, ready to put up a fight he couldn't possibly win. He was both an easy hit and a challenge." On the walks, Tommy would denounce everyone and everything, including Owens, including me. "He told me," Owens had written, "that if I was serious about my calling, I would go back to Montana, where I was born, and practice it there. 'This town is full of reporters like you, who try to cover it and can't even find Woodward Avenue.' When he wasn't raging at me, he raged at Rovere, at Mayor Jerome Cavanagh . . . at everything, really, from the New English Bible to cole slaw. He liked to write letters. 'More of that tripe . . . will mark you hopelessly as a pompous bumpkin, hogtied in ignorance,' he wrote once about a story of mine that displeased him. I don't know what I answered back, but Tommy's answer to my answer included: 'Continue praying. It's the only possible . . . escape for an oaf.' "

Sometime after Owens left Detroit, Tommy moved from the Royal Palm to the Four Freedoms, a retirement home run by the United Automobile Workers. He was resident there when, on December 22, 1971, he collapsed on a bus near Cadillac Square. A Fire Department ambulance rushed him to the Detroit General Hospital, where he was pronounced dead on arrival.

The anarchist had arranged for his body to be sent to Wayne State University Medical School.

# VIII

## John F. Kennedy

I was not one of those Washington correspondents who knew him well or saw him often. Before his nomination in 1960, I knew him only slightly and talked with him only briefly and formally. I now and then wrote about him as a Senator, but I never sought him out. I was, to be blunt, unimpressed. Although several of my friends were supporting him, his record seemed to me not much better than mediocre—though more honorable, to be sure, than that of his adversary, Richard M. Nixon. But he had, I thought, weaseled on McCarthyism, and I was not disposed to change this judgment when he reviewed my *Senator Joe McCarthy* for *The Washington Post*. He praised the book (which was published two years after McCarthy's death) but had few words in dispraise of its subject. I believe it was the only time he ever publicly committed himself, but the commitment was belated and minimal.

In the line of duty, I covered the 1956 and 1960 Democratic conventions and admired his and his managers' strategy, though I thought it ruthless. The first time I talked with him alone was on the Saturday before election day in 1960. He had had a wild day campaigning in and around Philadelphia, speaking in supermarket parking lots and riding in an open car through the most densely populated districts. He had shaken so many hands that his own right hand looked like raw beef. A woman had clutched at his right thumb to avoid losing her balance and had been dragged along for several yards; the thumb hurt badly and could hardly be moved. He was going to Washington to attend church in the morning (I doubt if he would have done this if he had not been in a contest in which the outcome was by no means certain) and found this a convenient time to talk with me. We must have been together for about an hour. We boarded his plane, the Caroline; about midnight, and he had a light supper served in his cabin. Clam chowder. Rather to my astonishment, he began talking about, of all things, motels and hotels. The Kennedy party, politicians and press, had been staying in a rather posh motel, the George Washington Motor Lodge, in King of Prussia, Pennsylvania, and he asked me what I thought of it—the architecture, the appointments, the food, the service, and so on. My surprise at his preoccupation gave way to a certain admiration. His interest was not that of a travelling salesman or a potential innkeeper; hotels and motels, in which he had been living for some time, were parts of our culture—as much so, though on a different plane, as literature, the theatre, or anything else—and I was rather pleased with the thought of having a President who saw things in this light, the more so since I did so myself. After a bit of this, I asked him how he felt about Nixon. "Until the last few weeks," he said, "I never thought about him one way or the other. I hardly knew him, and I can't say I disliked him as others did. He just didn't interest me. But then, at the first of the debates in Chicago, the son of a bitch began poking his finger at my eye, just the way he did to Khrushchev in that stupid kitchen in Moscow. Right before the cameras he poked and poked [here, for purposes of demonstration, Kennedy began poking *his* finger at *my* eye] and I hated the bastard's guts for that cheap way of trying to steal a scene." I was not taking notes and do not now recall what, if anything, else we talked about on the short ride. We parted company in Washington.

Not long after his inauguration, William Shawn asked if I would like to do a "Profile" of the President. I said I would. By then, Arthur Schlesinger, Jr., had joined the White House staff, and I asked him to ask Kennedy if he would cooperate. The President was agreeable, and it was arranged that I should now and then see him alone and spend some time with him in the

Oval Office. I saw him five or six times in all, and twice spent the better part of the day with him, leaving the office and repairing to that of Evelyn Lincoln, his secretary, only when he was in conference with others. I would get up to leave when the phone rang, but most of the time he would gesture to me to remain. I took careful and quite elaborate notes on these sessions and am confident of the accuracy of this account.

At our first postelection meeting, he said, "Arthur tells me you want to write an article or something." I said that was right, knowing, of course, that he knew perfectly well what I was up to. I had talked about the ground rules with Pierre Salinger, his press secretary, and I told Kennedy of our conversations. I asked him if he remembered John Hersey's articles about Harry Truman in *The New Yorker*. He said he remembered them well, particularly recalling Hersey's walks with Truman. I explained that this sort of thing seemed to me contrived and that I wished to avoid it as much as possible, that I simply wanted to talk with him at his convenience and that the time and place meant little to me, though it would be helpful, obviously, if I had some opportunity to observe him at work. We talked on about arrangements for a few minutes more. He seemed at least as much interested in journalism as in politics.

He was not one to stress the "burdens" of the Presidency, though he did say that he had a sense of its "isolation." "The news I get is unbalanced," he said. "The intelligence cables are all fire alarms. Everyone I see has unresolved problems. Of course, a lot of people come in claiming big successes, but I generally discount them because I know that what they really want is a go-ahead to work at some new crisis, perhaps an imaginary one. I guess some things do get solved, but I have to look through the back pages of the papers to find out about them." How did he estimate his own power to shape events? "I find," he said, "that it's easier to get what I want in this country than it is to get it abroad." I said I would have supposed it to be the other way around, but he said it wasn't—at least not in his experience. This was when he had been in the White House only a few months and had yet to encounter stiff Congressional opposition to his domestic program. That same day, he asked me if I would care to accompany him to a meeting in the Fish Room. I said I'd be delighted, having no idea of what kind of meeting it was to be. It turned out to be a gathering of Florida real-estate developers petitioning for federal approval and, I supposed, subvention for a plan to build a new city. I had no idea of how and why they happened to be meeting in the White House; it seemed to be absurd and also rather strange that the President should spend any time listening to a bunch of boosters. Listen is what he did— the talk was of the usual Chamber of Commerce variety—and he left quietly after about a half hour. Back in his office, I asked him why he had bothered. "I really don't know," he said. "I guess it's my way of learning how things work and what's on people's minds. People of that sort represent something, and if I can get a good cross section, I can learn from them—even learn how to fight them." He then began asking me about my work as a journalist and that of my friends, some of whom were also his friends. I was at the time Washington correspondent for *The New Yorker* and until recently had been United States correspondent for *The Spectator* of London. He followed both magazines quite carefully. "What do you know about Taper?" He asked. It so happened that I knew two Tapers—one, Bernard Levin, who used "Taper" as a pseudonym for his *Spectator* writing on politics; the other being Bernard Taper, a *New Yorker* staff writer. "I know two Tapers," I said. "I don't know which one you mean. "You know," he said, "the guy who writes the column on politics." I told him what I knew, which wasn't much. "If he comes over here, I'd like to meet him," Kennedy said. I said I was sure that this could be arranged. Then I explained that the other Taper had worked on *The San Francisco Chronicle* with Salinger. He was aware of this and said he had been disappointed in a recent *New Yorker* article by Taper on Pablo Casals because "it wasn't up to date. I figured he must have written it some time ago." I assumed that he had in mind something about the recent Casals concert in the White House, but that wasn't it.

It was that certain arrangements in Casals' life had changed: something about his house, something about his dog—my notes are unclear on this.

I was with him most of the day on St. Patrick's Day in 1962. A headline in a morning paper read:

PRESIDENT PLANS LONG
ST. PATRICK'S DAY
CELEBRATION

The story reported that the Irish Ambassador and a number of Irish-American Congressmen were calling on him and that he planned to end the day at the annual dinner of the Gridiron Club —an organization of reporters that has nothing to do with St. Patrick's Day. At any rate, I was amused by the occasion and wondered how the first Irish Catholic President would observe it. I noted that he wore a green tie with shamrocks of a somewhat deeper green, but I did not hear the occasion mentioned by him or by anyone else. Moving from his desk to his rocking chair, he picked up a copy of *Mr. Citizen*, by Harry Truman and asked me if I'd read it and what I thought of it. I said I had read parts of it and thought it less than a classic. He said he guessed that was how he felt, but he liked it because he liked Truman. This led him into another subject—the rating of Presidents in the order of effectiveness. He said that Arthur Schlesinger, Sr., and Henry Steele Commager, who had jointly been conducting a survey on this subject for many years, had recently been in to talk with him about it. "From what I've learned of the job," he said, "I'm skeptical of this sort of thing. For example, I've always had Truman high on my list, but now I'm not so sure. A President, I guess any President, does many things he simply can't avoid doing, and when they turn out well, he gets the credit. But why should he if there was nothing else he could do?" I said I thought the general rule in politics was that one got credit for what went right and blame for what went wrong, regardless. "That's the politicians' rule," he said, "but I don't think it's anything that anyone like you can go by. You have to figure out what the alternatives are, what the situation is in Congress, what the public will stand for and what it won't, what's likely to be the impact on the next election. I have a much stronger sense of all this now than I had before I was here." I had, later, the feeling that a lot of his thinking might have been influenced by the Bay of Pigs misadventure, then just a year in the past, but I didn't bring it up because, I suppose, it didn't occur to me to do so.

When I arrived at the White House that morning, one of his highest appointees was in line ahead of me. Kennedy saw him for a few minutes. Three or four times later, though, the same man phoned him, and when, on these occasions, I rose to go into Mrs. Lincoln's office, he motioned me to remain. I could see tremendous boredom in his expression and hear it in his voice. I was therefore not surprised to learn, a few months later, that the appointee had been given an even higher appointment—but one that made access to the White House a good deal more difficult. The influence of boredom on affairs of state is one to which I had not previously given much thought. But it can, I imagine, be considerable.

I lunched with him in the family quarters. For some reason not shown in my notes, I preceded him there by about ten minutes, and, while having a cocktail in the living room, looked around me and made some notes, which read as follows:

A stack of wire mail baskets—one labeled "Mail to Save," another "Clothes," the third turned over so I couldn't read. More disorder than I would have expected. Books in precarious piles on floor. Many children's books. Some tapes (for recorder) trailing on floor. Many photographs in wrong-sized frames and askew. Burned matches on carpet—picked them up. Pictures everywhere—many Italian watercolor scenes. Some pictures on chairs and floor too. Eleanor would say Kennedys not much better housekeepers than Roveres. . . . Tepid martini. . . . Commotion in the hall. Someone carrying crying baby. Caroline comes tearing in on tricycle: "My guest just left. If you're waiting for my father, he's right in there."

At lunch, there was more talk about my work and another "Taper" incident. "I ran into Kahn the other day," he said. Kahn? Kahn? Could he have meant Cahn? I knew several Kahns and Cahns and knew that he knew some of them. Besides, how in the name of God does a President "run into" anyone? "Which Kahn?" I asked. "Jack Kahn, on your magazine. He was in here doing a story about my going to the theatre in New York. Do you know when it's going to appear?" Ah—he meant E. J. Kahn, Jr., of *The New Yorker*. I told him I knew nothing about it. I later learned that Kahn had wanted to do a "Talk of the Town" piece on this subject but nothing came of it because the Secret Service agents would divulge nothing about the security measures taken to protect the President in New York. He wanted to know why I had given up the *Spectator* job and what I thought of Murray Kempton as a successor; I said I had quit to do other things and that I was glad that Kempton had taken over. "Yeah, I guess so," he said, "but he'll probably be giving me a hard time. Did you read that piece in which he asked what the hell kind of a revival of *American* culture is it that begins with having White House concerts by Pablo Casals, a Spaniard, and Igor Stravinsky, a Russian? That Murray—he's against anyone in power and for any Goddamned underdog who shows up, Jimmy Hoffa, Roy Cohn, the lot of them. Next thing you know, he'll be for Nixon." I said I doubted this and wasn't troubled by Murray's sympathy for losers. He didn't disagree but added, "I think Bill Shannon [William V. Shannon, then on the *New York Post*] would do a good job of it." I said I thought it would be hard to choose between them but that the decision had been made by Ian Gilmour, the *Spectator*'s publisher. "O.K.," he said. "I suppose Gilmour is pretty set up by the Liberal showings in the by-elections. I don't know how *I* feel about it, though."

We somehow got off on the question of the right wing in American politics. He asked my view. I said I thought it generated more noise than power. His reply: "It generates a hell of a lot of mail, too. I've had more letters on the Congo than on anything else. And I hear Nixon's having a hard time getting money since he started running down the John Birch Society. Of course, I don't take that too seriously. I'd like to see the day when Nixon won't know where the money is. But what does worry me is the polarization—the Birchers being equated with A.D.A. [Americans for Democratic Action] and other liberals."

More of my notes:

Before we left the table, I got back to a general conversation about the Presidency. How much self-awareness, how hard to bear in mind that things had changed, how much sense of remoteness. He again tended to make light of all this. After all, he said, he sees the same people pretty much, day in and day out, and they're mostly the people he's been seeing for years. Sometimes, though, difficult with others. For example, some of the crew of the PT-109 had been in a while ago, men he'd commanded in the Pacific and seen off and on for years, and they'd been awed and awkward in his presence. He found that sort of thing painful and troublesome. Contributed to sense of isolation. . . .

Nuclear testing (he had just announced the resumption of it after a long moratorium) much on his mind. "I'm anti-testing in my guts." But felt the case for it was close to unarguable. The scientists had told him underground testing was enough, but this proved wrong, even in scientists' judgment. "Everyone's for it now except Jerry Wiesner [his adviser on scientific matters]." The main anti-suspension man was Edward Teller. "He's crazy, of course. Pierre has proof." [By "crazy," he meant, as I understood it, that Teller had been demonstrably wrong in many of his earlier judgments.] He said he'd put off decision waiting for a show of some "give" by the Soviets; he would have taken just about anything as a signal—easing of pressure on Berlin or Laos, move toward general disarmament. But nothing came that would help him out. Said that most of new tests won't prove anything but that one or two may. Did not elaborate. As for consequences, we'd surely be hurt in Japan. Fallout problem no longer terribly important but people thought it was. His conscience in no particular agony, but [Harold] Macmillan's was, though Macmillan had to go along with British scientists. Pressure on Kennedy came from Congress—Joint Committee on Atomic Energy, from Atomic Energy Commission, and, of course, the Pentagon. Said, though, he wouldn't rank it among most difficult of decisions. "I thought it was one more case of having no alternative. All I can do now is see if we can't get some anti-test treaty with the Russians."

We stayed upstairs for a half hour or so, talking mostly about foreign policy. Of Laos and Vietnam, he said, "Two cans of worms." I gathered that he really had, at that moment, no idea of which way to turn. Later, of course, he would support heavier intervention. I didn't wish, on this occasion, to question him about his Secretary of State, but I did ask him about the military, and he—largely, I suppose, as a consequence of the Bay of Pigs—was contemptuous of the judgment of the generals and admirals. I went back down to the office for a while. He was a bit rushed because he was getting out a disarmament message a couple of hours before he had planned to—in order, I imagine, to get it out of the way so that the correspondents attending the Gridiron Club dinner could finish with it in a hurry. Still, he wanted to talk. "What did you think of that latest [Norman] Mailer piece?" I thought I might take this as my cue for leaving. I was about to say that I didn't want to take up his time talking about Jack Kahn, Bernard Taper, and Norman Mailer. "Mr. President," I said, "if I thought you had nothing better—" "I know," he said, "you think I wouldn't be much of a President if I sat around all day talking this way," which was close to what was on my mind, though I wouldn't have put it quite that way.

I thanked him and left. Outside, the White House was being picketed by antitesting and civil-rights groups, some of whose placards read:

WE HAVE CHOSEN LOVE AND NON VIOLENCE.
THIS IS NOT THE EASY WAY.

MR. PRESIDENT WE ARE WAITING

REMOVE EXCESSIVE BAIL FOR
FREEDOM RIDERS

For several months thereafter, I did not try to see him. I was writing some quite critical columns and did not wish to have to defend them in face-to-face encounters. Indeed, I was not sure that I wanted to do the articles about him that I had set out to do. I liked the man, and I liked his zestful, insouciant style in the White House. But I had several reservations about the way he exercised power and about his policies, and I felt I could not write much about him as a man until I formed some clear judgment of him as a national leader. Perhaps, I thought, it might be wiser to put off the whole thing until he was out of office. But I did not want to lose touch with him entirely, and I asked and got a late afternoon appointment on October 17. At almost the last minute, I was told that Mrs. Lincoln had been trying to reach me and had left a message. It said that the President was forced to cancel because of very urgent business. He was flying to Chicago and on to the West Coast that evening and had said I was welcome to "come along," joining him on Air Force One after Chicago. I was to learn that the "urgent business" was the visit of Andrei Gromyko, who assured him there were no Soviet missiles in Cuba. I made the trip, and was on hand the next morning to learn that the rest of the itinerary had been cancelled for reasons of health—an official lie. He returned to Washington to deal with the missile crisis.

Not long after that, I decided to put the project aside indefinitely. In the summer of 1963, I accompanied him on his tour of Ireland, England, Germany, and Italy and saw him occasionally but only to exchange a few words. I felt that I needed distance, perspective, a certain tranquility in which to reflect. More important, he needed time, time in which to establish himself as a national leader rather than as a spirited and often splendid rhetorician. The last year of his life provided little evidence that he would be able to do this, at least in his first term. It is all but idle now to speculate on what might have happened if he had lived and won a second term. His personal popularity continued to be high, and I think it almost certain that he would have won over Barry Goldwater or any other Republican candidate. But he would not have won as dramatically as Lyndon Johnson did in 1964, for Johnson's huge majority was in considerable part a memorial to the fallen leader, and Johnson's Great Society programs were a tribute as much to the country's grief over the loss of Kennedy as they were to the new President's mastery of legislative politics. I would like to think that Kennedy would have found a way of getting us out of Vietnam, but I see no evidence that he would have done much more than, as I later put it, merely have gone on "with a somewhat more elegant war." However that may be, I continue to find some consolation in the fact that in my time, we sent to the White House a man who cared about ideas, who was interested in every aspect of American life and culture, and who, though we now know that he had some rather tawdry liaisons, also had a strong taste for excellence in people.

# IX

## *Walter Lippmann*

Sometime early in 1950, I was telephoned by a young man who identified himself as being on the staff of *Flair*—a soon-to-be defunct magazine designed to appeal to what used to be known as the carriage trade—and asked if I would be interested in writing an article on Walter Lippmann. I was anything but enchanted by the prospect of appearing in that publication, whose principal contribution to world journalism was a hole in the front cover, but I said without hesitation that I would be very much interested. I had long admired Lippmann, but, although I had had some correspondence with him, I had never met him and looked forward to the opportunity of doing so. In time, I met with the editor of *Flair*, Fleur Cowles, and several of her colleagues in the magazine's offices in Manhattan. Mrs. Cowles was then the wife of Gardner Cowles, president of Cowles Communications, a corporation that owned several newspapers, magazines, and radio and television stations in the Midwest. After settling some details about length, deadline, and money, I was asked how I proposed to handle Lippmann's divorce from his first wife and his second marriage. I knew a bit about this—it had been a mild tabloid scandal in 1938—but I said that I had no intention of writing anything about it. I did not propose, I explained, to do Lippmann's biography, only an appraisal of his career and its impact on American politics and journalism. If gossip was what *Flair* wanted, it had better get in touch with Walter Winchell or Hedda Hopper, two eminent practitioners of the trade. This was taken with reasonably good grace, and by the end of the summer I had completed the article. It appeared in the last issue of *Flair*, and among my souvenirs is a copy of the magazine with Mrs. Cowles's signature framed in the famous aperture.

Soon after reaching agreement with the editor, I had written Lippmann, notifying him of my assignment. He replied that, while he did not care much for publicity, he would be pleased to see me at his summer home on Mount Desert Island, Maine. I found him gracious, less formal than I had expected, and one of the most stimulating conversationalists I have ever known. We remained good friends for the last quarter-century of his life. I cannot, however, say that ours, at least on my part, was an altogether easy relationship. At our first meeting, I was thirty-five and he was sixty-one, just my father's age. Perhaps because he had no children (only a stepdaughter, child of the former Helen Byrne Armstrong), it seemed to me that he often treated me rather like a son in need of instruction and guidance. This may have been partly my imagining, but others of my approximate age have told me they had the same feeling. As a consequence, I was somewhat more deferential than is normally my custom, and I tended not to challenge any of his views with the vigor I might have employed with a contemporary. But this was hardly a matter of importance, certainly not when measured against the fact that I had the opportunity to learn from a great teacher.

The side of Lippmann that I, like most people, was mainly aware of was the lucid analyst of men and events. But I soon became fascinated by other aspects as well. His interests were much broader than many people, even friends, realized. Before Lincoln Steffens snatched him away from Harvard and tried to make him a junior muckraker, he had planned to become an art historian. When he was a student at Dr. Julius Sachs Collegiate Academy in Manhattan, his parents took him to Europe, where, still in knee pants, he became a habitué of museums and cathedrals. Strolling through the Louvre one day, he came upon Mrs. Jack Gardner, the quintessential American art collector. This meeting led in turn to a lifelong friendship with Bernard Berenson, who became one of Lippmann's few real confidants. His passion for art—particularly classical art—never left him. He was also much interested in literature, philosophy, psychology, and theology. In the early twenties, he contributed some quite dazzling literary criticism to *Vanity Fair* and other magazines. (Some of this work, along with several political essays, is to be found in *Men of Destiny*, a book long out of print but one of his finest and by far the most entertaining. His appraisals of Sinclair Lewis and H. L. Mencken, written when both men were at the height of their vogue, are as perceptive as any done since and are, in places, extremely funny.)

At Harvard, Lippmann had been a protégé of George Santayana, and his undergraduate writing had attracted the attention of William James. His first book, *A Preface to Politics*, was published in 1913 when he was twenty-three. It was proclaimed by Ernest Jones, Sigmund Freud's leading disciple and first biographer, as the first Freudian treatment of politics. Hearing this, Freud said he wanted to meet Lippmann; they met once, in Vienna, but had no opportunity for conversation. Theodore Roosevelt read the book while hunting in the jungles of Brazil and expressed the same wish. He and Lippmann did meet, and for many years Roosevelt was Lippmann's beau ideal of a public man.

In this country, Lippmann was thought of primarily as a force in journalism and politics. Few regarded him as much of an influence in American intellectual life, but in Europe, at least in the early days, he was seen as a substantial figure in the intellectual community. Soon after leaving college he went to England and got to know many of that country's intellectual elite, among them H. G. Wells, George Bernard Shaw, Lytton Strachey, John Maynard Keynes, Harold Nicolson, and Rebecca West. He became a card-carrying member of the Fabian Society, and, as an editor of *The New Republic* and a talent scout for Harcourt, Brace, he recruited many of its members for the magazine and the publishing house. His interest in religion was a continuing one. He discussed it with me only in the most abstract terms, telling me of a plan to write a book about it. I have often been told, however, that at one point he seriously considered becoming a Roman Catholic. Whether or not this is true, one finds many touches of neo-Thomist thought in his writings.

A facet of his character that was even more deeply concealed from the public was his political activism. Indeed, whenever he advised other journalists on the duties and obligations of their profession, he would stress the necessity for keeping their distance from persons in public life. Fraternizing with politicians, he insisted, was destructive of circumspection. Addressing the International Press Institute in London in May 1965, he said:

The powerful are perhaps the chief sources of the news, but they are also the dispensers of many kinds of favors, privilege, honor, and self-esteem. . . . The most important form of corruption in the modern journalist's world are the many guises and disguises of social climbing on the pyramids of power.

And two years later he wrote:

Cronyism is the curse of journalism. After many years, I have reached the firm conclusion that it is impossible for an objective newspaperman to be a friend of a President. Cronyism is a sure sign that something is wrong and that the public is not getting the whole journalistic truth.

His practice, however, was far from his preaching. Throughout his half-century as a publicist, he intervened in government affairs far more frequently than did most of his colleagues. In the early years, he did so openly; in the later years, surreptitiously. In 1915 and 1916, he lobbied furiously for Senate confirmation of Louis D. Brandeis as Associate Justice of the Supreme Court. Although Brandeis, a labor lawyer from Massachusetts and one of the great American jurists, was Woodrow Wilson's choice, he had precious little support from other quarters—in fact a great deal of opposition. The common view, shared by many Democrats, by most Republicans, and by such generally enlightened organs as *The Nation* and *The New York Times*, was that his years as a labor advocate had made him a partisan and hence disqualified him for the Court. But Lippmann and Felix Frankfurter (who himself became an Associate Justice) were for Brandeis, as was *The New Republic*, of which Lippmann was a founder and editor. About the only other journalistic support came from some small populist papers in the Midwest and West, and a few trade-union journals. The struggle was hard and bitter. The fuss about Brandeis's past—in large part a cover for anti-Semitism—was led by William Howard Taft, then at the Yale Law School and bitter because he had not been appointed to the Court by the man he succeeded as President. (He was later, of course, to become Chief Justice.) In letters, articles, and conversations, Lippmann and Frankfurter worked tirelessly for Brandeis, who was confirmed only after prolonged and rancorous hearings. It was, perhaps, Lippmann's great triumph.

During the First World War, Lippmann was asked by Edward M. House, President Wilson's principal political strategist, to join the staff of The Inquiry, a nongovernmental and largely clandestine outfit that had been established—largely as a response to the British and French secret treaties with other powers —to draw up American peace terms. This was the group that compiled Wilson's noble but doomed Fourteen Points. Its putative head was Isaiah Bowman, a noted geographer and president of the American Geographical Society (not to be confused with the National Geographic Society). Most of the work, though, was done by Lippmann as executive secretary, and eight of the Fourteen Points were his. Wilson's six dealt with such abstractions as the freedom of the seas, the self-determination of peoples, and so on; Lippmann's were the hard, substantive ones, dealing with frontiers, demographics, sovereignties. While working on boundaries, he went to the State Department's Balkan desk and found the green eyeshades and shirtsleeves there using maps published in 1870. Back in the American Geographical Society's headquarters, he, under Bowman's occasional tutelage, gave himself a cram course in geography; in time he knew as much about it as did Sir Halford John Mackinder, the British student of geopolitics whose ideas were perverted by Hitler for his *Leben-*

*sraum* policies. The experience became central to Lippmann's political thinking; it was an enduring concept of his that on the baize-covered negotiating tables nations never yield so much as a kilometer that has not been won on the Champs de Mars. The idea was to serve him well in later years and later wars.

When the major phase of The Inquiry's work was complete, Lippmann was commissioned as a captain in the Army and served at General John Pershing's field headquarters. He is said to have contributed much to the modernization of psychological warfare— not the most attractive military field but certainly the least lethal. In the weeks after the armistice, he served on House's staff at the Paris Peace Conference, ostensibly as a public relations man for the Fourteen Points and for the President who was backing them. To him, as to many others, the Treaty of Versailles was a disillusioning experience. But he was not quite ready to give us his overt interventions.

In 1927, when the Mexican government nationalized the oil industry, Lippmann, like many others, foresaw the possibility of another war between Mexico and this country. As a way to head off any such development, he persuaded President Calvin Coolidge to appoint their common friend, Dwight Morrow, as Ambassador to Mexico, knowing full well that Morrow would make Lippmann his chief adviser. As he told it, it all came about as he had expected. The sovereignties involved were Mexico, the United States, and the Vatican, which was at the time distressed over the anticlericalism of the Mexican government and inclined to be partial to its opponents. Lippmann played by far the largest part in the crisis. He wrote letters to be sent from the American President to the Mexican President, Plutarco Elias Calles, and vice versa. He wrote letters for both to send off to the Pope and the Pope to dispatch to the two Presidents. The whole performance was widely admired, and it helped avert the possibility of war. When the crisis was past, Lippmann thought of a way to create a festive atmosphere: to have Charles A. Lindbergh, who had just made the first nonstop flight across the Atlantic, come to Mexico on a goodwill flight to visit several of its cities. Lindbergh accepted the proposal and in the American Embassy he met the Ambassador's family—including his daughter, Anne, who later became Mrs. Lindbergh.

After that episode, Lippmann seldom showed his hand in public affairs, but he never ceased to be active. He constantly—often without solicitation—offered his advice on appointments and policies. He helped write speeches and put ideas into heads that were largely barren of them. Reading his correspondence, now preserved at Yale, I learned that he was in large part the creator of Senator Arthur Vandenberg of Michigan. Vandenberg was a Midwestern Republican isolationist who, at a critical moment in World War II, became an internationalist and, politically, a bipartisan. His conversion brought him a reputation as a statesman and celebrity that he much enjoyed, both here and abroad. Two Democratic Presidents sent him to international conferences all over Europe and to the 1945 San Francisco Conference that established the United Nations. In reality, Vandenberg was a run-of-the-mill politician, a rather clownish one at that. But Lippmann, in collaboration with James Reston of *The New York Times*, talked him into his new position and provided him with some rather elegant language in which to express it. Lippmann was helpful in similar ways to many others—among them Alf Landon, Dwight Eisenhower, John Foster Dulles, Adlai Stevenson, and Lyndon Johnson—although none of these needed to be invented, as Vandenberg did. All of them profited by their association with Lippmann.

His last interventions were with John Kennedy. Lippmann had held off backing Kennedy until late in the 1960 campaign. He had nothing personal against the Democratic candidate, but he was distrustful of anyone connected with Joseph P. Kennedy, the candidate's father, who had been his close friend until late in Kennedy's tenure as American Ambassador in London. At that point, Lippmann came to think of Kennedy as pro-Nazi, and they were friends no longer. But he did in time come to support the Democratic candidate, and he watched with interest as John F. Kennedy, after his election, formed a cabinet. When he learned that the President-elect was considering the appointment of Dean Rusk as Secretary of State, he did all he could to prevent it. I do not know whether he had any personal animosity toward Rusk, but he certainly had political animosity—based in large part on Rusk's bellicose behavior at the time of the war in Korea, a conflict that Lippmann opposed from the start. His choice for Secretary of State was McGeorge Bundy, who, as it turned out, would hardly have pleased him either, since Bundy was for many years an ardent backer of Rusk's policies.

On another important occasion in this preinauguration period, Lippmann did prevail over Kennedy. Having almost completed the final draft of the speech he was to deliver after taking the oath of office, the President-elect took it to Lippmann's house to get his advice and consent. Lippmann advised but did not consent. He objected to Kennedy's use of the word "enemy" to characterize the Soviet Union, and suggested that it be changed to "adversary." Kennedy accepted this; it was a small change but an important one, and the fact that it was cheerfully made showed something about Kennedy's approach to U.S.–U.S.S.R. relations.

I had known Lippmann for about fifteen years before I was aware that he was much more than the standoffish political journalist known to the public. His services to President Wilson were, to be sure, a matter of public record (though his work on the Fourteen Points is still, as far as I am aware, known only to a few historians)—as was his brief service to the Socialist mayor of Schenectady, New York, shortly after leaving college. But I did not know the extent of his involvement in other matters until I gained access to his papers at Yale. (They were deposited there rather than at Harvard because a young businessman, Robert Anthony, had started a Lippmann collection of his own in his undergraduate days. When Lippmann learned of this, he added everything he could to it, and made Anthony the curator.)

This research at Yale came about while I was gathering material for a biography of Lippmann. For many years, publishers had urged him to write an autobiography, but he insisted that he would never do it. In 1950, he was persuaded by Allan Nevins, a colleague of his on *The New York World* in the twenties and head of the Oral History Project at Columbia University, to record a series of interviews about his life, but the transcript, though valuable, is an incomplete and in some ways unsatisfactory document. When some friends—particularly his publisher, Edward Weeks, of Atlantic-Little, Brown, and Arthur Schlesinger, Jr.—realized that further efforts at getting him to do an autobiography were futile, they cast about for a biographer. I do not know what other writers they approached, but in time I was asked to do the job, and accepted. At the start, Lippmann was agreeable but rather diffident. When I asked him about letters, he said that he had never been much of a correspondent and that, besides, someone had stolen many letters from his files. (This was true, but the purloined letters ended up in the hands of a book dealer; they were bought by a friend of Lippmann's and returned to his files.) Did he have diaries? Only appointment books, he said—not very interesting. But after I got into the archives at Yale, I quickly found that he was wrong on both counts. There were a great many letters, some of them fascinating. As for the appointment books, they were more than just that. Whenever any meeting seemed worth more than a note about the place and time, he would summarize the discussion in his tiny, cramped hand. And when he went abroad, he would dictate an account of each day's events to Mrs. Lippmann. A two-week trip would sometimes yield as much as two hundred typed pages. My awareness of this material, and of the light it cast on little-known aspects of Lippmann and of American life early in the century, led me to a procedural decision: to focus on him as an active participant in the political and social life of the time rather than as a political writer and thinker. His books and columns were interesting, but they could be dealt with by scholars whose main interest was in the content of his thought.

I do not know if I ever successfully communicated my idea to Lippmann, but I did discuss it with Weeks and Schlesinger, and they agreed with me. In my talks with Lippmann, therefore, I tried to concentrate on events rather than on political judgments.

I also tried to bring the Nevins oral history up to date in taped interviews of my own.

I think that what I was trying to do was sound in principle, yet in practice it did not work. Although I have never been particularly adept as an interviewer, I do not think that in this case the fault was altogether my own. At least in his later years, Lippmann was a man with what I can only describe as a profound distaste for the past—not the historical past, which delighted him, but his own past. It did not, I am sure, rest on any dissatisfaction with his professional career and his private life; both, to the best of my knowledge, had been satisfying to him. It was more a matter of a single-minded focus on the present and the future, which a man could attempt to mold, as he could not do with the past. This might have been a healthy attitude in a person as vigorous and busy as Lippmann was, but it was frustrating to a biographer, since a biographer deals only with the past. Most of the time, when I asked him to reminisce, he had difficulty summoning up details. Moreover, I learned that he had a very unreliable memory. His recollection of events was frequently contradicted by the evidence in contemporary letters and diaries, and before long I realized I could not use anything that was not confirmed in documents or by other people.

There were further difficulties. We had trouble agreeing on the terms of our collaboration. I was uneasy in the role of authorized biographer. I felt that I needed complete independence, and he always said that he, in a similar position, would settle for nothing less. I think, though, that he was troubled by the thought that I would find in the letters something either discreditable or of so private a nature that he would not want it revealed. I told him I thought his concern was groundless. For one thing, I had no intention of going into matters that were not part of the public's concern. For another, I had read enough of the letters and diaries to learn that he had a highly developed sense of privacy and never wrote of his private life to others. (He came close to doing this with Berenson, but the details he confided were mainly financial.)

I also assured him that I would show the completed manuscript to him and to anyone else he would like to have read it. I said that I would, of course, take most seriously and sympathetically any objections raised, and if his definition of privacy differed from mine, I would almost certainly accept his. I twice put a statement of all this into writing and submitted it to Louis Auchincloss, Lippmann's lawyer and a distinguished novelist. Both times, Lippmann said that he agreed and that all final decisions about content should be up to me. But then he would again be assailed by doubts. Once he proposed that we jointly appoint a board of arbitrators consisting of three men who were friends of his and of mine. Knowing whom he had in mind, I might have been able to accept the proposal, aware that the only trouble I would have would be the loss of time. But I didn't like the principle, and neither did two of the three proposed judges when I told them of it. In fact, they said they would have nothing to do with it. I did not speak to the third.

I foresaw another problem. Lippmann's health grew poorer, and I thought it likely that he would die before I finished my work. Mrs. Lippmann, who was eight years younger than he, could have been expected to outlive him, and not consider herself bound by the agreements (oral on his part) we had reached. But actually she died several months before he did. At any rate, I decided to turn the project over to a younger writer, a man who could make a fresh start. I found an ideal successor in Ronald Steel, who had been a Foreign Service officer and was also a first-rate journalist. He consented, and he is, he tells me, approaching the end of what I am sure will be a book worthy of the subject.

For several years after I turned the job over to Steel, Lippmann and I continued to be friends. He was a delightful companion, always entertaining and often, in conversation, as amusing as were those early literary criticisms I have mentioned. He had powerful likes and dislikes—a fact that I myself might have appeared to contradict in writing of him elsewhere. I quoted a famous exchange between him and Mabel Dodge, the mistress of a sumptuous salon in Greenwich Village, circa 1912. "What do you love?"

Mrs. Dodge once asked him, to which he instantly replied, "The living world." I rather rashly added the comment, "He liked everything." That was hyperbole; if it were not, he would not have been the man he was. What he meant, of course, was that he liked the experience of living and working and being part of his time. Life had been good to him in almost every way, and he had served his country—and, by extension, others—as perhaps no other journalist of the century has done. But he did not like everything, and he obviously did not like everybody. Although his mind was firmly fixed in the liberal tradition, he was essentially conservative—not in the sense of resisting change but in the sense of approaching it prudently and circumspectly. He liked order in life and society. He was skeptical of many democratic values and would, I think, have felt at home in a society in which hierarchies were more clearly defined than they are in this country. In 1955 he published a book, *The Public Philosophy*, in which he argued that too much authority was vested in representative bodies such as Congress, and too little in offices of consolidated leadership such as the Presidency. It seemed to me, and to many others who reviewed the book, that the trend was the opposite of what he held it to be. In this country, the executive branch was steadily gaining power at the expense of the legislative branch. I did not think that this was altogether bad, nor did most other critics; we simply felt that he had misjudged developments. The book got few favorable reviews, and he was so hurt by this that he gave up work for a few months.

I had a rather odd experience as a consequence of my own review of the book in *The New Yorker*. While I was critical of it, I paid tribute to Lippmann as a thinker and to the high quality of his other work. One day, soon after the review was published, I met the late Edmund Wilson in the corridor outside my office. He stopped me and said he had been deeply disappointed by my review. Assuming that he had read the book and liked it better than I had, I asked him what he liked about it. He said he hadn't read it, but had been put off by my general praise of Lippmann. I said that I admired the man very much, particularly in his latest phase, when he was bedeviling Eisenhower and Dulles for their foreign policy. "Have you been reading him lately, Mr. Wilson?" I asked. "Of course not," he said. "I haven't read him since 1926, when I discovered that he was an agent of the House of Morgan."*

This was a frequent charge, by liberals and radicals, against Lippmann in the decades before the Second World War, and Wilson's remark led me to think about it and look into it. There was a sense, a rather innocent one, in which the charge was true. In the twenties and thirties he, like many other columnists, was writing about economics and finance. Of economics he had a fine grasp, but he was an amateur in finance and needed expert help. In those days it was just about useless to consult anyone in Washington on such matters. The Treasury Department people were mostly businessmen who knew less about economics than he and not much about finance. At least until the New Deal, nearly all the financial experts were in Wall Street. Lippmann readily consulted the bankers there, particularly Russell Leffingwell, a Morgan partner. As it happened, Leffingwell was a liberal Democrat and, like most New York bankers, an internationalist. In the correspondence, I found instance after instance in which Lippmann had written Leffingwell asking him to explain and give his opinion on some current dispute. Leffingwell would oblige, giving a lengthy analysis—and not, as far as I could tell, a partisan one— and in a few days, that response, shortened and paraphrased, would turn up in Lippmann's column, "Today and Tomorrow," in *The New York Herald Tribune*. By inadvertence, perhaps, some of Lippmann's writings may have served the interest of the Morgan people, but "agent" was far too strong a word for the relationship.

Lippmann's association with the Morgan partners was often faulted on another ground altogether, particularly by fellow Jews

---

* As I subsequently learned, Wilson was, not uncharacteristically, exaggerating. In 1929, he wrote a respectful review of *A Preface to Morals,* and in 1931, when Wilson was an enthusiastic defender of the Soviet Union, wrote Lippmann an open letter charging him with failure to understand the nobility of the Russian "experiment."

who objected to his close association with what was, in the current parlance, a notoriously WASP firm. Lippmann had, after all, grown up in a Jewish community that had produced any number of distinguished bankers, some of whom he had attended school and college with—Kuhns, Loebs, Lehmans, and many others. He was frequently accused of anti-Semitism. In this, I am afraid, there was a modicum of truth. He was a German Jew whose family, a wealthy and cultivated one, had immigrated fifty years earlier than most of the East European (mainly Russian and Polish) Jews, and he shared some of the disdain of the one tribe for the other. He was never, to be sure, overtly hostile in what he wrote, but it was notable that he seldom wrote about Jewish questions and had rather little sympathy for Israel. He never visited that country, but he did visit Egypt under the Nasser regime, and the fact that he was allowed to do so says something about that government's attitude toward him. I know of only one instance in which he addressed himself to the condition of American Jews —an article entitled "Public Opinion and the American Jew," published in *The American Hebrew* in April 1922:

The fundamental fact in the situation [the rise in anti-Semitism in the early twenties] is that the Jews are fairly distinct in their physical appearance and in the spelling of their names. They are, therefore, inevitably conspicuous. . . . Thus, while the Jews are not sharper traders than the Greeks or the Scotch, and while they are not more blatantly vulgar-rich than among other stocks, sharp trading and blatant vulgarity are more conspicuous in the Jew because he himself is more conspicuous. . . . [The] rich and vulgar and pretentious Jews of our big American cities are perhaps the greatest misfortune that has ever befallen the Jewish people. . . . I worry about the Jewish smart set in New York. . . . They can in one minute unmake more respect and decent human kindness than Einstein or Brandeis could make. . . . That is the real problem of the Jew in America, the problem of his use of his opportunities. . . . What the American Jew needs is to develop the habit of self-criticism.

This begs several questions. Other ethnic groups are distinguished by physical features and the spelling of names. In the latter case, the Jews can hardly be said to be more "conspicuous" than, say,

the Greeks. Why should the "vulgarity" of Jews stand out in con-
trast to that of anyone else? I think he was trying to get at what
I consider a valid point, which is that what I call "otherness"—
in appearance, culture, religion, language, behavior—is often the
true explanation of racism. But the Jews are hardly unique. Lippmann's fallacy, it seems to me, was his failure to recognize that
anti-Semitism had deeper roots than mere "conspicuous" differences.

But the failing was a common one of the time, and Lippmann
was not, of course, anti-Semitic in any of his personal relationships. As I have noted, he made a valiant fight against the anti-
Semites who tried to bar Brandeis's appointment to the Supreme
Court.

Until 1938 Lippmann lived in New York. It was his native city.
His principal journalistic associations had always been with New
York publications—the *World*, *The New Republic*, the *Herald
Tribune*. New Yorkers, as I have pointed out, were better informed on many of the matters that concerned him than persons
he might have consulted in Washington. New York was, as in
most respects it still is, the intellectual capital of the country. But
Franklin Roosevelt's New Deal brought to Washington many people of a caliber rarely seen in preceding administrations—economists, historians, scientists, scholars of many kinds, not least
among them his friend Felix Frankfurter. The Foreign Service was
recruiting brilliant young men, as were most agencies of the executive branch, including the Treasury, which took on a number of
Lippmann's Wall Street friends. Although Lippmann was by no
means an enthusiastic New Dealer, he began to find the Washington climate intellectually more stimulating than he had ever known
it to be. He lived there until 1968, when he and his wife returned
to New York. At the time, he explained the move as "coming
home." It was more than that. He moved because he could not
stand the proximity to Lyndon Johnson. His dislike for the President was uncharacteristically passionate, amounting indeed to
hatred. The two had once been friends,. and the Lippmanns had
visited the Johnsons at the LBJ ranch. But the war in Vietnam

outraged Lippmann as nothing ever had before, and in time every facet of Johnson's personality became offensive to him. He made much of Johnson's Texas background (which always struck me as being largely an affectation, since Johnson, except in accent, was far more a product of Washington than of Texas and clung to the ways of his youth largely to give himself identity). He would often say something like, "What can you expect of a Texas jingo?"—a purely rhetorical question.

But withdrawal of support for a President he had earlier backed was a habit with Lippmann. Some incumbents, of course, he had never backed in the first place; but, except for Wilson, who could not be faulted for his terminal illness, he ended up hostile to every President from the first Roosevelt to Richard Nixon. He was a bit of an idealist: he expected more from those he chose to favor than they could possibly deliver, and disappointment was thus inevitable. In commitment and subsequent alienation, he was perhaps little different from other journalists, except that he was one of the few who made public endorsements. With other journalists, it is generally possible to tell from the tone of their work whom they favor, but few feel impelled to announce their support publicly, thus averting any need to announce their withdrawal of it. But I suppose Lippmann's practice of declaring himself was a function of his activist side.

One of the warmest and most sensitive of the tributes paid him after his death was by James M. Cain in *The Washington Post*. Cain, author of the classic *The Postman Always Rings Twice* and other novels, had worked under Lippmann on the New York *World* in the early twenties and had observed sides of him that I had not, although I assumed they existed. One was his perfectionism, sometimes carried a bit far, in the matter of writing. Once, for example, something of his that appeared in *The Washington Post* contained a sentence urging the country to revert to the "status quo." Seeing this in print, he shot off a letter to the editor of the paper asserting that his copy had been manhandled and that the phrase should have read "statu quo." Cain thought this nitpicking. "True, the dative use of *status*, in Latin, is *statu*, but who cuts it so thin?" At the same time, Cain was pleased to be "working for the one man in the newspaper business to whom such things mattered." And he goes on to explain that it was his, Cain's own passion for rhetoric that led Lippmann to hire him for the *World*'s editorial page in the first place. "As he told me later, when we compared notes, 'When my ear caught the participles that didn't dangle, the infinitives well buttoned in, the pronouns all with antecedents, it occurred to me that you could take [Maxwell] Anderson's place.' " In similar circumstances, I should have felt the same way. Purism was characteristic of Lippmann, in substance as well as in form. There were times when he may have had a poor case or none at all, but he rarely overstated or understated.

Another aspect of Lippmann that did not strike me until I read Cain's article was his physical strength and grace, even though I had been impressed by his vigor. Into the last decade of his life, he was a tennis enthusiast, regularly playing with competence a game that I had given up in my forties. When I first met him in Maine, he was a tireless walker, and despite being twenty-six years younger, I had a hard time keeping up with him. Cain cites an instance in which Lippmann's strength saved his subordinate's life. The two were on the sidewalk in front of the Pulitzer Building, where they both worked, and Lippmann said, "Jim, I think it's up to the few to keep civilization from being torn down by the many. Don't you?" Cain was startled by this remark, as well he might have been. "I was so astonished my head snapped around, and at that moment this iron hand caught my arm, to pull me, almost lift me, back from the curb, as a taxi shot by within inches. If it hadn't been for that hand, I would have been killed. It was that kind of hand, and he was that kind of man."

The remark that threw Cain off balance seems perfectly in character. Lippmann was an elitist. When he was misled, it was almost always because of an undue respect for established authority. The most famous case was in 1927, when he accepted uncritically a report by the Lowell Commission (chaired by A. Lawrence Lowell, president of Harvard) on the verdict that led to the execution of Nicola Sacco and Bartolomeo Vanzetti, two Massachusetts radicals charged with a payroll robbery and murder. The commission had been appointed by the Governor of Massachusetts and was staffed by the kind of persons—New Englanders, Harvard men, estimable public servants—in whom Lippmann had an instinctive trust. It led to an ugly rupture of relations between him and Heywood Broun, another ornament of the profession, who refused to accept the report and was forced to leave the *World*. In time, it was revealed the report was riddled with simple factual errors—some of the commissioners had not even read the transcript of the testimony—and Lippmann quickly and apologetically reversed himself, but by then the damage was done. One more example: in 1949, when Alger Hiss, a former State Department official, was accused by many of treason and was tried in federal court for perjury, I spent an afternoon walking with Lippmann in Washington. We were discussing the cause, and he said, "I know Alger Hiss. He couldn't be guilty of treason." I said that I didn't understand his use of the word "couldn't." I said that, without judging the merits of the case, it seemed to me that anyone was capable of treason, depending on how the term was used. I pointed out that if I told him someone had betrayed a friend, or a wife, or a husband, he would probably accept the statement as true and, since that sort of thing happens every day, think nothing more of it. In my view, I went on, betraying a fellow human being is never justifiable, whereas betraying a government may be an act of virtue, as I thought he must assume it was in this country in the Colonial period or in the case of those Germans who plotted Hitler's destruction. I added that in the not impossible event that I became convinced that my countrymen would be served by an act of treason, I would, if I could summon up the courage to face the consequences, commit one. I am sure I made no impression on him.

If any man was a member in good standing of the Establishment, Lippmann was. But he served it well and, with few exceptions, critically. When he discovered that he had made an error of judgment, he was quick to acknowledge it. And he made far fewer mistakes, even of prophecy, than his detractors have claimed. Back in the sixties, the Pentagon, whose operations he was criticizing in almost every column, put some researchers to work on his writings over the years and circulated a document detailing what the military men regarded as faulty appraisals and forecasts. In some cases, the Pentagon was itself misinformed as to his opinions; in others, the errors were trivial. One mistake that was far from trivial was his 1968 estimate of Nixon. In early October of that year, following his customary procedure in Presidential elections, Lippmann endorsed the Republican candidate and announced his acceptance of the view that a "new Nixon" had emerged. (By my count, this would be at least the eighth announced incarnation.) "I believe," he wrote, "that there really is a 'new Nixon,' a maturer and mellower man who is no longer clawing his way to the top, and it is, I think, fair to hope that his dominating ambition will be to become a two-term President. He is bright enough to know that this will be impossible if he remains sunk in the Vietnam quagmire. . . . And at home, he must, as he knows well, move out to find common ground with the active minorities who are dividing and might paralyze the nation." It did not take him long to recognize and regret this spectacular misjudgment.

Reviewing his work as a whole, I found most of it stood up far better than I had expected it to. I recall rereading, about ten years ago, two of his books—*U.S. War Aims* and *U.S. Foreign Policy*—published in the war years of 1944 and 1943. I approached them with the expectation that they would be full of false assumptions about the future. They were, for one thing, prenuclear. They were written before the Communist domination of China and the Soviet domination of Eastern Europe and before the formation of the United Nations. Yet Lippmann, drawing on his geographical theories, foresaw that the Soviets would establish a military and political presence from the Baltic states to the Balkans. He recognized the instability of the Chinese Nationalist government. And when the Truman Doctrine—a kind of global application of George Kennan's "containment" thesis—was promulgated, he saw its dreadful consequences immediately.

It is impossible to assay the impact on events of any individual in or out of politics. But Lippmann's influence was surely greater than that of any other journalist in this country's history. He was not the most widely read of political writers, but he was the most widely respected among his colleagues and among enlightened politicians, here and abroad. At one time or another, he was consulted by every President in his time and by most high government officials. When he traveled abroad, his views on American affairs were sought by foreign leaders, and he often served, as he did in the Mexican affair of 1927, as an unofficial ambassador. Talking with him and with State Department officials in the middle and late sixties, I got the distinct impression that he was serving as a kind of broker between Lyndon Johnson and Charles de Gaulle; it was a period when de Gaulle appeared to be very anti-American and would give almost no time to our people in the Paris Embassy. But Lippmann always saw him and had lengthy talks with him on his European travels and thus became one of Lyndon Johnson's prime sources on what the French President thought and on what Franco-American relations de Gaulle did and did not favor. I suspect that when we know more about the history of the sixty years between 1913 and 1973, we will see Lippmann as a frequent and forceful intervener in affairs of state.

I believe that the history of the period would have been somewhat more dismal than it was if he had not now and then intervened. On most things, he was far ahead of his time. He saw the fatal weaknesses of our post-1945 foreign policies sooner than any of his contemporaries. His reason for opposing our participation in the war in Korea in 1950 was, essentially, that it would lead to precisely the kind of disaster we were later to meet in Vietnam. Though always an internationalist, he never believed in a global conception of our national interest. Though less than a passionate democrat, he understood the strengths and weaknesses of the system well. In 1922, he published *Public Opinion*, a seminal study of a subject on which many millions of words have since been written, few of them adding or subtracting much from those in Lippmann's spare, modest volume. His *The Good Society*, published in 1937, was a critique of the New Deal that many liberals then thought reactionary; today, though, it seems a perfectly reasonable critique of certain practices that few liberals any longer defend.

But I think something valuable would be lost if we thought of him simply as a pillar of social and political wisdom. He was far more than that. He embodied most of what was best in the liberal and humanist traditions. He brought a new dignity to American journalism and practiced it as if it were one of the learned professions. As a stylist, he should be studied not only by other journalists but by anyone interested in English prose, for he was surely as much a master of it as any modern American writer. A humanist with remarkable powers of logic and clarity, his departure leaves our world less rational and murkier.

# X

## Biographies, Profiles, Problems

Five of my books can loosely be described as biographies, and I
have written, I suppose, close to two hundred magazine articles
of a biographical nature. Both as a reader and as a writer, I find
the form congenial. I by no means hold with Emerson that "There
is properly no history; only biography." It was only the great
whose lives he thought worth recounting, and no anthropocentric
view, even one that embraces the masses, can serve as a basis
for understanding history. The proper study of mankind may be
man, but it cannot be the study of man alone. Besides humanity,
there are also the other forms of life on the planet; there are, too,
the inanimate resources on or below the surface, the climate, the
tides, time itself. Biography is a less than adequate means of
tracing the flow and flowering of the ideas—the religions, the
truths of myth, the sciences, the social and economic doctrines—
that go into shaping of societies. There are many splendid lives of
Marx, Freud, and Einstein, but the best of them tell us little about
economics, psychiatry, or physics. Still, I know of no single genre
—fiction and poetry apart—that tells us more about ourselves and
our condition, and for me there is no work in English literature
that is as constantly rewarding or as replete with truths about
myself and the world as Boswell's *Life of Johnson*, and I have
been more influenced by Johnson's *Lives of the Poets* than by
most of the poets themselves. In any case, nothing I have written
has given me more satisfaction than books and articles dealing
with the lives and characters of individuals.

This may be a rather pretentious way of introducing the notes that follow and the three *New Yorker* "Profiles" that follow, for I hardly qualify as a professional biographer, being far less a scholar than a journalist, and my mini-biographies of Bruno Furst, John Gunther, and Henry Blackman Sell illuminate no great truths. But the work has been important to me, and the subjects have all become part of my life. The relationship between biographer and subject is a peculiarly intimate one. Friendships and enmities develop, and tensions may arise as in marriage and family life. I have probably written more about public events and controversies than about lives, careers, and personalities; the events recede in memory, the controversies are settled or subside, and it becomes difficult to recall their substance. But if one writes a biography, its subject becomes either a transient or permanent member of one's household, like children and parents. This can be true even of dead subjects. I would never have chosen to share the same quarters with Senator Joe McCarthy, about whom I wrote a book two years after his death, but he has been a presence in my life for most of the last two decades, and will be for the rest of my life. He is only one of several dead subjects I recall more vividly than many friends of the past; though I hope I shall not be called upon to write about him again, I shall never stop speculating on his motivation, the nature of his character. In my consciousness, Lyndon Johnson will always be a larger figure than George Washington, and Wendell Willkie larger than Woodrow Wilson. The least of my subjects have been preceptors, teachers of one sort or another, even what one might call antiteachers. I am sure that my views on American foreign policy owe no more to Walter Lippmann, of whom I was an admirer and to a degree a follower, than to John Foster Dulles, my study of whose mind and career helped bring into focus views and values I felt unfounded and insupportable. And I am sure that my life and my outlook on life itself would have been in several ways different if I had not had associations and dissociations of this sort.

As it happens, I did little of this kind of writing through most of my first decade as a journalist. In those years, I was more an editor than a writer, and as a writer I was more a polemicist than a reporter—first on the Communist *New Masses*, then as an anti-Communist liberal on *The Nation* and *Common Sense*. (Of the three, only *The Nation* survives.) I wrote about local and national politics, foreign policy, the labor movement, ideologies I supported or opposed. But I had little talent for editing (though I did acquire some aptitude as a rewrite man) and a few years of it persuaded me that my future, if I had one, lay elsewhere. And, though I remained a liberal, I wearied of liberal journalism. To be sure, *The Nation* and *Common Sense* were less doctrinaire than *The New Masses* and were captives of no political organization. But in their own somewhat looser ways, they were as tendentious; ideological soundness, as the editor construed it, was the highest value, at least in my day. I somehow cannot imagine the late Freda Kirchwey, editor and publisher of *The Nation* when I worked for her in the early 1940s, behaving, as elsewhere in this book I describe Harold Ross as doing: expressing revulsion at what a staff member had written yet agreeing to its publication because he felt committed to the writer. Nor did those magazines have much room for the kind of writing under discussion here. Their view, to borrow from Emerson, was that there is no history, only mass movements and the faiths they live by. They were interested less in the people whose names turned up in their pages than in the gospels those people propounded.

At any rate, in 1944, I left *Common Sense*, which was to cease publication little more than a year later, and retooled as a freelance writer. My hope, like that of so many others of my generation, was to write regularly for *The New Yorker*, which I then thought of, as I still do, as the best magazine of general circulation in the country. My interests were extending far beyond politics, and those of *The New Yorker* seemed to have no limits. Its editors were hospitable to almost anything—including politics, though less so than they were later to be; if it was neither conservative nor liberal, it was committedly humane. It had nothing to sell but good writing, imagination, and wit—and, of course, Ross's passion for fact. But, although I had a few friends who had written for the magazine, I knew none of its editors, and I did not think that anything I had done up to then would commend me to them. I managed to get an assignment to write an article for *Harper's* about Vito Marcantonio, a member of the House of Representatives and a power in New York social and political life, especially in East Harlem, which in those days, as now, was also known as Spanish Harlem, despite the fact that there were as many Italians as Spaniards in the population. A protégé of the explosive and unpredictable Mayor Fiorello La Guardia, Marcantonio was a unique figure in the history of American politics. He ran and was regularly elected as a Republican and in Congress just as regularly espoused and voted the Communist Party line. This was a phenomenon that could not be understood merely by a study of his bizarre record; it required a knowledge the man, of his patron in City Hall, and of the sociology of East Harlem. I produced an article—"Vito Marcantonio: Machine Politician, New Style"—which appeared in the May issue of *Harper's*; this, I thought, was close enough in content and texture to a *New Yorker* "Profile" to call to the attention of the editors. I sent a copy to William Shawn, then Ross's deputy, and asked for an appointment, which was granted. I found him as courteous and gracious as I had been told he was and have always found him to be. But he was then, as now, firm in his opinions and unmovable in his decisions, and our meeting was brief and discouraging. "We don't print exposés," he said—an assertion that now has a certain irony, since the magazine, under his editorship, has published as many exposés, some of them by me, as any magazine in the country. For my part, I had not thought of the article as an exposé. What I had described as Marcantonio's political role in New York and Washington was news to no one in either city. The article seemed to me a portrait of a rather exotic New Yorker and a description of aspects of life in one of the more interesting sections of the city—the kind of thing *The New Yorker* so frequently offered its readers. But Shawn thought otherwise, and that was that. I gave up hope of satisfying *The New Yorker*, at least for a while.

But I had pleased *Harper's*, and, except for *The New Yorker*, I knew of no magazine for which I would rather write. It was going through a spirited period under Frederick Lewis Allen, assisted by Russell Lynes and George Leighton, and Allen said he would take an article a month for an indefinite period. (*Harper's* did not pay as well as *The New Yorker*, but writing regularly for it, I could support my family somewhat more comfortably than I had when I was a salaried editor.) My first assignment was an article on Thomas E. Dewey, then Governor of New York and far ahead in the race for the Republican nomination for President. I got in touch with James C. Hagerty, Dewey's press secretary who was later to perform the same service for Dwight Eisenhower, and was told that while the Governor would not receive me, he had agreed to admit me into his presence while he heard arguments for and against granting a reprieve to a murderer sentenced to die in the electric chair at Sing Sing. I thought the very suggestion told a lot about Dewey, and since I had some research to do in Albany anyway, I accepted the macabre offer. Dewey decided against a reprieve.

My article appeared in *Harper's* for June, and it had several odd consequences, some gratifying, some revealing. The most gratifying one was that Shawn, having read it, called me into his office, told me he had liked the piece, and offered to take me on as a writer of "Profiles." I had not sent him a copy of the article because I thought it as much an exposé as the one on Marcantonio and assumed that his rule would still hold. But some quality of it had impressed him, and, in late May, I was signed on as a *New Yorker* staff writer, which I have been for a bit more than thirty-two years. I then went through an agonizing period of two or three months in which I did nothing for the magazine except send Shawn a few memoranda on possible "Profile" subjects. Either my ideas struck him as unusable (often because some other staff writer had "reserved" one for his own future work) or his ideas struck me as in one way or another beyond my scope. Shawn wanted me to write "Profiles," and I wanted nothing more, and we must have considered dozens of names in those weeks, but none seemed right to both of us, and I began to wonder if *The New Yorker* was really the right magazine for me. In time, we agreed on Newbold Morris, another La Guardia protégé who was at that time President of the New York City Council—an agreeable, idealistic, and thoroughly uncontroversial man.* I had hoped to get away from politicians, but I was not yet able to until another year or so, after I had written another "Profile" on Edward J. Flynn, one of Franklin Roosevelt's main political advisers and strategists, and a two-part one on Peter J. McGuinness, a charming old Democratic district leader who gloried in his role of "boss of Greenpoint," an industrial and almost solidly Irish district of Brooklyn.** After that, I did not lack for subjects, political and nonpolitical.

In the period in which Shawn and I could not agree on a "Pro-

---

* Uncontroversial in 1944 but the center of a national storm eight years later. In 1952, the administration of Harry S. Truman was plagued by corruption, actual and alleged. The Republicans, who had mainly been basing their hopes for victory that year on the unpopularity of the war in Korea and McCarthy's charges of Communist infiltration, began saying that Truman and his associates were not only wicked but crooked. In desperation, Truman sought a Republican lawyer of high repute to look into what the newspapers were calling "the mess in Washington" and clean up whatever he found. He finally settled on Morris, whom he had been told, accurately, was an incorruptible man from what many believed was the most corrupt of American cities. Morris accepted, was appointed a special assistant to the Attorney-General, J. Howard McGrath, and given an office in the Department of Justice, which, he did not seem to understand, was the den that housed most of the thieves. He was allowed to investigate nothing of consequence and, in addition, was quickly accused by McCarthy of being part of the Communist conspiracy. His noninvestigation lasted two months. He was fired by the Attorney-General and repudiated by the President. The failure of his patrons to cooperate only contributed to the impression that much was rotten in Washington and to the Eisenhower victory later that year. Two days before his departure on April 4th, he asked me to serve as a kind of press secretary, my only venture in that line of work. Together, we tried to air his side of the story and scored another nonsuccess, the only account of the episode being an article by me—"Mr. Morris Goes to Washington"—published in *The New Yorker* of May 10, 1952, and later in *The American Establishment*.

** Published under the title "The Big Hello" in *The American Establishment*, 1963.

file" subject, I continued to write about politicians for *Harper's*. From the *Harper's* piece, I learned what every biographer, every writer of biographical pieces, sooner or later comes to know, which is that the consequences of such work cannot be foretold and are often very different from what the writer intended. The message it conveyed to most readers and the one I thought was based on the facts was that Dewey was not the candidate the Republicans needed and not what the country needed in the way of a President. Though he had been a reasonably efficient Governor —this was not difficult in wartime, when the states had little to do but enjoy the prosperity—his grasp of national and international affairs was weak, and his instinct was to play it safe on everything, taking only those positions that had overwhelming support in the public-opinion polls. He was, as I saw it, a determined opportunist whose best features were perseverance (as a special prosecutor in New York City, he had convicted a large number of gangsters, and he had later been an effective District Attorney) and a certain tidiness as an administrator. Sensing uses for the article that had been no part of my plan, Dewey's Republican opponents made it an overnight sensation by ordering thousands of reprints for intra-party distribution, and one of them, John Bricker of Ohio, a man whose shortcomings were far more glaring than Dewey's and who was to become the party's 1948 candidate for Vice President, had a copy of the article placed on the chair of every delegate and alternate at the convention. (Meeting the editor of *Harper's* at a party in New York, Herbert Hoover, a Dewey supporter, told Allen he considered it beneath contempt that the magazine would publish such an article.) Later, when Dewey was the nominee, the Democrats gave the piece even broader circulation.

It should not have surprised me that the anti-Dewey Republicans, some of whom might have fared more roughly at my hands than the Governor did, sensed support in what I had written, as, of course, did the Democrats. But more than a few *pro*-Dewey Republicans read the article as a handsome tribute to their man. A month or so after the appearance of the *Harper's* piece, I was approached by a member of the Women's Republican Club of Wilbraham, Massachusetts—my wife's home town—who told me that the members had been so pleased by the article that they wished me to address them about Dewey. It took me a while to recover from the shock. After all, the article contained such judgments as the following:

Search through [Dewey's] life, and you will find no part that is not consonant with every other part. He has wasted no years, sowed no political wild oats. He abandoned his only youthful enthusiasm, singing, when he was forced to perform with a sore throat; according to his mother, the thought then dawned on him that his earning power would always be dependent on two fragile vocal cords. If any . . . cause, wise or foolish, has ever lured him from the pursuit of his own career, the record does not show it. He had to be entreated for months before he would take up the lance against crime; he was making, at thirty, more than $25,000 a year and was troubled by the prospect of having to scale down to $16,995. He is . . . an immensely hard worker who works for himself. . . . [It] is impossible to conclude that the mainspring of his life has been [anything but] personal ambition.

In time I understood. The qualities I found distasteful were regarded by some readers as high virtues. The driven man, striving for upward mobility, having a sharp eye for the main chance, was what the Wilbraham clubladies wanted in a husband and what they wanted in a husband they wanted in a President. What, after all, is wrong with "personal ambition" as the mainspring of a man's life? I had pointed to such Deweyite bromides as "We need not be afraid of the future, for the future will be in our own hands. . . . We shall have our freedom as long as we are all free." Weren't these unexceptionable statements? I had subtitled the article "The Man in the Blue Serge Suit" and had questioned as excessive Dewey's concern over appearances—his own personal appearance and the air of bustle and busyness he sought to convey wherever he went. But in the world of those I was being asked to address, one cannot be too attentive to the impressions one creates in others.

I was to find myself more deeply embroiled in the 1944 campaign than I cared to be. When the *Harper's* article came out, I was approached by Nelson Poynter, the publisher of the St. Petersburg (Florida) *Times* and the head of a Washington organization named Press Research, and asked if I would undertake a far more extensive report on Dewey's record. I was still without a *New Yorker* assignment and the money Poynter offered was hard to resist, so with a friend, Esther Chasan, helping me on the research I quickly turned out a study the size of a short book, of which Press Research distributed tens of thousands of mimeographed copies. Like the article, it created an almost immediate stir—one not at all to my liking. In his dealings with me, Poynter had not told me that he was functioning on behalf of the Democratic National Committee and the C.I.O.'s Political Action Committee, and it was for the benefit of these groups that my study had been commissioned. I only learned of this when I read in the newspapers that the Democratic leaders had ordered the burning of all copies of the document because they could not tolerate a party publication that contained so many unflattering reports on them. I had used terms like "ward heeler" and "boss" to describe some of the politicians and labor leaders I had been unwittingly working for. Since I had not signed the report—the attribution was to Press Research —my name was not mentioned in connection with the study that went up in flames.

I had written about Dewey without having exchanged a word with him—in the hour-long clemency hearing I attended, he did not once speak—and I have done the same with many other living subjects. In some cases, they have not wished to see me; in others, the decision has been mine. Among those who refused interviews were Douglas MacArthur, about whom Arthur Schlesinger and I wrote a book in 1951,* and Ezra Pound, both suspecting that what I wrote would be hostile. In Pound's case,** he was, as he later

---

* *The General and the President,* reissued as *The MacArthur Controversy* in 1965.

** The poet was then being held in St. Elizabeth's Hospital in Washington. He had been charged with treason for his wartime broadcasts from Italy. He had clearly been a deranged man for the better part of two decades, and my feeling, as well as that of the editors of *Esquire,* which published the article in September 1957, was that no good end would be

acknowledged, very much mistaken. With public figures in general, my feeling has been that the advantages of acquaintance are often more than offset by the disadvantages and that in general it is best to confine oneself to material that is fixed in the record and cannot be repudiated. In 1955, I wrote, for *Harper's*, a study of the career of Richard Nixon, whom I had often observed in Washington and elsewhere but whom I had never met and never sought to meet. When, in 1956, I boarded his campaign plane, he asked me how I could pretend to judge a man I had not met. I said that I had written much about people who had died before I was born and asked if he thought that Carl Sandburg should have abstained from writing about Abraham Lincoln because he had not known him. I added that millions of voters who would never know the then Vice President would have to appraise him on the basis of his record and that my job, as my editors and I conceived it, was to assemble the kind of material that would enable the electorate to make a fair judgment. He shrugged and moved on. As a rule, the personality shows in the record. (In Nixon's case, it most emphatically did.) Talking with politicians privately, nearly all of what one gets is a rationalization for what they have done in public, and this, when not irrelevant, is almost always manifest in what they have said, how they have voted, and whom they have befriended or attacked. I have not applied this rule inflexibly. In 1950, when writing about Dwight Eisenhower, I felt it imperative to meet and talk with him—partly because there was so little in the way of a record, partly because it *was* his personality that made him so attractive to the public. I had known few military men and wanted to make my own judgment on what he might be like as a civilian leader. In other cases, I have sought out my subjects largely to satisfy myself about them; Adlai Stevenson, John Kennedy, and Lyndon Johnson struck me as unusually interesting human beings, more than the sum of what they projected to the

---

served by trying him or by further confinement. (He was a physical menace to no one.) My article was used in Thurman Arnold's successful plea for his release in 1958, a legal brief that had the distinction of being rewritten by Robert Frost.

public, and I was eager to meet them, but except for the Kennedy memoir I wrote in 1975, I relied almost exclusively on what was available to any journalist.

After I had been on *The New Yorker* for a while, I developed a considerable interest in law, especially criminal and constitutional law; indeed, the interest was so great that, in my thirties, I seriously considered going to law school and was dissuaded principally by the difficulties I foresaw in supporting my wife and three children while preparing for the bar. The next best thing, I decided, was to study law by observing its operations in the New York criminal-justice system at the expense of my employers. For several weeks, I spent nearly all my working hours in Manhattan's Criminal Courts Building, which housed both the County Courts and the District Attorney's offices and was connected by an elevated bridge—the Bridge of Sighs—to the Tombs, or county jail. I consorted with judges, prosecutors, defense attorneys, defendants, witnesses, bailiffs, bondsmen, and the courtroom buffs, the afficionados whose morbidity, if not their zeal for justice, make them guarantors of the right to a public trial. The District Attorney then, as for more than three decades to follow, was Frank Hogan, a Democrat who had been chosen by Dewey as his successor, and was returned to office term after term with no Republican opposition. He was a gentle, unpretentious man of unquestioned integrity, a skipper who ran a tight ship, and he gave me the run of his office, on the workings of which I wrote for *The New Yorker* a long account. In the course of my researches on the past of the D.A.'s office, I became intrigued by references to the exploits of two spectacularly and unabashedly crooked turn-of-the-century lawyers, William F. Howe and Abraham H. Hummel, partners in the Centre Street firm of Howe & Hummel, just across from the old Tombs. Howe handled the criminal end of the business, and successfully represented more than a thousand accused murderers and a large proportion of the city's most notorious felons. He was a burly, raucous Englishman of suspicious background, notable for his flashy dress and the diamonds he sometimes used to distract jurors and cause temporary blindness among them. His mastery of courtroom histrionics, of fixing judges and juries, and his enormous ingenuity as a defense strategist helped keep the prison population down and made him a much-revered figure in the underworld. Hummel, a small, sedate figure who always wore funereal black, took care of the civil end and had a clientele drawn largely from the stage; he was a pioneer in developing alienation-of-affection and breach-of-promise litigation, and hundreds of ladies of the chorus and ladies of the evening improved their lot in life by suing or threatening to sue wealthy and promiscuous young men who had, Hummel and his clients charged, first promised bliss, then reneged and broken innocent and trusting hearts. He was the mastermind of any number of blackmailers, confidence men, gambling rings, and bucket-shop operators. So popular was this pair that in 1891 they were given a place, alongside President Harrison, Queen Victoria, Buffalo Bill, the actress Lillian Russell, and the pugilist John L. Sullivan in the Hall of Fame sponsored by the *National Police Gazette*, which distributed large sepia portraits of the members to be part of the decor of pool parlors, game rooms, barbershops, and hall bedrooms throughout the country. But the barristers had, it seemed to me, been inadequately celebrated by posterity, and I felt that if the justice they so often obstructed was to be done them, it would have to be done by me—and quickly since, in 1946, there could be only a few survivors of their epoch. I retired from the Criminal Courts Building to the New York Public Library and similar institutions elsewhere; simultaneously, I sought to find people who had known them in their great days, mainly lawyers who had worked for and against them and journalists who had written of them. I found several whose memories were vivid and richly detailed, and from those memories and my research I produced four *New Yorker* articles, which were published in the fall of 1946 and in book form—*Howe & Hummel: Their True and Scandalous History*—the following summer.

It was my first venture in biography of more than article length, and in doing it I learned something of the art, if that is what it is, and something about the attitude toward such work of American publishers and readers. When it appeared in *The New Yorker*, several publishers expressed an interest in doing it as a book, and I was, of course, pleased. At length, it ran to about thirty thousand words, or considerably less than most current biographies. To me, this seemed in its favor, since it has always been my view that any book should be as short as its subject will allow and its author can make it. But the first publishers I talked to took the view that it ought to be longer, that readers were suspicious of any book that lacked a certain heft. I explained to them that even if I wanted to lengthen it, I did not think I could do so. I had included everything of relevance I was able to learn by library research and interviews, and I had excluded everything that struck me as unilluminating or repetitive. All I could do was to put back the chaff I had so diligently sought to separate from the wheat. "But couldn't you," I heard from many, "make it a portrait of the period, of the New York in which Howe and Hummel lived?" The period, I said, had already been portraited to a fare-thee-well. The libraries I had worked in were well-stocked with books on the Gilded Age, the Mauve Decade, the Gay Nineties. If this was what readers wanted, they could find it in plenty of other books. Mine was not an exercise in nostalgia; if it was a portrait, it was one of a pair of men who would have been interesting in any period, and part of my aim was to demonstrate this. But I kept running into the same argument—that the book needed more bulk, and that the simplest way of getting this was to turn it into a period piece. I decided that I could not in good conscience pad it with the cotton wool that so many publishers seemed to want and that I would turn it over to any reputable house that would accept it as I had done it. Fortunately, the firm of Farrar, Straus, then in its infancy, saw things my way. The slender book was a modest success; it reached the middle rungs of several best-seller lists and did moderately well in several paperback editions. Whether it would have done better if it had been fatter, I do not know and, at this distance, do not much care. But I felt that I struck a blow for what I regard as sound doctrine for writers and simple justice for readers. It was hardly a famous or a lasting victory, for it still seems to me that most American books in most categories are, like so much else in American life, fatter than they have any need to be. As a reader, I object to this, and as a writer I strive first of all to please myself.

I have started and abandoned at least as many biographies and *New Yorker* "Profiles" as I have completed, the reasons for the breakage being numerous and varied. After *Howe & Hummel*, Ross began to think of me as a specialist in crime. He was intrigued by the doings of a band of hoodlums to whom the press had given the collective sobriquet Murder, Incorporated, or, for headline purposes, Murder, Inc. Its high command was a pair of industrial racketeers named Louis Buchalter and Jacob Shapiro, known to their comrades and the public as Lepke and Gurrah. Both had been convicted of first-degree murder and punished by electrocution before Ross thought of having me write anything about them, but many who had been associated with them were still alive, some in jail, some at liberty. The label Murder, Inc., had been applied because it was widely believed that they would contract for murder in the public market; they would kill anyone whose death was sufficiently desired by anyone in a position to pay the hit man's fee. Actually, this seems to have been myth; there was no record of Lepke or Gurrah or any of their confederates doing in anyone outside their own mob. But it was quite a story anyway, and Ross thought he had a good source in his friend William O'Dwyer, then the Mayor but formerly the Brooklyn District Attorney who had prosecuted several members of the gang. He *was* a good source, but he turned out to be just about the only one, and the story could not be told simply by talking to the chief prosecutor; fairness seemed to require that I heard the other side's story. I managed to get in touch with a few but found, on the one hand, that they would tell me nothing that might incriminate any of them and, on the other, those who were willing to reveal anything would do so only, as was said to be their practice in undertaking murders, for a stiff fee. Stiff or otherwise, such payments were out of the question. I approved the policy but was disappointed by the loss of the material. The only one who would say anything without a down payment had a touching story to tell. When, as he was about to leave my office, I asked him what had led him to get out of a lucrative racket, he said, "I was getting pretty high up in the Knights of Columbus, and my wife thought it would be held against me if the Knights knew I'd worked with Lepke and Gurrah."

There are ideas that, like some love affairs, simply don't work out. At one point, Ross wanted me to finish a "Profile" on Harry Houdini, the magician, that had been started several years earlier by James Thurber. As a young reporter, Thurber had covered Houdini's death and funeral and had formed a friendship with Mrs. Houdini, who gave him Houdini's letters and other papers. Thurber was enthusiastic about doing a Houdini "Profile," but blindness overtook him soon after he started work on it. I thought I would enjoy taking up where Thurber had left off; I had no great interest in magic, but I was intrigued by Houdini's crusades against the occult and supernatural. Soon after he got me the material, Ross died; when I talked to Thurber, I found that his approach and mine were completely different. He thought I should not concern myself with Houdini's ideas but solely with his genius in his profession. My interest, never as great as his, began to cool, for I could not see myself writing the kind of articles he could have approved. I did not realize, though, that I had antagonized him until I read Burton Bernstein's *Thurber*, in which a letter on the subject to E. B. White appeared:

. . . I haven't heard anything about the Rovere pieces, since he is busy blowing up criticism like a tire, but if he hasn't started to work, I'm going to take the pieces away from him. This I'd do in the name of Harold Ross, who created a good magazine by staying away from the Roveres. . . . They are carrying on . . . all right . . . even though everybody I meet seems to suggest that it should now be called "Momentum."

I had never heard from Thurber after our first talk. There was nothing to take away; by 1952, when Thurber wrote White, I had long since decided that Houdini was not a suitable subject for me.

On occasion, the kind of intimacy I often sought to avoid with politicians proved the undoing of what seemed at the outset a promising project. This, as I explained in the chapter on Walter Lippmann, was largely the reason for turning that biography over to Ronald Steel. Even the most large-minded and free-spirited of people develop a strong proprietary interest in the material of their own stories and become apprehensive when a sympathetic biographer wants to reserve to himself the right to deal with the material as he and he alone sees fit. But intimacy is not the only reason for jettisoning such an undertaking. While still in my law-and-lawyers phase, I wanted after finishing with *Howe & Hummel* to write about a criminal-court judge, and I was given the name of James Garrett Wallace, who was then on the Court of General Sessions and who, although a product of Tammany Hall, was regarded by many as one of the fairest and most craftsmanlike of American judges. I sought him out and found him impressive and altogether delightful. He was a gallant, charming, civilized New Yorker of Scotch-Irish background, respected by his fellow jurists, by the lawyers who practiced in his court, and even by such anti-Tammany zealots as Governor Dewey, who had tried many cases before him, and the scourge of Tammany, Mayor La Guardia. He was full of Irish wit, often exercised in writing parodies and librettos, some of the latter finding their way into musical comedies. He was a most cooperative subject and we were close friends until his death in 1957 (more than a decade after I first approached him about a "Profile") but after spending a good deal of time in his chambers and in his court, I decided that I could not, in an article or articles on him, get at those aspects of the law that I wanted to write about. I had by no means been misled about his distinction as a judge. His knowledge of the statutes was immense; he had an enviable record in having his rulings and decisions survive appeal in the higher courts; better than most of his colleagues, he maintained dignity, order, and decorum in the courtroom. But my interest now was in the theory of criminal law, in the conflict of principles in juridical thinking, in justice in the abstract rather than in particular cases. Admirable public servant that he was, Judge Wallace did not have the kind of mind that concerned itself with such questions; his approach was that of a highly skilled technician, and since this was not really what I wanted to study, I had better save his time and mine by dropping the idea of the "Profile."

Doing so confronted me with a problem of a kind that my colleagues and I have often had to face—how to tell him of the mistake I had made. Nearing the end of his career when I first met him, Judge Wallace, like many subjects, had come to feel that what I wrote would serve as a kind of monument to his life and work. Telling him the truth—that he was not the kind of legal thinker I had been in search of—would, I knew, be painful for both of us. I gave myself two or three weeks in which to decide on what would be the most tactful, the least distressing way of telling him that the monument would never be built. But the difficult task was abruptly taken from my hands. I had told several friends that I was not going ahead with the Wallace "Profile" and of my reasons for not doing so, and one of them must have told Leonard Lyons, who wrote a gossip column, one that was unusual in being insipid rather than malicious, for the *New York Post*. It was soon brought to my attention that Lyons had an item to the effect that I had decided against writing what I had planned because I was disappointed in Judge Wallace and embroidering this important bit of intelligence with the assertion that I had "torn up" my notes and a preliminary draft. (I know of writers who tear up notes and manuscripts, but I think there are few of them, and I, a magpie by nature, never do so, my theory being that a day may come when I will find some use for work put aside in midstream.) Certain that the Lyons item had been brought to the judge's attention too, I asked if he, would consider writing an introduction to my forthcoming *Howe & Hummel*. Up to then, I had felt no need for an introduction to the book, but I could think of nothing else that would ease his disappointment. He accepted and wrote a graceful series of anecdotes about the New York he had known as a young lawyer, none of them related to the content of the book. As in politics, there are payoffs at times in journalism, and gossip is a complicating feature of life in both professions.

I still wanted to write about judges and the law, and I thought I had an almost perfect subject in Jerome N. Frank, a judge on the United States Circuit Court of Appeals. A brilliant and colorful man, Frank had been a highly successful corporation lawyer in Chicago, one of the architects of the New Deal's economic policies, and one of his generation's most influential legal thinkers. His 1930 book, *Law and the Modern Mind,* was the manifesto of the young, mostly radical lawyers who espoused what they called "legal realism"—which held that the old doctrine of *stare decisis,* or abiding by the precedents, was inadequate and that the law had to be conceived as part of the social and political process. He was perhaps the most widely read man I have ever known, and he spoke and wrote in a muscular, unlawyerly style. His main interests, like mine, were in criminal and constitutional law. But this project, too, had to be abandoned, for, I found, after spending a good deal of time with him, that his private life was so tangled and troubled and that he often contemplated—and once attempted—suicide. His neuroses were so numerous and deep-rooted that when he was being psychoanalyzed in Chicago in the 1920s, he had gone to his analyst twice and sometimes three times a day. There are times when it is possible for a writer to separate a subject's private life from his professional or public one, but in Frank's case the two came together at so many points that it was impossible, or so at least I felt, to do so, and I put still another project aside. Both Judge Wallace and Judge Frank died in 1957, and my notes form the bases for eulogies I delivered at memorial services at the New York County Bar Association.

The three *New Yorker* "Profiles" I have excerpted here were written and published at a time when "Profiles" were regarded by the magazine's editors as a kind of centerpiece for each issue, and a week in which there was none to feature was considered a failure of the system. Now months may go by without the appearance of one. There are several reasons for this. Most of the obvious subjects have been done, some more than once. To be sure, people die and are succeeded by others, but often what is written is not so much about individuals as about the roles they play. For example, my articles on Newbold Morris were as much about the office he held—President of the City Council—as about him, and although quite a few others have held it since, the job has changed little, and what I wrote was not far short of exhaustive. Also, under Shawn the magazine does not concentrate on life in New York to the degree that it did under Ross, and much of the space once devoted to people is now devoted to ideas and now and then even to polemic. But most important, I think, is the fact that Shawn is a fundamentally gentle man and not given to having fun at the expense of others. Very often the "Profiles" that worked best and the ones that writers most enjoyed doing were those that deflated their subjects and sometimes savaged them. It is not that his *New Yorker* is less acerbic than Ross's; on the contrary, it is probably more so. It was with his full approval and collaboration that Richard Harris and Jonathan Schell zeroed in on Richard Nixon, John Mitchell, and the whole cast of Watergate. But he is less inclined than Ross to give the same treatment to lesser charlatans, and it was these who often made the best "Profile" copy.

The first *New Yorker* "Profiles" were short enough to make the title an apt one. A "profile" is by definition an outline, a silhouette, and the early ones were just that—a few hundred words, a few columns in length. In time, their length multiplied tenfold or more—never to the elephantine bulk that has become fashionable in American biography but to something much more than a sketch. *The New Yorker* is often credited with having developed the form that has been so widely adopted—and often crudely imitated—by other magazines. Actually, the very short ones go back as far as Plutarch, and a modern progenitor of the longer ones was Lytton Strachey's *Eminent Victorians*. (Before that, there was the superb *English Men of Letters* series.) *The New Yorker*'s contribution was, in part, to apply the method to the lives of many persons who were not in the least eminent and to infuse it with some of the qualities of fiction. Joseph Mitchell, as fine a stylist as anyone who has contributed to the magazine, has written movingly of many on the underside of life in New York and indeed some of his subjects have been creatures of his own invention. There have also been *New Yorker* "Profiles" of places and institutions—Central Park, the American Museum of Natural History, the American Institute of Arts and Letters (all by Geoffrey Hellman)—and of such inanimate objects as oranges (by John McPhee). My own efforts broke no new ground, but I think they captured something of the period, the half decade after the Second World War. Like most postwar periods (at least for the victors), it seemed a period of considerable promise, and because of that one could write with a kind of lightheartedness and insouciance that in most of the years that followed would have been mere flippancy. I do not think that today I could recapture the voice in which these articles were written, but I am glad that once I had it.

## I. DR. BRUNO FURST

Sometime in the summer of 1945, on a train from New York to Springfield, Massachusetts, I found myself seated beside a man who identified himself as Bruno Furst, a mnemonist, or memory expert, who was on his way to deliver a lecture on his specialty to the Rotary Club of Springfield. Never having met a memory expert, I asked him how he became one and what he did with his expertise. He was only too pleased to spend the next two hours or so satisfying my curiosity. He also invited me to attend his Springfield lecture and to visit his School of Memory and Concentration in New York. And I was only too pleased to accept, for I sensed that I had the subject for a *New Yorker* article.

I also sensed that I had met a charlatan. But there were hundreds of *New Yorker* readers who felt, after reading about Dr. Furst, that they at last had the name of a much-needed therapist. And I learned once again that irony seldom pays. I had intended, among other things, to tell any readers who might be concerned about their faulty memories that they would find no remedies in Dr. Furst's mnemonics, that they would do better to live with their disability than to further addle their brains with Dr. Furst's silly, impossibly complicated codes and methods of association, which, I felt, could only make matters worse for them. But almost immediately after the article appeared, hundreds of letters began arriving at the office asking such questions as how to get in touch with the miracle worker and what he charged to improve bad memories. I believe that nothing I have ever written drew so large a response—nearly all of it from people who felt some need to be saved by Dr. Furst. And within weeks, I learned, his preposterous school had more applicants than it could accept. Sales of Dr. Furst's books spurted shortly after publication of my article. Later, he began an extensive advertising campaign, featuring some of my ironies as endorsements. I never saw him again, but for several Christmases after publication, which was February 23, 1946, I received from Dr. Furst a case of champagne, which, though I disapprove of accepting such gratuities from businessmen, came in handy on New Year's Eve.

## How To Forget Nussing

Dr. Bruno Furst, an intense and ferret-faced man who used to be a criminal lawyer in Frankfurt-am-Main, is probably the best all-round mental athlete of the century. If there were an intellectual Olympics, Dr. Furst would win the decathlon. Nothing cerebral is beyond him. He is a mental telepathist, a hypnotist, and a mnemonist, or memory expert. His limber and absorbent brain frequently receives flashes of precognition and psychometric intelligence. He has developed his powers of concentration so well that he can focus his attention on the head of a pin for five or six minutes. By sheer mental effort, he can regulate the beat of his heart, increasing and decreasing the tempo as he wishes. He can relax his mind so completely that he is able to suspend thought altogether and fix on infinite nothingness for minutes at a time. His eyes and his mind coordinate like a thoroughbred's shanks. Professor Norman Lewis of New York's City College, the author of *How to Read Better and Faster*, considers him the second-best and fastest reader he knows. Dr. Furst is also a professional graphologist, or handwriting analyst. He is a chess player of tournament rank and a first-class performer in every kind of quiz and card game. He enjoys bridge and would be a champion if people would play with him. Few do, on the reasonable ground that his mnemonic systems and his highly developed extrasensory perceptions would enable him not only to communicate with his partners but to know what cards everyone held. If he wanted to, he could also cheat by means of prestidigitation, a nonmental hobby with which he amuses himself on the rare occasions when his mind is tired from too much concentration or relaxation.

Naturally, a man who sprints, hurdles, and broad-jumps with his brain must, like one who conquers space with his feet, spend a good deal of time practicing. Dr. Furst seldom lets a day go by without transferring several thoughts, memorizing many facts and figures, and inducing a trance or two. For seven years, however, or ever since he arrived in this country from Czechoslovakia, where he had been living, a refugee from Germany, he has devoted most of his professional activities to mnemonics, the field in which he feels that, at least for the time being, he can make his most substantial contribution to American life. After a year of study, he memorized enough English to lecture in the language, and he has since been conducting a relentless crusade against American forgetfulness. He has assaulted the grasshopper mind in countless lectures on the Rotary and Kiwanis circuits. He has written two books on the science of memory—*Use Your Head*, published in 1939, and *How to Remember*, published in 1944—which have drawn a steady stream of self-conscious wool-gatherers to Brentano's and Macy's and have electrified such authoritative reviewers as Dale Carnegie, May Lamberton Becker, of the *New York Herald Tribune*, and Orval Graves, M.A., F.R.C., of the *Rosicrucian Digest*. In his School of Memory and Concentration, on the sixth floor of Steinway Hall, underneath the campus of the University of Advanced Metaphysics, Dr. Furst teaches hundreds of absentminded New Yorkers, in a ten-week course, how to remember not only their own telephone numbers but as many others as they want. Since he reached this country Dr. Furst has worked out a dozen or so brand-new mnemonic systems. He has devised a method for learning the International Morse Code in fifteen minutes (once the Furst Code has been mastered), a scheme he perfected just a few months too late to be of use in training men for the war. He has also solved several rather special problems brought to him by people who feel called upon to make more than normal demands on their memories. Thanks to Dr. Furst, there is now one hotel manager in New York who has an infallible system for remembering the names of all his guests and for associating each name with the right room number. The New York *Daily News* now has an advertising solicitor who can quote all the rates and discounts of his publication without reference to a rate card (something no other salesman on a metropolitan paper has ever been known to do), as well as all the rates of all the other papers in town and of three in Brooklyn and Long Island as well. There is an official of a local wholesale drug firm who knows the number of drugstores in every American city large enough to have a number of drugstores. Most of the formulas for such miracles have been worked out by Dr. Furst; some of them, however, have come about as a result of experiments in applied mnemonics conducted by the Dr. Furst Memory Club, which is both a kind of honors society for Dr. Furst's best students and a research organization whose work promises to open new frontiers in human retentiveness.

Dr. Furst does not look like a wizard. He is fifty-four, of medium height and build, slightly paunchy, nearsighted, half-bald, conventional in dress and manner, and anything but swift in conversation. He has a pointed, rather eager face that shows a measure of intelligence, but the face and the intelligence might just as well belong to an alert waiter or a thoughtful dentist. As far as can be determined from such usually reliable sources as *Mind Digest, The Psychic Observer*, and the Classified Telephone Directory, Dr. Furst is the only professional mnemonist active in New York and one of the only two in the entire country, the other being a man named Nutt, who operates out of Greensboro, North

Carolina, and is known as the inventor of the Nutt Mental Filing System. There is a good reason that memory experts are scarce. It takes no training at all for a man to set himself up in business as a personality builder or a soul vibrator, but a memory teacher, who is expected to produce tangible results, has to develop his own memory before he can go to work on the memories of others. Mnemonics is a difficult and seldom cultivated field of human knowledge, and a mnemonist's life can be a strenuous one.

When Dr. Furst began his work in New York, in 1939, the local memory market was in the hands of Bernard Zufall, a General Electric salesman who had memorized large sections of the *Saturday Evening Post* every week for fifteen years, had pretty well mastered the 1935 *World Almanac* and the Winter 1935 Manhattan Telephone Directory, and was well along toward the fulfillment of his great ambition, which was to memorize the whole of *Webster's Unabridged Dictionary*. Zufall kept going until a few years ago, when, for fear that his head would burst if he persisted in stuffing it with definitions, he began to taper off. He is now down to a few dozen a week and has passed on the torch to Dr. Furst, to whom he now refers all prospective students. There seems to be little danger that Dr. Furst's head will burst, for he has never punished his memory so brutally. Except for certain material that he has memorized to use in demonstrations, he has gone in for more digestible information than the sort that is found in the *World Almanac* or the Telephone Book, and even for his lecture demonstrations he prefers the brief, flashy feats of memory to the recital of massive bodies of knowledge. One of his favorite tricks is to fan out a deck of freshly shuffled cards, study it for a few moments, and tell the sequence to the audience from memory. He always has some of its members check him by examining the deck. He can do two decks in slightly more than a minute. Another stunt is memorizing several pages of any morning paper in whatever city he is appearing in. It generally takes him no more than a day to forget the card sequence or the news stories.

Despite his emphasis on the fleeting but spectacular, Dr. Furst's mind is well stocked with permanent information. No one has ever been foolish enough to try to take an inventory of the contents of his brain, but if this could be done it would almost certainly show that Dr. Furst knows more than all the quiz-show experts put together. Generally, he has let his interests, professional and recreational, lead his memory where they will. When he was practicing law in pre-Hitler Germany, he memorized the entire German Civil Code, which then comprised 2,385 paragraphs of legal language. Even today, he can cite the law in any given paragraph of it or, given a law, cite its paragraph number. He has also stored up six languages, thousands of telephone numbers and street addresses, hundreds of poems, dozens of plays, and a score of novels. He likes to point out that for a man with an educated memory, being caught on a train ride or a dull weekend visit without anything to read is no problem. When Dr. Furst, whose lecturing involves a lot of tedious bus and train travel, finds himself on a long journey without a good book, he remembers one. He can recline in his seat, close his eyes, and enjoy Goethe, Heine, Thomas Mann, or any of the other authors in his large portable library. He is greatly interested in geography, and can instantaneously recall most of the vital and geographical statistics about the earth. He knows to the mile how far it is from Murmansk to Mozambique, what mountains and bodies of water lie in between, how high the mountains are and how deep the waters, the names and populations of all principal way stations, and all the points of natural and historic interest en route. As a sort of patriotic gesture to his adopted country, he has learned the population and area of every state in the union and the population of every American city of over a hundred thousand. For Dr. Furst, Paterson, New Jersey, is a city not of 140,000 but of 139,656. He knows every date worth knowing, and he can give the day of the week of every date after the institution of the Gregorian calendar. If, for example, he were giving Andrew Jackson's birthday, he would say, "March 15, 1767. Now ledd me see—ah, zo, that was a Sunday." On the whole, Dr. Furst is not as proud of his collection of geographical and historical facts as he is of his work with abstract material. He feels that his most notable achievement is his mastery of the powers of two up to the hundredth power, which is, if anyone cares, 1,267,650,600,228,229,401,496,703,205,376.

Not all the students who attend Dr. Furst's School of Memory and Concentration have faulty memories. Occasionally someone enrolls because his recall is so nearly total that he thinks a little study will make it perfect. Aside from people like this, the school's student body is a roster of the worst memories in New York and its environs. People who can't even remember their own telephone numbers and street addresses are common. Many of them complain that they have difficulty in recognizing members of their own families when they encounter them away from home. Now and then, someone actually has trouble with his own name. Not long ago, one desperate woman, giving up the struggle with the school's application form, which asks routine questions about home and business addresses, phone number, employer's name, and so forth, wrote across the blank, "Goodness, if I knew all this, I wouldn't be here!"

Every ten weeks, when Dr. Furst is ready to repeat his course, he gives a memory demonstration in Steinway Hall. The event is not widely advertised in the press, but news of it seems to travel rapidly by grapevine among the city's forgetful, and as many as 200 may show up. (Hundreds of others undoubtedly start off for the demonstration but forget where they're going and never arrive.) From the group of 200, one or two classes of from 30 to 40 students each are formed. What Dr. Furst's students find comforting in his demonstrations is not so much his admirable memory as the astounding and heartening news that it was once very feeble. Like a great many people of extraordinary development in a special direction, Dr. Furst has built up his long suit from a weakness. His capacious memory and all his other mental powers are an example not of the wonders nature can work in man but of the wonders man can work in improving on nature. Thus, Dr. Furst has the same appeal for the scatterbrained that Charles Atlas, the World's Most Perfectly Developed Man, who at seventeen was, in his own words, "a ninety-seven-pound runt, skinny, pale, nervous, and a prey to bullies," has for males of inferior physique. If Dr.

Furst had been endowed with a good memory, if he had been anything like John Stuart Mill, who at the age of ten is said to have known by heart Gibbon's *Decline and Fall* and Hume's *Human Understanding*, his memory demonstrations would be a mockery rather than an inspiration to the sufferers who seek him out. When Dr. Furst was ten, he always tells his students, he was still having trouble with the alphabet, was at sea in the multiplication table, and was screaming for help in history and geography. He was then a schoolboy in Metz, where he had been born, in 1891, and where his father, the proprietor of one of the city's large department stores, was a citizen of considerable substance. Furst was, he says, a rather intelligent boy, but neither his intelligence nor his father's social position protected him from the derision of his schoolmates. "It was terrible," he tells his classes, who nod sympathetically and chuckle knowingly. "I could remember nussing. My glassmates were way ahead of me. My teachers said I would never amount to anysing. That was before I learned that the memory could be trained like a muscle."

The idea of the memory's being trained like a muscle, becoming taut and quick in response, eventually bulging with power as the result of properly directed exercise, always appeals to Dr. Furst's students, and he uses the metaphor often. The man who gave him this idea and served as Dr. Furst's memory coach was the late Ludwig Poehlmann, of Munich. Poehlmann was best known on the Continent as the inventor of methods for teaching languages quickly, but he also jacked up puny memories. Dr. Furst studied under him for a year, starting in 1911. By this time, Dr. Furst, who eventually took a doctorate in jurisprudence, was a candidate for a law degree at the University of Munich, a fact which may suggest that his descriptions of the sievelike memory of his youth are at least slightly exaggerated. At any rate, Dr. Furst gives Poehlmann the credit for transforming him from a student who could scarcely remember his teacher's name into the only lawyer in all Germany who kept the Civil Code in his head rather than in the five fat volumes in which it was published. Poehlmann equipped his students with fewer remembering devices than his protégé does, but he was an excellent teacher of concentration. Dr. Furst learned to concentrate so well that he was soon branching out into telepathy, hypnotism, speed reading, and a good many other forms of endeavor that are based on the capacity for intense concentration. It was not Poehlmann, however, but Adolf Hitler who was responsible for Dr. Furst's devoting himself wholly to the life of the mind. From 1912 until 1933, Dr. Furst, whose family had lost its money ,when, after the First World War, the French regained Alsace-Lorraine, devoted himself most of his time to building up a practice in criminal law in Frankfurt. More or less as a hobby, he kept his memory in trim, conducted telepathy experiments, and wrote about all this for learned journals. Surprisingly, he found few ways of using his side interests in his profession. Occasionally, in cases involving identification, he would trip up a witness against one of his clients by submitting the witness to an impromptu memory test, but that is a procedure often used by lawyers who have had no traning in mnemonics. Hypnotizing witnesses was, of course, against the law. Telepathy might have come in handy as a lie detector, but at that time, unfortunately, Dr. Furst's mind was better at concentrating than at relaxing, an unsatisfactory state of affairs for this sort of work. In telepathy, the sender's mind concentrates and the receiver's relaxes. Dr. Furst might have been able to transfer thoughts to witnesses—he says that his sense of ethics prevented him from doing it—but he had not yet become receptive to the brain waves of others, particularly others who would be none too eager to beam the truth his way. In recent years, Dr. Furst, having'learned to relax, has improved as a receiver, but he is still better as a sender. "Dr. Furst can send thoughts all over town," one local telepathist says, "but, if you ask me, he doesn't seem to receive very well except from people in the same room."

Dr. Furst came to New York by way of Prague; being a Jew and an active anti-Nazi, he had decided in 1933 to leave Germany. Like most émigré lawyers, he had to give up his profession when he gave up his nationality; unlike most, he had an avocation that ·

turned out to be as remunerative as his vocation. In some ways, Prague was better than New York for a man of Dr. Furst's abilities. Whereas New York is slightly better for his pocketbook, it is not so good for his ego. In Prague he was a celebrity in the scientific and business worlds. Mnemonics, telepathy, and hypnotism were considered important scholastic subjects there, and Dr. Furst was engaged to teach them at Masaryk University, the Czechoslovakian Harvard. He was also in wide demand outside the university as a lecturer on all these subjects. Conventions of writers and scientists invited him to appear before them and transfer thoughts. He had a brisk private practice in hypnosis therapy, exorcising the phobias and inner conflicts that result in nail biting, eye twitching, watch-chain twirling, and similar manifestations. He was retained by a number of banks and corporations to appraise the character and ability of prospective creditors and employees by examining specimens of their handwriting. Dr. Furst felt that these diversified activities gave him a well-rounded intellectual life, and he thought that he would lead much the same sort of life in this country. He didn't know his America. He was shocked to discover that the curiosity of the average American about such phenomena as hypnotism and telepathy is mild enough to be satisfied by an occasional magazine article and that the accustomed place for men gifted with such extraordinary mental powers as his is not in institutions of higher learning but in night clubs. It pained him to learn that in this country graphologists are mostly not on corporation payrolls but working in carnival booths and at charity bazaars. But, being highly perceptive, he also learned quickly that the average American, while he may not know what he is missing by being unable to send thoughts through space, is always willing to put out cash for anything that sounds like self-improvement, especially for anything that sounds like self-improvement in business. It might be said that for Dr. Furst the beginning of wisdom, as far as America is concerned, came with the removal from his prospectus of the School of Memory and Concentration the statement that his course is "a great aid in making the knight's move in chess" and with the substitution of the testimonial "SALESMAN SAYS: At least forty percent greater efficiency since taking Dr. Furst's course."

When Dr. Furst lifts the hearts of his beginning students by telling them that he too once had a weak memory, he might logically go on to say that he still has a weak memory. So far as is known, a man's memory, like his intelligence, remains just about constant most of his life. Nothing can be done to increase its power, and only the deterioration of the brain cells because of age or disease can subtract from it. Most memories, however, like most intelligences, operate far below capacity, and even the poorest memory, if properly used, can become the repository for surprising quantities of information. This is where Dr. Furst comes in. He cannot increase the power of anyone's memory, but he can enable a person with a poor memory to make the best use of it. He cannot rebuild the motor, but by overhauling the ignition, adjusting the carburetor, and cleaning the spark plugs, he can get more speed and mileage out of it.

Mnemonic science antedates automotive science by more than two thousand years, and, though much further advanced in some respects, its development has tended to be uneven. It has developed a method by which a person can memorize every name, address, and number in the telephone book, but it has not evolved a foolproof system for remembering even one face. Faces give a lot of trouble to many of Dr. Furst's students, but the best he can do is tell them to look hard and long at the faces they wish to remember. "Look at a face from every angle," he said in a recent lecture. "Study it. Observe every feature carefully. Look at it and compare it with other faces. If you can draw, make a picture of the face. If not, write a description of it. Also, try to limit the number of new faces you see at one time. If you are going to a party and you want to remember the people, always arrive early so you will see them one by one." Not only do these instructions result in some queer social deportment on the part of Dr. Furst's students but the prescription doesn't always work. The failure of mnemonics to deal successfully with the face problem has worried him; he feels that he ought to do something about it. He thought for a long while, in his earlier days, that Freudian psychology might be of some assistance. While he was still in Europe, he had several talks about face-remembering with Carl Jung, Alfred Adler, and others prominent in psychoanalysis. "It was really useless," he says. "I wanted them to discuss remembering. They would discuss only forgessing."

In arranging the curriculum for his school, Dr. Furst has put such matters as face remembering toward the end, so as not to discourage his students at the outset. As a rule, he starts off with a lecture on the rudiments of association. Association is the basis of almost everything in mnemonics, and Dr. Furst's students soon learn to be speedy associators. As soon as they hear a word—house, let us say— they begin to make associations: louse, mouse, grouse, wall, door, foundation, fraternity, and so forth. As they become acquainted with the Furst memory devices, they are unable to see a canoe without recalling that the *star boarder* is always *right*. If they go to the store to buy cake and ketchup, they fix their shopping list in mind by thinking, rather unappetizingly, of a piece of cake spread with ketchup. The scheme of using association as an aid to memory is not, of course, the exclusive property of students of mnemonics. It has long been known that the human mind, when it wishes to retain something, finds it easier to retain something else and to associate the first thing with the second. For some perverse reason, it is easier, as Dr. Furst tells his students when he is teaching them to remember the names of the states, to recall Idaho by thinking of a girl named Ida, of an idea, or of a potato rather than by thinking of a large Western state named Idaho.

The difference between a man with a homemade memory and a trained mnemonist is that the untrained person makes up his associations as he goes along and the mnemonist has a system, or several systems. The most elementary system that Dr. Furst teaches is what he calls the "chain method." It could as well be called the Simonidean method, for, according to some historians of mnemonics, it was invented, circa 500 B.C., by a Greek poet named

Simonides. He had attended a dinner party but gone away early, and after his departure the roof of the house had fallen in, killing all the remaining occupants. When the authorities asked Simonides for a list of his late companions, he could at first remember only a few. Later, he discovered that by forming a mental image of the dinner table at which all the guests had sat, he was able to compile a complete list. According to one historian, Simonides, using this experience as a basis, set to work devising a system of remembering which became very popular among the early Greeks and Romans and which the Greeks named after Mnemosyne, the goddess of memory and the mother of the Muses. Simonides reasoned that if a dinner table could be an aid to memory, an entire house could be of even greater assistance. He experimented and found that he could greatly increase his retentiveness by forming a mental image of a house and furnishing it with information. A whole series of slippery facts might be made skidproof simply by assigning each separate fact to a particular room, or a wall, or a table, a chair, a statue, or anything else a Greek house might reasonably contain. A sequence might be recalled at any time by mentally proceeding through the house, from front door to attic. When Simonides' house became overcrowded, he began to make mental maps of entire towns; he would lay out facts along every street, tethering them to every tree, and storing them in every attic.

The science of mnemonics has gone far beyond Simonides and his many disciples in developing the technique of systematizing association, but even the earliest methods are still useful. Dr. Furst, for example, teaches his students to remember the first ten amendments to the Constitution, the Bill of Rights, by associating each amendment with a piece of living-room furniture. Free speech can be associated with the radio, over which speeches are commonly heard; the right to bear arms may be thought of in connection with a chair, because a chair has arms; a lamp can suggest security against unwarranted search, because lamps are often used in a search. The method is wholly adequate for projects like the Bill of Rights, but it is not much good for telephone numbers or heights of mountains. Dr. Furst teaches his students to remember numbers, or facts that can somehow be related to numbers, by what he calls the "hook method," sometimes referred to as the numerical code. This is without question the greatest triumph in the history of mnemonics. The method has been in the process of development ever since 1492. Just about the time Columbus was sighting San Salvador, a German scholar named Conradus Celtes conceived the idea of using letters and numerals as an aid to memory. In the centuries between Simonides and Celtes, the only progress in mnemonics was the dubious scheme of using the signs of the Zodiac and the degrees of the circle as guides. Celtes' revolutionary idea is the foundation of the method which has today just about taken the ceiling off the human memory. When Dr. Furst or one of his students decides that a numerical fact is worth remembering, he does not, as a rule, make any effort to remember the figure itself; instead, he translates it into a word, or series of words, in accordance with the numerical code, and this, when it is translated back, gives the coded fact. Thus, when Dr. Furst wants to remember the population of a city or the area of a state, he does not recall any of the digits involved; he remembers a sentence which gives him the key. One of the statistics at his command can be translated into "Hitler in Chicago wore a stylish brown rose." Another is "For heavenly chipmunks, whiskey is pleasant." By a process of thought no more difficult than translating from one language into another, these sentences become figures of twenty-one and twenty-five digits, respectively.

The numerical code is as essential to modern mnemonics as the theory of relativity is to modern physics, and it is almost as complicated and as difficult to grasp. Several two-hour lectures by Dr. Furst are necessary merely to explain it to his students, to say nothing of teaching it to them. However, at least an inkling of its principle, and its intricacy, can be grasped from an examination of how it is first applied to a fortunately simple telephone number that Dr. Furst has frequent occasion to call. The number is BUtterfield 8–7878, and the phone belongs to Dr. Sidney Goldberg, a lung specialist who is a close friend and disciple of Dr. Furst and the author of Furst's school song, which contains the bracing lines

"And once you know mnemotechnics, You'll find it will lessen the strife." When Dr. Furst wishes to get in touch with Dr. Goldberg, he dials him at "Buf cough cough." "Buf cough cough" is code for BU 8–7878. In the code, every digit from zero to nine is represented by a consonant. One, for example, is "t," two is "n," three is "m," and so forth. However, when two consonants have the same sound, such as "s" and soft "c," or when the sound of a consonant (say "j") may be simulated by what the phoneticists call a consonantal diphthong (in this instance "ch") the second consonant or the consonantal diphthong may serve as an alternate. Using these consonants, or their alternates, in place of the digits of, say, a telephone number, it is possible to construct pronounce-able words simply by adding whatever vowels are needed. (Vowels, in this system, don't represent any digit at all, so as many as are needed can be used.) A set of figures can, moreover, be represented by several words or even series of words. This makes it possible to devise something as appropriate as "Buf cough cough" as the code for the telephone number of a lung specialist. In codifying BU 8–7878, Dr. Furst converts "BU 8" into "buf" by adding "f," the symbol for "8," to "bu." He arrives at "cough" by using the alternative hard "c" for 7 (instead of "k," the customary symbol) and "gh" for 8 (instead of the usual "f") and by throwing in the vowels "o" and "u." Any suspicion that the difficulty of this system may outweigh its practicability is dispelled by considering its amazing adaptability. If Goldberg were in the cloak-and-suit business, "Buf cuff cuff" (the second member of a double consonant ordinarily has no value) could stand for BUtterfield 8–7878. If he had something to do with restaurants, hotels, night clubs, or the like, it could be "Buf café café." If he owned a boat, lived near the water, or liked to fish, "Buf cove cove" would be suitable. If he were a drinker, it could be "Buf quaff quaff," and if he were philanthropic it could be "Buf give give." These are only a few of the possibilities.

Dr. Furst is convinced that a good head for telephone numbers is one of the marks of an educated man. "Make this your firm resolve: I will never look up a number twice," Dr. Furst has written in *How to Remember*, the Memory School's textbook. He scorns the obvious arguments against this position: that the wide distribution of directories and the efficiency of the Information operators make the effort of remembering unnecessary, and that the mental storage space taken up by telephone numbers could better be given over to knowledge of a more enriching character. He is contemptuous of the notion that it is possible for the human mind to become overcrowded; he believes that every fact, of whatever nature, the mind adds to its store makes the brain that much more receptive to the next fact that comes its way, just as each new sensory perception prepares the senses for the next one. The reason so many of his students are eager to remember telephone numbers is that they have a profound desire to get ahead in business. Businessmen, it seems, are greatly impressed by employees who can save precious time by dispensing with telephone books. Employers, apparently, are also impressed by people who can remember birthdays, the first names of wives and children, odd tastes in ties, and other useful trivia. It appears that an employee with a good memory for such facts is often rewarded with promotions, raises, and bonuses.

Not long ago, one of Dr. Furst's students, a travelling salesman with an especially low-caliber memory, used Dr. Furst's teachings as the foundation for a memory project of staggering magnitude. By combining the hook and chain methods, he worked out a system for remembering everything he does; he imprints on his memory, at the end of a day, a mental diary of all his activities— where he has been, what he has seen, what transactions he has conducted, and so forth. These gossamer notes will, or so he hopes, stay put until the end of his life. "This is probably the greatest thing that has ever happened to me," he explained to a friend recently. "Why, you just can't believe how much good this has done me. You see, in the old days, when I'd call on a customer, I'd always try to open up our conversation by reminding him of the last time I'd called. I'd walk in, and I'd say, 'Well, now, let's see—I guess this is the first time I've called since last March, or maybe it was early April. As I remember it, you gave me a pretty big order then. Hope we can get together again this time.' It wasn't such a hot line, and besides half the time I was wrong. I hadn't seen the man for two years, and he hadn't given me any order at all. I made a lot of bad impressions that way. But now, thanks to the Doctor, I have a whole new line, and it works wonders. Let's say we call my customer J.B. I walk into his office and say, 'Well, J.B., remember when I was in here last? I bet you don't, but I do. It was June 26th. A nice, sunny day, not a cloud in the sky. And I remember that steak we had at Barney's. I certainly enjoyed that filet. And those french fries and garden peas. How about joining me for one of Barney's steaks today, J.B.? And I hope you'll come across with another order like the last one—thirty-four hundred and fifty, you remember. Oh, and I hope Edith got over that nasty grippe she had last time I was here. By the way, it's getting near her birthday, isn't it, J.B.? Did she like those Flora Mir chocolates I sent her last year? I sure hope so, because she'll be getting some more of them in a few days.' Well, you can see the effect that sort of approach is going to have. With Dr. Furst's system, it takes me about fifteen minutes every evening. I don't know how long it will stick, but I've been doing it now for over a year, and I haven't forgotten anything yet. Just pick a date and ask me what I did on it. I'll tell you."

It takes six of the school's ten weeks for Dr. Furst to teach his students all the variations and the innumerable applications of the numerical code. The remaining sessions are devoted to face remembering, observation and concentration, and other less systematized branches of mnemonics. The numerical code can help the student of it to remember nearly anything, from the hour of his next appointment with the dentist to the most complex formulas in nuclear physics, but there are a few minor worlds it has yet to conquer. The only way to memorize even the simplest piece of prose is to sit down and memorize it. Neither the Gettysburg Address nor a sales talk will yield to any kind of mnemonic codification. For plain out-and-out memorizing, concentration is the only possible aid. Dr. Furst is quite successful at teaching the art; one of his female students has become so accomplished a concentrator that she is under contract to a publisher to do a book on the subject, tentatively titled *Ten Minutes in One*. The Doctor's methods are deceptively simple. His procedure in teaching observation is to admonish his students to observe; he teaches them concentration by advising them to practice it. He suggests that they begin exercising their powers of concentration by concentrating on some simple object, like a pencil, and that they gradually work their way up to a long train of thought, such as the course of an argument with a friend. "When you are concentrating on one sing," he says, "you must let nussing else enter your mind. At first this will be difficult. But if you keep trying long enough, you will improve, I assure you." His students discover, often to their surprise, that he is right.

## 2. JOHN GUNTHER

The late John Gunther—he died in 1972—was probably more widely read than any other political journalist in American history. Among his colleagues, though, he was not widely admired. Indeed, he was regarded by them as something of a fraud, a kind of high-grade, high-level gossip columnist, and frequently as inaccurate, though never as malicious, as some of them. I felt this way when I undertook to do this article. I found his work superficial and sometimes irresponsible, and I felt that someone ought to show him up for what he was.

That was what I intended to do, and perhaps it is to an extent what I did. But not to the extent I planned. For when I met him in 1947, I found him not enjoying the life that his ill-gotten, as I saw it, gains had made possible but a man sunk in misery. He was still lamenting the breakup of his first marriage and enduring the tragedy that befell the issue of that union, Johnny, a brilliant and charming boy of seventeen who was dying slowly of a malignant brain tumor. I also found him an extremely modest man, one who disparaged his own work as thoroughly as I had planned to. Johnny was in Columbia Presbyterian Hospital then, and it evidently meant a lot to John to have someone, me, around who would get him talking of other, better days. I decided I could not write the article I had planned. But if I could not at that time pour salt on his wounds, neither could I console him with flattery, which he would not in any case have wanted. So I finally turned out this piece—not fiercely critical but critical nonetheless—and it was published in the issue of August 23, 1947. It is, I think, the only example of such a compromise in my work, and as I reread it recently, it seemed to me that I had made my central points about him in language that would not cut as deeply as the language I might otherwise have used.

While working on the piece, I went often with John to visit Johnny in the hospital, and Johnny, in terrible pain and sedated much of the time, sensed that I might not be the friend his father thought I was. In his account of Johnny's ordeal, *Death Be Not Proud*, John quotes Johnny as saying I might be a "hatchet man," which was somewhat too strong a word for the role I had expected to play. When the article came out, many of John's colleagues and mine accused me of having been too soft on my subject. I could only tell them of the circumstances.

## *Insider*

John Gunther, the author of *Inside Europe*, *Inside Asia*, *Inside Latin America*, and *Inside U.S.A.*, is sick and tired of people who steal his trademark and of people who ask him when he is going to write a book called *Inside Gunther*. Since the publication of *Inside Europe*, eleven years ago, there have been about thirty *"Inside"* books by other writers, or enough to fill up a couple of bookshelves in Gunther's New York apartment. Only a few small and undeserving countries have missed having *"Inside"* books written about them. There are three called *Inside Germany*. There are, besides, a dozen with such titles as *Inside the Department of State, Inside the F.B.I., Inside Our D-Days, Inside Vermont,*

*Inside California, Inside Dover*, and *Inside Medicine*, a popular
work about the intestines. The magazine and newspaper adapta-
tions of the idea run high into the hundreds. Since *Inside Europe*
appeared, scarcely a week has passed that some editor has not
rested his brain by putting an "Inside" title on one of his articles.
For several months after the Allied landings in France, various
dispatches from the Continent were datelined "Inside Europe."
As for *Inside Gunther*, Gunther can't bear to estimate how many
people have asked about it. In fact, when he meets someone
who does *not* bring up *Inside Gunther* within the first five minutes, he is willing to put him down as a person of high intelligence.
Gunther is one of the gentlest and most amiable of men. He
would sooner pass up a subcontinent than hurt anyone's feelings.
When he is asked the awful question, he cringes inwardly but
manages to produce a chuckle or two before saying that he really
doesn't expect to write an autobiography. Despite all his for-
bearance, the situation grows worse and worse. Some are now suggesting that he call the book *Inside Out*. He tells them that three
wits have already used that title for their own books. Some men
dread medical examinations because of the bad news they may
hear; Gunther dreads them because of the bad jokes he may hear.
"You can imagine what happens when I need an X ray," he says.
"It's ghastly." Whenever Gunther plays poker, someone is sure
to bring up the matter of an inside straight. The thing has gone
so far that when he wires a hotel for a reservation the reply will
say something like "Expecting you inside us April 24th."

Gunther's plight is one of the odder consequences of the fact
that in an age that has elevated its journalists above its poets and
philosophers, he is believed by some to be the world's foremost
journalist. He is certainly the foremost world journalist. The
entire planet is his beat. He is a society reporter for all mankind.
He still has some mopping up to do on a couple of outlying
continents, but he will get to these in due time. He is already pric-
ing elephants and pith helmets for the travels that will result in
*Inside Africa*, which his publishers figure will be the international
best-seller of 1950. *Inside Australia* should follow in 1952. He

may lump the Arctic and Antarctic together in one omnibus volume. These books will help to keep alive Gunther's reputation, but they cannot greatly add to it. He may pick up a few new fans with *Inside Africa*, but most literate Luos and Ibos already know of him. It's the same thing everywhere. A few Eskimos of the more provincial sort may read Gunther for the first time when he gets around to their race, but for most of them the chief interest will be to see how they stack up alongside other peoples in Gunther's estimation.

Gunther is one of the half-dozen or so authentic international celebrities. There is a bar in Bagdad named after him, and the Texas legislature once convened a special session in his honor. He is on easy terms with all the world's important potentates except Stalin. He hopes to remedy that. The late George II of Greece made him a Virgin Eagle, Second Class. In 1937, the Viceroy of India, the Marquess of Linlithgow, threw centuries of precedent aside and invited Gunther, who bore no credentials beyond a reporter's police card, to bunk in the Viceroy's palace. A couple of years ago, when Gunther got through interviewing the Governor of Oklahoma, the Governor took out a pad and pencil, explained that he was a columnist himself, and begged permission to interview Gunther. In Amman, King Abdullah of Trans-Jordan let Gunther see his most treasured possession, a set of Coney Island distorting mirrors. When some of the Dutch Royal Family were at the White House, the Roosevelts presented them to Gunther. There is no cause for alarm in the fact that Gunther has not yet struck up a friendship with Stalin. Wendell Willkie said that when he visited the Lenin Library, in Moscow, he was treated very coolly until, passing a stack of Gunther books, he remarked that the author was a good friend of his. His standing now is excellent.

Until recently, Gunther was better known in most foreign countries than at home, but his reputation in this country is impressive enough. Each of his large surveys has been distributed by the Book-of-the-Month Club. *Inside Latin America* and *Inside U.S.A.* were regular choices; *Inside Europe* and *Inside Asia* were dividends. It is, of course, honor enough to be tapped once by the Club, but to be tapped four times, and on two of those occasions to be a book dividend, is, according to Club officials, to achieve a particularly desirable state of grace. It is like having a monument erected to one during one's lifetime. In book-club circles, a dividend has more cachet than a monthly selection, even though it is likely to be less profitable. "I'd say that having been both a dividend and a selection is really the most striking part of his record," a Club executive said recently. "The dividends are mostly classics, you know—Longfellow, Omar Khayyám, that sort of thing. The judges have nothing to do with picking dividends. We pick them right here in the business office. Most often, we offer our readers Dickens, Tolstoy, treasuries of art masterpieces—the very best stuff. Well, when we give them Gunther, right along with all those big fellows, he steps right out in front. The people want him." Gunther is now in such good standing with the Book-of-the-Month Club that practically as soon as there is a rumor of an impending Gunther book the judges suspend their normal practice of choosing books already written and settle quickly on Gunther. *Inside U.S.A.* became the Club's June 1947, selection in November 1946, when Gunther still had twenty chapters to go. The judges read thirty-two chapters and a brief outline of what was to come. The deal on *Inside Latin America* was closed when Gunther had written only half of it. "Of course, you couldn't do that with your average writer," Harry Scherman, the president of the Club, has explained. "Some of them start out like winners and then break down halfway through. But with a fellow like John, you don't run that kind of risk. If he's good on Texas and California, you can be pretty sure he'll be good on New York and Pennsylvania. I read only one chapter of *Inside U.S.A.* myself, but then I'm not one of our judges."

Altogether, what with the books the judges read all the way through and the ones they didn't, the Club has distributed a million and a quarter copies of Gunther's books. Another million and a quarter have been sold in the conventional way. No single Gunther book has done as well as *Gone With the Wind* or *How to Win Friends and Influence People*, but there was a distinct flash-in-the-pan quality about those books; their authors never did it again. Each book by Gunther sells just about as well as another. He has stability. His name has been on the best-seller lists seven of the last eleven years. A few years back, to establish Gunther's position once and for all, his publishers, Harper & Brothers, put up a prize of twenty-five dollars for any statistician who could prove that any other author had ever done better than that. The money is still in escrow.

Although Gunther has never set a record for sales with any one book, it looks as if he might do it with *Inside U.S.A.* It has already set a few minor records. Its first printing was 125,000, the largest ever ordered by Harper's. This, of course, was on top of the Club's order of almost 400,000. On Saturday, May 31st, three days after it was published, it accounted for ninety percent of the day's book business done at Macy's. Nothing like that had ever happened before. It would be rash to set a ceiling on the heights to which Gunther may soar with his latest book. He is not subject to the economic laws that operate against other authors. The market for books is what economists describe as "inelastic." The classic example of the inelastic market is the casket business. No one can use more than one casket. If there were more coffins in a country's stockpile than there were people in the country, the coffin industry would be well advised to shut down operations for ten or fifteen years. The demand for any book, no matter how remarkable, is inexorably limited: no member of the reading public needs more than one copy of any one book. As soon as a reader buys a book, he is permanently retired from the market for it, unless he can be talked into giving away copies for Christmas, in which case he retires other people from the market. None of this has any bearing on the sales of *Inside U.S.A.* When it reaches its saturation point, perhaps a year or two from now—that is, when everyone who wants and can afford a copy already has one—Harper's will begin selling readers their second copy. Harper's has discovered that Gunther books can be sold the way dress manufacturers sell dresses and automobile makers sell cars—by changing the model. The experiment has already proved successful with *Inside Asia* and *Inside Europe*. It will be done on a much larger scale with *Inside U.S.A.* There were seven models of *Inside Europe*. There was a 1936 model, a 1937 model, a 1938 model, a "Peace" (or "Munich") model, two "War" models, and a model with illustrations. "*Inside Europe* . . . was a sensational departure in publishing," a Harper's archivist has written. "It was a book that kept pace with history. For the first time a publisher and an author collaborated to keep a book on current events completely up to date." For a while, Harper's considered putting out a loose-leaf edition and merely selling new parts every so often. The idea was soon abandoned. It would have been as foolish as if, when fashion demands longer skirts, dress manufacturers sold women an extra piece of material with which to lengthen them, or as if, when an improved windshield wiper was devised, Chrysler just sold new wipers to be installed in old cars. Far better to sell a whole new dress, a whole new car, a whole new book. Harper's advertising began to play on the theme that there was something backward, if not downright *infra dig*, about having last year's edition of *Inside Europe* around the house when next year's was on the market. The man who hung onto his "Peace" edition after war had been declared was living in a dream world. There was at first some sales resistance, but Harper's overcame it with a device used by Ford and General Motors. The buyer of a new Gunther book got a trade-in allowance on his old copy. If a man with a "Munich" edition, not wishing his friends to get the wrong idea, went to his bookstore for a "War" edition, he was allowed fifty cents on his old copy, which was either given to a hospital or orphan asylum or sold in the second-hand market. The seven models of *Inside Europe* ran to ninety-five American and foreign printings and sold, altogether, better than a half-million copies. The first model of *Inside U.S.A.* has already gone over a half-million copies. Assuming that the book keeps on at this pace and that it goes through as many models as *Inside Europe* did, it will sell in the neighborhood of 13 million copies, which would be 300 percent higher than the record made by *Gone With the Wind*.

Gunther's worldwide popularity is probably greater than that of any other living writer. A few authors may outsell Gunther in one or two countries, but nobody comes up to him as an all-round international favorite. His following is a delayed rebuke to the Rev. Sydney Smith, who in 1820 could get no satisfactory answer to the question "In the four quarters of the globe, who reads an American book?" Today the answer is, in all four quarters, millions do. There are plenty of Letts, Hondurans, and Outer Mongolians who, even if they have heard of Chaucer, Shakespeare, Wordsworth, or the Rev. Smith, have surely never read any of their work, but who queue up at their bookstores as soon as a new Gunther appears.

Gunther is not a revolutionary force in his own country, as he is elsewhere, but he is still a force. Perhaps he cannot inspire political unrest, as he has in other countries, but he can inspire civic reforms. In *Inside U.S.A.*, he said that he had found the streets of Indianapolis in an unkempt condition. Other visitors had noticed this before and had remarked on it, but Indianapolis had been apathetic. A few hours after reviewers' copies of the book reached the Indianapolis newspapers, Gunther was advised by telegram that, spurred on by the press, the citizens were massing for a great antidirt campaign. This striking example of the influence of Gunther's pen is meagre beside what he accomplished in Ecuador. He happened to say, in *Inside Latin America*, that he had been quite favorably impressed by a statesman named Galo Plaza, and that he was such a flashy performer that he would almost certainly get to be President eventually. Several Ecuadorians had had the same idea for quite a while, but they had been waiting for a revolutionary situation to develop. When they read *Inside Latin America*, they thought a revolutionary situation had developed. Once it got around that Gunther thought highly of Galo Plaza, they felt certain that peasants and proletarians would begin stampeding into the Galo Plaza movement. A few months after the book was published, a Galo Plaza revolution began. It was beaten down, but some of the revolutionaries have said that it would have been a success if they had waited until *Inside Latin America* had become the all-time Ecuadorian bestseller. It is conceivable that someday Boston will ban a book by Gunther, but it is unlikely that it will ever honor him with a Tea Party. Panama did. When an issue of *Reader's Digest* containing a Gunther article that disparaged the administration of the republic appeared on the newsstands there, the government confiscated all the copies and had the Panamanian navy dump them into the sea, just far enough out so that they would not block the Canal.

Gunther is forty five, but he looks a good deal younger. In fact, he looks like a recently graduated football star from a Corn Belt university. He is tall and blond, with a bulldozer frame, blue eyes, a ruddy complexion, and incongruously delicate features. A man who gets around a lot among kings, rajahs, and generalissimos, and is a literary celebrity too, might be expected to develop regal and commanding ways. Gunther hasn't. He is not an enthusiastic participant in the Gunther craze. "Those books of mine," he will sometimes say, "they're fun to write, and people like them, but they're *so, so* superficial." By his own analysis, his personality is compounded of aggressiveness and shyness in almost equal parts. "I'm like a man who crashes a party and then sits moping in a corner all evening," he has said. Fortunately for him, the demure and self-effacing side of his nature does not assert itself in critical moments. On the one hand, he is constantly belittling his own work; on the other, he has the temerity to take on the world a continent at a time. He has a theory that his success is founded solidly upon ignorance—his own and that of his readers. "You know, I'm really naïve," he says. "When I tell a story, I put in everything—even the facts the readers ought to know already. That's probably why people read me. Other writers act as though their readers had absorbed everything in the encyclopedia, so they go on to tell them what isn't in the encyclopedia. I know very little myself, and I figure my readers know as little as I do. It nearly always turns out I'm right." Sometimes, he admits, his ignorance exceeds that of the average reader, and it becomes necessary for his publishers to edit him up to the general level of ignorance. "Cass Canfield had to cut wads of stuff out of *Inside U.S.A.*," he said the other day. (Canfield is the chairman of the board of Harper's, and Gunther's editor.) "For instance, if I'm writing about cow country, I'm as likely as not to explain that cows are four-legged, and that they are the source of steaks and milk, and that they eat grass and are sheltered in barns. There were whole reams of stuff like that that Cass had to cut out so I wouldn't look like an ignoramus. But of course I am an ignoramus."

Gunther's success may be a tribute to ignorance, but it is certainly also a tribute to daring and ingenuity. For example, by taking on the job of writing about his own country after twenty-three years as a foreign correspondent, he boldly inverted a pattern so firmly set that it had acquired almost the status of a folkway. According to this pattern, the American foreign correspondent starts out in this country as a police reporter or sportswriter and gradually works his way up, through city halls, county seats, state capitals, and Washington, to the big jobs overseas. Gunther began as a foreign correspondent and gradually worked his way back to the city halls and county courthouses. Between 1924 and 1936, he represented the Chicago *Daily News* in twenty European capitals, and between 1936 and 1945 he interviewed everyone of importance in Asia and Latin America, all in preparation for his assignment of soliciting the views of the mayor of Provo, Utah, and the governor of West Virginia for *Inside U.S.A.* To begin with, there is a good two hundred dollars a week difference between covering the city hall of Vienna, say, and the city hall of any American city, and then, as Gunther has lately proved, the man who has covered Vienna can, when he begins to feel the pull of hearth and home, go back to Main Street and clean out the banks by writing courthouse news.

Gunther was born in Chicago on August 30, 1901. His father, Eugene McClellan Gunther, was a moderately prosperous real-estate dealer, and his mother had been a schoolteacher. John spent his boyhood in a kind of middle-middle-class neighborhood on the North Side and attended the public schools and the University of Chicago. In his sophomore year, he became a campus hero on the strength of a recondite essay. In those days, the writing of essays was a sure way to ostracism in college, but Gunther's performance made him the social equal of a shotputter or a saxophonist. His entry in a campus essay contest was a dissertation on James Branch Cabell. The judges, all professors of English, felt that Gunther's composition had certain merits of style and perception, but they seemed not to have heard of Cabell, and they thought that the prize, fifty dollars, should go to an essay dealing with a really well-known literary figure, like Elkanah Settle or Thomas of Erceldoune. Gunther sent the rejected essay to *The Bookman*, which bought it at the usual space rates, according to which, it turned out, the piece was worth fifty-one dollars. It was the fifty-first dollar that made Gunther famous on the campus. If he had won the contest, he would have gotten nothing more than some perfunctory applause on Commencement Day. If he had sold the piece to *The Bookman* for forty-nine dollars, he would have lived on in obscurity. But the dollar by which he topped the professors' fee gave the student body a sense of gratification, a vicarious thrill of revenge. It was as though the coach had put him on the scrub team but he was nevertheless chosen for All-American.

After his success with *The Bookman*, Gunther began to see himself as a Sainte-Beuve or Matthew Arnold. He wrote to twenty-five or thirty Eastern book publishers, telling them that John Gunther, of Chicago, was ready to deliver his critical opinions on contemporary books and suggesting that any books they thought worthy should be forwarded to him. His letters sounded so important that dozens of complimentary copies of the latest books began to arrive. He published his opinions of them in the college paper, *The Daily Maroon*. Seeing no good reason why, in an age of syndication, his views on literature should be available only to the readers of one publication, he sent a prospectus of the Gunther book service to a selected group of sixty or seventy newspaper editors around the country. Several of them accepted, at three-fifty a week, and by the time hé was nineteen he had his own column, which he distributed through his own syndicate. Harry Hansen, then the literary editor of the Chicago *Daily News*, liked the way Gunther wrote and had him do occasional book reviews, in addition to running his syndicated column. Once established as a book reviewer, Gunther tried to move in on dramatic criticism. When he learned that Percy Hammond was leaving the Chicago *Tribune* for the New York *Tribune*, he applied for Hammond's job. Twenty-five plays had been performed in Chicago that year, and Gunther had seen them all. The night he learned about Hammond, he sat down and wrote—refreshing his memory from the programs, which he had kept—long reviews of all twenty-five. He sent them to Edward S. Beck, then the managing editor of the *Tribune*. The theatre lost Gunther to world reporting by a hair. Beck replied that the reviews were good enough to hold the job but not quite good enough to get it.

The book-reviewing syndicate might have grown into an international cartel if Gunther had not been so much influenced by the books he was reviewing. The First World War had ended a couple of years before, and the best American writing was being done in Europe. Gunther decided to go there. He liquidated his syndicate, gave up his job on the *News*, left college several weeks before graduation, and shipped across the Atlantic on a cattle boat to begin a twentieth-century version of the nineteenth-century grand tour. The university mailed him his diploma; the Phi Beta Kappa chapter there is still holding his key for him. Gunther did not think of himself as a journalist then. He had no interest in politics. The day Mussolini marched on the city he arrived in Rome in a sleeping car. In fact, his train pulled into the station just a couple of hours ahead of Mussolini's. Gunther paid as little attention to Mussolini as Il Duce paid to him. Gunther was completely wrapped up in art. He had elected himself a member of the Lost Generation. To show what he could do, he worked out, in 1922, a brand-new wrinkle in Lost Generation novels. It was *High Sat White Helen*, which had the same plot as *This Side of Paradise* but had a woman instead of a man as the principal sufferer. Some literary agents in New York thought they could make a killing for Gunther with this ingenious twist, but Gunther, who has always been his own best critic, decided not to let the book be published. Later in his career, however, he wrote several other novels that were published. Most of them were written on the Riviera or in the Alps, on vacations from his newspaper work, and all of them were ninety-proof Fitzgerald and Hemingway. In one of them, for example, a mixed group of groping souls spends a riotous night in a bank vault and goes out early in the morning to grab gallows-side seats at a hanging.

Gunther had some trouble getting started as a foreign correspondent. In 1922, having seen Europe and having decided that he wanted to settle down there, he made a brief return visit to this country and joined the staff of the Chicago *Daily News*, with an eye to getting himself sent back to Europe. The *News* tried hard to squeeze him into its mold. Its convention-ridden editors held that a man ought to have some experience with local news before taking on world events. For several months, Gunther covered municipal politics, crime, and other routine assignments. Pretty soon, however, he told his editors that he thought he ought to be sent overseas. They told him not to be silly; he was only twenty-three, and there were men twice his age on the waiting list for jobs abroad. Gunther resigned. He had just enough money for a third-class passage on the *Olympic*. When he got to New York, he learned that the Prince of Wales was to be a fellow-passenger, and he talked the United Press into raising his passage from third to second class in exchange for some interviews with the Prince, which he got. Then he got a hundred dollars from Reuters for some other shipboard interviews. He reached London broke. It occurred to him that the *News* office there might be more astute than the home office. He went around and asked for a job. Someone was leaving, and it seemed easier to take on a replacement who was already on the scene than to send back to Chicago for one. Gunther lasted only a few weeks; when his name turned up on the payroll submitted to Chicago, the London office was or-

dered to fire him. It was felt that it would be demoralizing to the
staff if a man who couldn't get what he wanted at the home office
had merely to show up at one of the branches to get it. Gunther
went down the street and got a job with the United Press. He '
didn't like it there. It wasn't long before he was back with the
*News*'s London office, which took the view that his period of
service with the U.P. put him in a new category.

When Gunther first worked for the *News* in Europe, he had no
regular assignment. He was a kind of utility infielder, or swing
man. He was used to replace colleagues on vacations or leaves of
absence. The job was invaluable preparation for writing *Inside
Europe*. Gunther hit every city on the Continent and built up a
first-class collection of potentates. He interviewed everyone from
Lloyd George to Leon Trotsky, from Eamon De Valera to Ad-
miral Leon Horthy, the Hungarian dictator. After a few years of
circuit riding, he worked for longer periods in London, Paris, and
Vienna. Gradually, he became one of the best known of all the
American foreign correspondents, though not for the reasons the
others had achieved celebrity. For one thing, he was not much of
a hand at spot news. It is widely believed that the quickest way
to get ahead in newspaper work is to gather lots of news and to
report it quickly. Gunther showed this to be mere superstition. "I
never really got a big scoop in my life," he says, "and the little
ones I got were just plain accidents. I wasn't one of those reporters
who managed to be on the scene when big things happened. I was
generally somewhere else. Matter of fact, I never really gave a
damn about spot news. The idea of beating the Associated Press
by six minutes bored me silly." Gunther made his reputation
mainly with his background stories. When a story was news, he
was almost bound to muff it, but after it had been kicked around
a while, he could work wonders with it. High-school and college
textbooks are full of Gunther's background stories. Anthologies
that illustrate "the topical essay" with selections from Bernard
Shaw and Walter Lippmann invariably illustrate "the background
story" with something by Gunther. He developed the entire scheme
of his books while writing his articles. Whenever his work for the

Vienna bureau would allow, he headed for Bulgaria or Greece or wherever and wrote for the *News* a series of simple, precise little pieces, peppered with readable anecdotes and designed to explain to the uninformed American public the mysteries of Balkan politics. After a while, *Vanity Fair*, *The Nation*, and the *Saturday Evening Post* began asking him to write for them. Often, he and M. W. Fodor, then the dean of Central European correspondents, went together on hunts for people who could provide them with lively copy. Long before the Anschluss, they went to Braunau, the Austrian town in which Hitler was born, and talked with a number of people who had known Hitler before the world knew him, including the midwife who had delivered him. Another time, at a resort on the Danube, Gunther turned up a waiter who had made a career of waiting on persons engaged in political intrigue; the man had listened in on their plottings, saved their tablecloth jottings, and even had a menu stained with the blood of an archduke who had been assassinated just as he was ordering dinner.

As a correspondent, Gunther wrote large chunks of *Inside Europe* without knowing it. But when publishers began proposing the idea of doing the book, he didn't like it. The proposals were made because of the success of the *Washington Merry-Go-Round* books by Drew Pearson and Robert S. Allen, which were published, anonymously, in 1931 and 1932. They were the first nonfiction books in years to offer serious competition to novels. It occurred to a number of people that the *Merry-Go-Round* formula could be applied to Europe as easily as to the United States. One publisher even whipped up a symposium of European political gossip called *Not to Be Repeated*, to which Gunther contributed the chapters on Central Europe. The book didn't do especially well. Gunther's wife, a New Yorker named Frances Fineman, whom he married in 1927 and from whom he was divorced in 1944, thought that her husband might do better with a book all his own, and kept encouraging him to try one. He didn't think he should. He still looked upon himself as essentially a novelist, and he wanted to limit his book-writing to fiction. To the publishers who broached the idea of a European *Merry-Go-Round* to him, he said that the only man who could do it was H. R. Knickerbocker, the best known of the Hearst correspondents. They went to Knickerbocker, who said the only man who could do it was Gunther. Gunther then tried to shoo the publishers away by demanding too large an advance. He said he wouldn't take on the job for anything less than five thousand dollars on account. That was an immense advance in those days, and it did scare off most of the publishers, but finally, in 1935, Harper's and Hamish Hamilton, the London publisher, put up the money. Gunther accepted it reluctantly, put aside his novels, and went calling on the few kings and prime ministers he had not already interviewed. He worked on the book that summer and autumn, and excerpts from it appeared in *Harper's Magazine. Inside Europe* was published in January of 1936. The first American printing was five thousand copies, and Hamilton put out a small edition in England. "We figured the book ought to sell just about five thousand," Cass Canfield said recently. "That way, we'd have paid off our part of the advance and have made a fairly decent profit." In seven months, it went through fourteen large printings, and during that time it was taken by the Book-of-the-Month Club as a dividend. The Club alone distributed two hundred and forty thousand copies, and, all told, Gunther hit a jackpot that was estimated to be something over a hundred thousand dollars.

Gunther did not immediately realize that what he had done for Europe he could do profitably for every other continent. It was not until the middle of 1937 that he started work on a book about Asia. Even when he was halfway through, he wasn't fully aware of what he had got hold of. He thought for a while of calling the new book *Outside Asia*, on the theory that in the Orient he was a visiting student rather than an established authority. His publishers sensibly overruled him. It was probably about then that the grand design began to take shape in Gunther's mind. This, as he describes it, is an attempt "to chart in continental segments the known political world of today." There are very few works with which it may fairly be compared. There is H. G. Wells's *Outline of History*, which might be called a sort of vertical Gunther, but the comparison does not really stand up. Wells's four volumes amount to only 1,395 pages. The first volume of *Inside U.S.A.* is almost that long. Arnold Toynbee, with his first six volumes of *A Study of History*, is a few pages up on Gunther at the moment, but Gunther will go into the lead with his next book. Toynbee, like Gunther, has three or four volumes to come, and the race may be neck and neck the whole way. Any impartial referee, however, would disqualify Toynbee on the ground that he cheats by filling in many pages with documents and quotations. When all this padding is removed, as D. C. Somervell recently demonstrated in his one-volume digest, Toynbee looks like a bantamweight. He could, in fact, be stripped down to the size of *Inside Latin America*, Gunther's skinniest book.

Few of Gunther's rivals come anywhere near him in the expenditure of creative energy. Toynbee and Wells drew largely on the books of other men in writing their own. Gunther has gathered his material first-hand, chalking up records not only as a writer but as a world traveller and interviewer. An excellent case can be made for him as the most widely travelled man in history, and an unchallengeable case can be made for him as the leading interviewer of all time. No doubt, many sailors, aviators, and railroad men have more mileage to their credit than Gunther, who estimates his total at well over a million miles, but it is doubtful that anyone in any of these trades has visited so many places in the world. Sailors go mainly to seaports, fliers to airports, railroad men to railroad towns. Travelling salesmen follow the markets; explorers shun civilization; Gunther goes everywhere. Where trains, boats, and airplanes cannot take him, he goes in sleighs, gharris, droshkies, rickshaws, bullock wagons, seilbahns, and charabancs, and on the backs of elephants, asses, and camels. He has never been south of Dakar in Africa, but he plans to go there next year. Aside from that, a list of places he has not seen would consist principally of insignificant suburbs, inaccessible mountaintops, and utterly worthless stretches like the Dakota Badlands. Generally speaking, Gunther and Nature have neglected the same places. He has been to every country on four continents and to nearly all their important provinces, states, and cities. He has cut corners only twice. He acquired the franchise in Tibet and Afghanistan simply by driving up to the borders of those countries in an automobile and walking ten or fifteen yards into them. He did not go to Lhasa or Kabul, but then very few outsiders ever have. He has no idea how many people he interviewed for his four *"Inside"* books, but the count, quite apart from a vast number of men in the street, runs well into the thousands. He has talked to practically everyone in the world who has ever made the cover of *Time*. Illness, weather, and revolution have caused him to miss an emir or pasha here and a minor cabinet member there, but no one living has talked to the heads of so many countries as Gunther, and before his time no one could have got around fast enough to do all that he has done.

Gunther works himself at what would for most other men be a brutal pace. *Inside U.S.A.* was only twenty-seven months in the making. He spent thirteen months travelling, fourteen writing. He visited more than three hundred towns and cities, interviewed from two to twenty people a day, and took more than a million words of notes, an average of twenty-three hundred words a day. The book itself is a half-million words long, or roughly two-thirds the length of the Bible. It was a lot longer before his editors cut the sections explaining about things like cows eating grass. Each chapter was set in type as he finished it, and he was going over the proofs of his last chapter as he wrote his next. He did all his own fact checking and research. Most writers would be lucky if such an ordeal gave them nothing worse than ulcers, but it did not bother Gunther. Luckily, he does not find writing the dispiriting chore that most writers do. He just sits down at a desk and writes. Alice Longworth once called him "a self-wringing sponge." To finish *Inside U.S.A.* on time for the Book-of-the-Month Club, he had to work on a fixed schedule of ten to twelve hours a day at the typewriter. When he was not working, however, he enjoyed himself. Except for some occasional art collecting, he is a hobbyless man and, in spite of his rugged appearance, an unathletic one. Most of his spare time is spent with his friends, who are mostly people he met and worked with in his newspaper days—Raymond Swing, William Shirer, Whit Burnett, Dorothy Thompson, Walter Duranty, Jay Allen, Hamilton Fish Armstrong, Vincent Sheean, and Sinclair Lewis.

Since 1938, when he came back from Asia, Gunther has made New York his headquarters. He does most of his work in an office on Forty-ninth Street, off Madison Avenue. He has an apartment on Park Avenue in the lower Sixties. He likes New York and plans to go on making it his base of operations. Right at this moment, he is working up a kind of postscript to *Inside U.S.A.* He had a few hundred folders of notes— mostly on people in national politics— left over when he finished up last March, and he is putting them together into a book that he will probably call *Inside Washington.* Then he will be in the clear to tackle Africa. There is always, of course, the question of what Gunther will do when he runs out of continents. If he goes on at his present speed, the supply will be exhausted in five or six years, when he will be in his early fifties and still good for millions of words. After having dealt so successfully with the great land masses, he might find any subject he could think of a comedown. One solution remains. The last time he revised *Inside Europe* was in 1941. Europe has changed so much since then that another revision is out of the question. His publishers, however, have been urging him to consider starting another continental series, the first volume to be called *Inside Europe Today.* He could work on that for a couple of years and then start running through Asia, Latin America, and so on. By 1961 or 1962, it would be time for an *Inside U.S.A. Today.* That way, he could go on forever.

## 3.  HENRY BLACKMAN SELL

It was either John Gunther, the journalist, or Jerome Frank, the jurist, who first introduced me to the exotic subject of this period piece. Both had known Henry Sell in Chicago in the nine-

200 Arrivals and Departures

teen-twenties, and both had followed his career with fascination and some admiration. Hearing about it, I, too, was taken by it and decided, in late 1947, to try writing about Sell for *The New Yorker*. I ended up with three articles, which led Harold Ross, on reading them, to write William Shawn a startled note, saying, "Three articles about this man? He may be interesting, but he isn't Herbert Hoover." But Ross, who would never have printed three articles about Hoover, accepted them, and they were published in March and April of 1948.

What follows is a distinctly abridged version of what I first wrote. In condensing, I have tried to retain those passages which seem to me to tell something of the period, or periods, in which Sell lived and worked. He helped to create them and was himself largely created by them. His decades were the twenties and thirties, the frivolous and the earnest, and both were part of the makeup of this man. He never stopped being a huckster and faddist, but he did develop a social conscience, and he became a figure of integrity in a field, merchandising, in which integrity is rare.

### Specialties

Henry Blackman Sell, the maker of Sell's Liver Pâté, Sell's Corned Pork Hash, and several other tinned products, a line known collectively as Sell's Specialties, is a man of letters turned meat packer. History offers no parallel to this remarkable evolution. Many men, of course, have done it the other way. Shakespeare was a butcher boy who became a great writer. H. G. Wells served a brief and reluctant apprenticeship behind a meat counter. George Horace Lorimer went from the Armour packing houses to the editorship of the *Saturday Evening Post*. Sell, however, is unique in having gone from prose and poetry to beef and pork. Now a trim, dapper, rapid-speaking man of fifty-eight, he was the literary editor of the Chicago *Daily News* back in the days when H. L. Mencken was calling Chicago the literary capital of the world. While Chicago was the capital, the Daily News Building was the royal palace, and Sell sat on a mighty throne. With the merest flourish of his sceptre, he could make or break a literary reputation. Some authorities still regard him as a pivotal figure in American criticism. "Sell?" one veteran of the literary wars, a still erect and ruddy old soldier, said recently. "Why, Henry Sell is the fellow who took criticism away from the *North American Review* and gave it back to the people." Sell has long since put all that behind him. Now he lives for meat, or, more properly, for his work as a canner of meat. Ordinarily blithe in manner and a bit on the arch and skittish side in conversation, he becomes grave and metaphysical when he talks about meat. "I only hope," he sometimes says, "that when I die, people will remember me for the excellence of my meat products."

Meat, though substantial as a food, offers frail hope for immortality. The world has a short and ungrateful memory of the men who have kept it supplied with edible flesh. School children learn the names and dates of important figures in such lines as gunpowder, wheat harvesting, printing, and sewing machines. They are taught nothing about the great men of meat. The city of Springfield, Massachusetts, has honored its leading founder, William Pynchon, by naming a handsome museum after him and in many other ways, but, though everyone pays tributes to his exploits as a pioneer settler in the Agawam country, the fact that he was the father of the meat-packing industry is always politely overlooked. As far as posterity is concerned, Sell, a native of Whitewater, Wisconsin, would be better off if he had stuck with literature and attached his name to books rather than to minced chicken and braised beef in gravy. After all, people everywhere know that the writing Swift's first name was Jonathan, but who knows or even cares to know that the meat-packing Swift was Gustavus? Sell, though, is not the sort of man who believes that because it was ever thus, thus it will ever be. He feels that he has a revolutionary program for meat and that the world will someday thank him for it. "What I want to do," he says, "is reexamine the whole structure of meat from top to bottom. I want to forget everything we've ever done with meat and start right in from scratch. I want to treat meat as though it were an entirely new problem, as though it were some precious raw material that had just been discovered."

Our attitude toward meat, Sell says, is largely conditioned by tradition, complacence, superstition, and bigotry, and in some respects we have made no progress since the Stone Age. It is true, to be sure, that there have recently been great advances in the breeding and feeding of meat animals, but these, according to Sell, have been of benefit principally to the producers of meat, not to the eaters of it. As to what we actually put into our mouths, we aren't much better off than we ever were. We just pull the meat off the animals and cook it as is. "Oh, sure," he says, with the impatience of a man anticipating a stock argument, "I know that we salt it down a bit and treat it with a few chemicals now and then, but that's just to make it keep a little longer and chew a little easier. What we do is terribly superficial, really. The fact is that we just go along being smug and satisfied about the kind of meat Nature has given us. There's a lot of good in meat and a lot of bad. I want to see if we can get rid of the bad and make the good better. I think science can do things with meat the world has never even dared to dream of, and I won't rest till I've proved it."

Sell got into the meat business just seven years ago, after compiling a spectacular record as a trailblazer in other fields. Writing and packing are merely the opposite poles of his experience. He was once an influential figure in interior decoration. It has been said that the genteel tradition that dominated the art showed its first signs of grogginess after the publication, in 1916, of *Good Taste in Home Furnishing*, a book that he and his wife, Maud Ann Sell, wrote. He eased gradually away from belles-lettres by becoming, in 1920, the editor of *Harper's Bazaar*, and then, in 1927, assistant to the chairman of the board of the Butterick Publishing Company. In ladies'-dress circles, some people have gone so far as to claim that Sell is the inventor of the fashion magazine as we know it. He is also hailed for his vigorous crusade in behalf of the mannish tailored suit, the cloche hat, and the Grecian drape. While still working for Butterick, Sell bought the Blaker Advertising Agency, which he made into one of the prominent firms of the period. In the early thirties, he abandoned journalism to concentrate on advertising. In some respects, his career from then on resembles that of the late William Wrigley. Wrigley was a soap manufacturer who gave away clocks, insurance policies, and whatnot—to encourage his soap sales. Sometimes he got so excited about one of his sidelines that it became his chief interest. He worked through all of these things and several others, among them lamps and baking powder. He ended up in the chewing-gum business. One day, Sell picked off for his agency the account of a firm making vitamin pills. He got so engrossed in vitamins that he became a manufacturer himself of a line called Vitamins Plus. Vitamin men agree that Sell's campaign to put over Vitamins Plus helped enormously to make the taking of vitamin capsules, up to then the ritual of a few health faddists, a national pastime. "It would be interesting to know," a man who gets around a lot in the B-complex world said recently, "exactly how much industrial productivity increased as a result of Henry Sell getting the idea of putting vitamins on cosmetics counters." From the vitamin business, it was only a step to the meat, or protein, business. He took the step in 1940, selling Vitamins Plus to the Vick Chemical Company and putting the proceeds into meat. He still has the advertising agency, but he himself now handles only one large account —that of Elizabeth Arden, an old friend.

In addition to all his careers, Sell has had a number of subcareers. Several of these have been involved with the entertainment industry. In 1912, he was a theatrical press agent, representing the Abbey Theatre, the Irish Players, Morris Gest, and several others. In the early days of the movies, he was part owner of an open-air theatre in Dayton, Ohio. For a while, when the last depression was at its worst, he was a doctor for ailing hotels and night clubs. His chief contribution in this field was the idea of using Social Register girls as café singers. This was considered a brilliant innovation, not from the standpoint of music but from the standpoint of nightclub earnings. The theory, amply confirmed in practice, was that if rich girls performed in nightclubs, their rich friends would come to see them and leave part of their riches behind. Then, after his fashion-magazine days, Sell was the American public-relations representative of a half dozen of the large Parisian dressmakers. For his work in behalf of French couture, he wears the red ribbon of a chevalier in the Legion of Honor. Chevalier Sell was also, briefly, the American representative of the wine-growers of the lower Rhine Valley, and in 1939 he served a short hitch as a Brain Truster, being a special consultant to the Secretary of Agriculture. Since he got into the meat business, he has twice branched out, trying his hand once as a soap manufacturer and once as the producer of a cereal food, Extendo. He quietly abandoned both these projects.

Sell, who feels that he is only now on the threshold of his great adventure with meat, has already enjoyed some notable triumphs. For example, by devising Sell's Liver Pâté, the first and the most successful of his specialties, he has come as close as any man in history to actually making a silk purse out of a sow's ear. Messing around in a laboratory with a lot of pig muscle, lard, wheat germ, soya beans, defatted milk, and other substances of a wholly un-appetitzing nature, he and some associates finally concocted what many gourmets feel is the perfect appetizer, a canapé paste of unusual taste and delicate bouquet, as well as an ideal accompaniment for truffles, aspics, and squab on pedestal. "We were digging for coal when we came upon gold," Sell says. Sell's Liver Pâté is a result of its inventor's tour of duty in the Department of Agriculture. He had dinner one night at the home of Secretary Claude R. Wickard. Among the guests was Dr. Robert S. Harris, head of the National Biochemical Laboratories at the Massachusetts Institute of Technology, who got to talking about the coming protein shortage in Europe. He expounded the theory that it would be possible, after a little experimenting, to turn out a compact, concentrated food that would not take up valuable space in ocean freighters and that could be shipped without refrigeration. It should be of high caloric and protein value and provide everything else required for a well-balanced diet. Sell was momentarily out of challenges, and he found this one to his liking. He rounded up some of his vitamin researchers and set them up in a laboratory in Brooklyn to dope out a formula. He worked right along with them. Dressed in white duck butcher aprons and high rubber boots, he and his men slopped around in animal blood, soup stocks, skimmed milk, and grease for almost a year. In that time, stirring these elements up into various combinations and permutations, they made five hundred and six mixtures, in batches of two hundred and fifty pounds apiece, which they tried out on the laboratory's white rats. Finally, using pig liver as the base, they came through with a formula on which the rats grew exceptionally powerful and acquired I.Q.s that qualified them for Princeton. The stuff bulged with protein, exuded carbohydrates, and bristled with calories. Its riboflavin, pantothenic acid, biotin, calcium, iron, and pyridoxine made it, compared to natural foods, a Triton among the minnows, a blockbuster among cap pistols. The Red Cross took a million tins a month and put one in every prisoner-of-war package. Reports began to come in about escaped Allied prisoners who had lived for weeks in jungles, in deserts, and in lifeboats on nothing but Sell's Liver Pâté and had got through their experiences as fit as if they had been eating three square meals a day back home in East Orange. CARE and most of the other agencies that send food to Europe and Asia use Liver Pâté as one of their staples. All this, of course, is exactly what the preparation was intended for. What was unexpected was that a foodstuff supercharged with niacin and thiamine, and selling for the price of a can of beans, should turn out to be a menace to the foie-gras and caviar interests. "It was just our good fortune," Sell says. "When you're looking for something to keep people alive and healthy, you don't think first of all about their taste buds. We wanted our product to be palatable, so that people could get it down, but we weren't exactly looking for a filling for calla-lily sandwiches." Not since the ancients found that sick whales could be useful in the production of the headiest of perfumes has there been anything to match Sell's discovery that hog liver combined with hydrolyzed plant protein could be used to advantage in assembling gnocchi, cheese dreams, and mousses. Never before, it is safe to say, has a multipurpose food achieved so wide a range. A couple of years back, Alfred Knopf, a gourmet of great repute and an ardent consumer of Sell's Specialties, published a book by June Platt, the former food editor of *House & Garden*, called *Serve It and Sing: Forty-four Simply Delicious Ways of Serving Sell's Liver Pâté*. This is probably the only book ever devoted, without a tieup of any kind, to a single commercial product. Mrs. Platt's recipes are grouped under six headings: Sandwiches; Canapés, Appetizers, and Hors-d'oeuvre; Soups; Luncheon Dishes; For Dinner Time; Cold and in Aspic.

Sell now markets two million tins of his Liver Pâté a month, but he worked out the formula in a spirit of philanthropy, never anticipating that he would be making the stuff himself. As soon as he was satisfied with the formula, he asked some of the established packers if they would undertake the preparation and canning of it. The defense boom was getting under way then, and the established packers were so busy with their established meats that they couldn't be bothered with anything new. As it turned out, this circumstance made Sell a very happy man. He rented some vacant corners in packing houses here and there and went into the pâté business for himself. The foreign and Red Cross orders provided an excellent backlog, but he decided that he also wanted to tackle the domestic market, which meant that he had to have a merchandising organization. A merchandising organization, like a train, can carry several passengers as easily as one, and the more passengers it carries, the less the overhead per passenger. Sell therefore branched out as soon as he could. He determined to put out several pâtés. His first experiment was leaving the liver out of the Liver Pâté and putting in chicken meat. He called the result Minced Chicken. He followed that with Corned Beef Loaf, Beef Stew, Braised Beef in Gravy, Corned Pork Hash, and Beef Steak & Kidney in Gravy. All of these have been hugely successful. He plans soon to add two pâtés, one with ham and one with tongue as the base, and a Chicken & Rice. In terms of finance, Sell is not a giant of the industry. His business grosses between five and six million dollars a year, and he ranks well down the scale in size.

In terms of five-star ratings, blue ribbons, and gold seals of approval, he may rank first. *Gourmet* has described his work as "inspired canning." *Woman's Home Companion, Mademoiselle, Town & Country*, the Food Research Laboratories, Inc., Department of Agriculture officials, and several consumer-research organizations have used up all their superlatives on his foods. Clementine Paddleford, of the Herald Tribune Home Institute, has come right out and called Sell's Corned Pork Hash a "heavenly hash," saying that she liked not only the meat in the hash but the potatoes. Sell feels that his Corned Pork Hash is a stunning example of what can be done with meat if one refuses to be intimidated by precedent. "Of course, the conventional thing for us to have done," he says, "would have been to see if we couldn't make a better corned-beef hash. But we started right in at the beginning. We didn't say, 'How can we make a better corned-beef hash?' We said, 'Is corned beef really the stuff for hash, anyway? Why does it have to be corned-*beef* hash? Maybe some other meat would be better.' We took the whole problem into the laboratory and reexamined it. By the time we were through, the whole idea of corned-beef hash seemed pretty droll. Beef is fine for braising and stewing, but in a hash it hasn't got half the distinction pork has. We found that what you want in a hash is tender fibres and a succulence that survives the processing. There's just no question about it—pork was made for hashing."

The market for meat being what it is these days, it takes a man with a will of forged iron to prevent a five-million-dollar business from becoming several times that large. Sell is determined to keep his concern small because he feels that otherwise he and his co-workers might forget their high ideals and slip into the old, easy, mass-production way of doing things. "I want to be a pacemaker in meat," he says, "and for that you've got to stay lean and supple." He can't think of a happier, more useful life than being a pacemaker in meat, and he declares that he enjoys this work more than anything else he has ever done. His friends take a tolerant but skeptical view of this enthusiasm. They have heard him talk the same way about his other careers. "I give Henry another two or three years of this sausage grinding," a friend of twenty-five years' standing says. "Then—who knows? Maybe he'll move in on plastics or plywood or something like that. Maybe he'll revolutionize undertaking. Maybe he'll buy a race track. He's been showing a lot of interest in horses lately. I've been a bit suspicious about that, but I guess it's really the racing he likes." Sell insists that he's in meat for the rest of his life. It fascinates him and gives him scope, and has provided him, he says, with his pleasantest personal relationships. He has spent most of the last thirty-five or forty years moving among the celebrated and the accomplished in many spheres. The range of his friendships is enormous. The dowager Duchess of Sutherland and Philadelphia Jack O'Brien both have been his friends. He is probably the only living man who admires and is admired by both William Randolph Hearst and Henry Agard Wallace. His literary acquaintanceship has run all the way from William Butler Yeats to O. O. McIntyre. Among his Continental friends have been the Duchess de Gramont and the Three Flying Codonas, the great Spanish aerialists. Others he has known intimately are Carl Sandburg, Lucien Lelong, Gene Tunney, Rabindranath Tagore, and the Black Brothers, self-proclaimed kings of the Hungarian fiddler gypsies. Sell enjoys this vast assortment of friends, but he maintains that there is some special excellence, some real, though perhaps intangible, distinction that sets the meat crowd apart from the rest.

Of the twelve tinned meats that now carry the Sell colors, the pâtés are the most striking tributes to Sell's program for bringing together meat packing and laboratory science. Science has helped in the development of the others, but only marginally. The beef that goes into the Beef Stew and into the Braised Beef in Gravy is not beef that has been taken apart and reassembled according to scientific principles. It is pretty much the same sort of beef our fathers ate and our grandfathers before them. Even the pork in the Corned Pork Hash is merely a superior grade of hog meat, something Sell hopes someday to improve upon. It is true that he has jacked up the nutritive value of his Corned Beef Loaf by adding milk powder and powdered yeast, but, aside from that, the meat is otherwise unfortified, is undefatted, and is generally un-tampered with. Most of the contributions he has made so far have to do with the cooking and canning processes. "What we're trying to do is get control over our meat," he says. "Control is the es-sence of the scientific method. It's also the home method. But it hasn't been easy in canning, because once the product is in the can there isn't much you can do about it—and many canners do cook in the can." In his Braised Beef, he feels that he has pro-duced a superior and more homelike taste by braising the beef before canning it. This sly maneuver, which no one else has bothered with, apparently because of its tediousness, gives the man who takes it a chance to sear in the juices. According to Sell, who is getting to be something of a historian of meat packing, the principal reason for the tastelessness of most canned foods is to be found in the canner's fear that the cans will suddenly start to go off on the pantry shelves like Chinese firecrackers. If a can of food is not cooked long enough to be sterilized, the contents will ferment, producing gases that may eventually rip open the can. This happened quite often in the early days of the industry. Doc-tors were frequently called to attend to housewives lacerated by flying tin or temporarily blinded by spraying pepper pot. To avoid these disasters, most canners took to cooking tinned foods longer than was necessary for safety and, Sell says, longer than was de-sirable for good eating. By consulting three or four laws of thermo-dynamics, Sell has found that it is possible, by some complicated fussing around with temperatures and timing, to put up food that will not explode and at the same time to make it possible for the palate to distinguish between his pork, his beef, his chicken, and his liver.

Sell looks astonishingly like Charlie Chaplin, who, as it hap-pens, is only a few months older. Sell is five feet nine, which is quite a bit taller than Chaplin, but the men are of approximately the same build. They both have full, slightly pouting mouths and broad foreheads of medium height. Sell's hair is as thick as Chap-lin's and as wavy, and it has grayed at the same pace. Sell is well known to headwaiters in New York, where Chaplin is often mistaken for him, but elsewhere he is constantly being mistaken for the actor, which is all right with him, since Chaplin is a high-priority man in hotels and night clubs. Seventeen years ago, when Sell was in Moscow on business, word leaked out through the Hotel Metropol busboys and charwomen that Charlie Chaplin had arrived in town. Within a half hour, there was a mass of admiring peasants and workers in the streets around the hotel. The place became a forest of Stalin banners. They were about to call the tanks and the girl athletes out by the time it was learned that the newcomer was not Chaplin but an American who looked like him.

Sell's life is governed by two principles, and the Liver Pâté is an expression of both of them. One is high living; the other is healthy living. He is simultaneously a sybarite and a health crank, a lounge lizard and a physical culturist. He is an ascetic world-ling. One of his standard luncheons is two champagne cocktails, followed by boiled lobster, served hot or cold (with lemon and olive oil), and ending with a snowcapped mountain called Palm Beach Cake, which is always on the menu at the Waldorf Astoria, where he often eats. He has this kind of food four days out of five. On the fifth day, he fasts. He has nothing but a little fruit juice and perhaps a wafer or two to keep his stomach from wrin-kling. Sometimes the Braised Beef man will taxi perilously down-town through snow and sleet, if need be, for zucchini fried with olive oil and garlic, and his eyes will brighten at the thought of an hors-d'oeuvre collation of artichoke, sardines, Greek olives, and cold beans. Each morning, however, he forces down six whole yeast cakes; setting his teeth and putting all thoughts of zucchini from his mind, he also gets down some wheat-germ oil, and then six more yeast cakes before going to bed. In a way, he is an anachronism. So few people bother with raw yeast cakes nowa-days that the only way Sell can be sure of his twelve a day is by having a Fleischmann truck deliver them to his office once a week. Besides all this, he takes, every day, vitamin concentrates amount-ing to fifty times the quantity recommended by the American Medical Association.

These extremes are characteristic. The sybaritic Sell is strictly an eiderdown-cushion man, and the eiderdown had better be the real stuff from Iceland, plucked in the spring by the birds for their nests, or he will have none of it. His apartment, on East Fifty-seventh Street, and his office, on Madison Avenue, are furnished with some of the most yielding and relaxing mediums of repose that the upholstery world can contrive. The apartment, though, also contains a wooden inclining board, as rigid as hundred-gauge steel, on which Sell lies for fifteen or twenty minutes a day while he goes through some masochistic yoga exercises for the improvement of body tone. Once, in the twenties, when Sell was the chief party-giver for the Hearst organization and was considered one of the greatest men in the field since Lucullus, he borrowed the Ile de France for a night and gave a huge dinner party aboard her. While planning the function, he was suddenly horrified by the thought that he would be inflicting cruel and unusual punishment on his guests by asking them to walk from their cabs and limousines all the way down Pier 57 to the main salon of the boat. He imported twenty wheelchairs and twenty wheelchair pushers from the Atlantic City boardwalk. "It was a wonderful idea," he says. "Everyone was so wide-awake and ready for fun when they got there. They weren't all tuckered out from the walk." That is the sybaritic Sell talking. The ascetic Sell is a hiker who is proud of his calf development and always wears a pedometer. He checks the pedometer every week, and if it shows that he has walked less than twenty miles, he hits the road right away and stays there until his pedometer has registered the proper mileage.

Sell was born in Whitewater, Wisconsin, on November 14, 1889. Whitewater, in the southeastern corner of the state, is a small town that had then, and still has, a population of about thirty-seven hundred. Sell's father was the Reverend Dr. Henry Thorne Sell, a high functionary of the Congregational Church, the editor of a Congregational magazine named the *Advance*, and a big Sunday school man. He is one of the men whom millions of American children can thank for the present-day short, informal Sunday-school sessions, in which finger painting, sex talks, and group play have replaced responsive readings, recitations, and half-hour doses of hymns. He was also a lecturer on the old Chautauqua circuits and the author of *Sell's Bible Study Text Books*, a monumental work of twenty-one volumes, cross-indexing the Holy Scriptures. Few men, before or since, have tried to do such an all-out cross-index of the Bible. The work is still in print, and the name of Sell is still an honored one among the harassed clergymen who anxiously grope through it on Saturday nights for texts. Revolutionizing Sunday schools, competing with musical-saw artists and talking horses on the summer circuits, and rubricating every common and proper noun from Genesis through Revelation left Dr. Sell little time for family affairs, but his son saw enough of him to acquire a deep respect for him. Although the younger Sell's attitude toward tradition is one of thoroughgoing contempt, he sometimes seeks the comfort of continuity by comparing his career in meat with his father's career in theology. "Sell's Specialties and *Sell's Bible Studies,*" he will say. "It's almost as though Father and I were an act. My products are supplemental feeding for the body. His were supplemental feeding for the soul."

Sell's mother, the former Mary Blackman, was the daughter of the richest man in Whitewater, the president of the local bank. "Grandfather *was* Whitewater," Sell says. "He was the Old Man there, the one who lived in the Big House on the Hill." Sell's mother was gay, careless about money, and a bit scatterbrained. It is possible that Sell's urge to improve the lot of mankind with good reading, good clothes, and good food is a variant of his father's liberal evangelism. His urge to improve the lot of Sell and to enjoy himself in elaborate and generally expensive ways could be a legacy from the Blackmans, who loved luxury as much as he does. Although the family was a pioneer one, having settled in Whitewater in the middle of the nineteenth century, and although Mrs. Blackman was a first cousin of Buffalo Bill, the life the Blackmans led followed an Eastern Seaboard rather than a Middle Border pattern. They travelled a lot, visited for long periods in Boston and New York, and patronized most of the polite arts. Even in the cheese country, Sell says, they always managed to look as if they were on their way to Sunday dinner at Delmonico's.

Sell went to high school for five years, but he did not graduate. His formal education was really the only unsuccessful project he has ever undertaken. He was a quick-witted boy but impervious to the current educational methods. "I've never had any head for organized knowledge," he says. "I don't think I ever passed an examination in my life. I crumpled up whenever I took one." After the public schools had washed their hands of him, he was sent, in 1906, to Culver Military Academy, where he stayed until 1909, when he was nineteen. Except in his studies, nearly all of which he failed, he did well at Culver. He eventually became president of two or three societies, editor of the student newspaper, and the school's official guide and greeter. He was good-looking and rather courtly, and whenever celebrities or the parents of prospective students visited the campus, he was shown off to them as an example of what nice, clean-cut, well-spoken boys went to Culver. It was never explained that this overage paragon was in his fifth year of first-year Latin. In the spring of 1909, the commandant sent Sell's father a friendly but candid letter. "I regret having to say that the end for Henry is still nowhere in sight," he wrote. He said he doubted that Henry could ever be admitted to Yale, for which he had been intended, or to any other self-respecting college, and that while he was a decorative and engaging fixture at parties and receptions, it was well known that money came hard to a clergyman and it seemed inadvisable to sink any more of it in a lost cause. Dr. Sell took the advice, and Henry left Culver that June with an indeterminate academic status. Culver has nevertheless used him as a kind of advertisement, claiming him as a distinguished alumnus of the Class of '10. This pleases Sell, who has shown that he is not against education for others by helping subsidize university projects for nutrition research and by recently establishing a scholarship in sociology at Syracuse University.

Following his emergence from Culver, Sell had a series of newspaper jobs. He and a boyhood friend, the late Hiram Motherwell, knocked around the Middle West picking up reporting jobs and holding them briefly. Then they bought a small movie house in Greenwood, Indiana. Sell managed the theatre, and Motherwell played the piano. The venture was a success, so they sold out and moved on to Dayton, Ohio, where they bought a larger, open-air theatre. Everything went fine until the cops descended on the place one night and ran Sell and Motherwell out of town for showing indecent films. The pictures were conventional ones, Sell says, but Dayton was in the hands of Philistines. After a while, Sell and Motherwell returned to Dayton, reopened the theatre, and showed a series of inspirational films chosen by a hurriedly formed committee of local ministers, who were glad to be of help to the son of the author of *Sell's Bible Studies*. Ticket sales, however, never regained their old briskness, so Sell and Motherwell went back to newspaper work.

One of the newspapers Sell worked on was *The Indianapolis Star*. He was its gypsy editor. Indianapolis was a gypsy mecca in those days. Its metalworking shops had plenty of jobs for gypsy tinkers, fortune-telling was legal and popular, and the town was a great horse-trading center. The *Star* had a section devoted to gypsy advertising, in which occult wares were described and fortune tellers announced their talents. It was Sell's job to solicit gypsy advertising and gather gypsy news. He wrote his stories and took in his ads in a broken-down Gilded Age mansion on the edge of town occupied by Queen Zenora, a wrinkled old Rumanian who claimed descent from the royal family of Egypt and who was the acknowledged social leader of the Indianapolis gypsies. When Zenora had no paying customers, she used to look into Sell's future for nothing. He believes that Zenora influenced his life and that she inspired in him the confidence to plunge into so many unrelated careers. "She told me I was failure-proof," he says. "She gave me a feeling of indestructibility and convinced me I could succeed at anything I tried." Sell has been a confirmed friend of the gypsies ever since, and a fairly regular patron of fortune tellers and astrologers. He doesn't exactly believe in their powers, but he doesn't exactly disbelieve, either. Being rather touchy about the subject, he insists that he has no faith in tea leaves, palmistry, and the zodiac but that he has respect for gypsy wisdom. "Those old gypsies," he says, "have been watching life for a long time to see how things work out. If I know a gypsy isn't lying for the sake of a few extra dollars, I'll play her hunches any day."

In 1913, Sell went to Chicago. He became a glove salesman at Marshall Field's. He sold plenty of gloves from the start—enough, in fact, to go from basement gloves to main-floor gloves in a week —but he had to stand all day on his feet, which made them ache. He had distressing visions of a million dollars in the bank and his feet in a pail of hot water. He got transferred to a sitting job in the store office, but this didn't suit him either, so he tried to get on the staff of the Chicago *Daily News*, which he admired. The *News*, however, did not admire him. It was typical of Sell's career in journalism that what he was unable to get from the editorial department, he eventually got from the business department. He decided to get on the staff of the paper by working up a project with business appeal.

He studied the Chicago papers and discovered what he thought was a weak spot in them, then went to the *News* offices and told the business people that the paper was missing a big thing by not making a special appeal to the immigrant groups in the city. Before he was through, he had the mouths of the circulation men watering as he told how the newsstands would be mobbed by clamoring hordes of Poles, Italians, and Bohemians once Henry Sell started a department on Polish, Italian, and Bohemian life in Chicago. The business office told the editorial office that a great new journalist had been discovered. The city editor didn't think so, but he agreed to buy three articles from Sell, at twenty-five dollars apiece. Sell wrote them in a week. He continued to produce at that rate for more than three years, by which time *News* readers had made the acquaintance of just about every barber, grocer, priest, and bartender of foreign ancestry in Chicago.

Successful though he was, Sell was not put on the regular reporting staff of the *News*. The paper had some distinguished journalists on the payroll, and the editors felt that property values would be lowered if a nobody like Sell was admitted into such company. All sorts of riffraff might come in after him. This was all to Sell's benefit. The distinguished journalists got around thirty-five dollars a week, and Sell was making twice that by working only half time. In addition, he had the leisure for a number of other activities. He did some free-lance writing for art magazines, and he became a theatrical press agent, handling all the shows that came into the Fine Arts Theatre and all the Chicago appearances of the Abbey Players, the Manchester Players, the Irish Players, Morris Gest's companies, and a number of others. For a couple of years, Sell was stagestruck. He wrote a short book in defense of the "New Theatre" called *What Is It All About?* and also served as a super with the Chicago Opera.

In 1914, Sell married a young actress, Maud Ann O'Harrow. The Sells decided to retire from the stage and set themselves up as authorities on interior decoration. Sell worked an evening or two a week in the Marshall Field furniture department. There he supervised the pushing around of some tables and chairs until their arrangement pleased his eye, then took pictures of them and wrote about them for the Field house organ. This was better than standing behind a counter in the glove department, because he could drop into a chair whenever he pleased. He also became the paint-and-wallpaper expert for the *Ladies' Home Journal*. Every month for several years, he and Mrs. Sell had their four-room apartment completely decorated for a hundred dollars a room and then wrote an article on how to redecorate a four-room apartment for four hundred dollars. In 1916, a ground-breaking book by the Sells, *Good Taste in Home Furnishing*, appeared. Its ideas seem to be a mélange of a once-over-lightly reading of William Morris, the notions of Frank Lloyd Wright, then one of their close friends, and some thoughts of their own. It is hopelessly dated today. ("I am not in any way presupposing," Sell wrote, "that electricity is the final triumph of illumination, but it is in general use, and has a certain adaptability not to be found in gas or oils.") Nevertheless, it was a revolutionary manifesto in its time. It sounded a battle cry against the revolving whatnot, it put the finger on curly maple and dark woodwork, it described shiny floor surfaces as an "abomination," and it courageously debunked Oriental rugs. The book sold over a hundred thousand copies and established the Sells as authorities in the field. Sell abandoned the field at once.

That same year, Sell stopped writing his *News* feature articles and became the book editor of the paper, a job he held until 1920. Carl Sandburg and Ben Hecht were on the *News*, and Sherwood Anderson, Edgar Lee Masters, Theodore Dreiser, Floyd Dell, and Vachel Lindsay were all Chicagoans. Margaret Anderson's *Little Review*, which claimed to have sponsored "twenty-three new systems of art," and Harriet Monroe's *Poetry*, both published in Chicago, were the liveliest literary magazines in the country. But although literature was being produced in Chicago, it had to go to New York and Boston for approval or disapproval. Journalistic criticism was dominated by a few Eastern magazines and newspapers, most of whose reviewers were either Ivy League professors or elderly gentlemen of means. Few of them were sympathetic to the roughhewn stuff being turned out in the Middle West. Sell decided that the *News* should have a book page to give Chicago writers a sounding board. He went to the editors of the paper and told them that he could provide them with a first-class book page. The editors weren't interested. He went to the business manager and told him he could make a lot of money on book ads. The business manager put over the idea for him. The section was published every Wednesday. It consisted of as much advertising as Sell, who was his own space salesman, could get; a column of literary gossip and opinion, written by Sell; a cartoon or caricature, by Gene Markey; and three or four book reviews.

When the book page was at its height, H. L. Mencken called it "the only civilized book section in this Presbyterian satrapy." However that may be, it was certainly as unrestrained a book section as has ever been published anywhere. It represented no known school of critical theory. Sell's reviewers ran all the way from police reporters, whose prose style was pure Race-Track Final and who saw no need for shifting gears as they went from the works of Johnny Torrio to the works of James Branch Cabell, down to flowing-tie aesthetes and lady poets, who wrote lacy little pieces sprinkled with Pateresque epigrams. Sell permitted, even encouraged, unbridled logrolling. Ben Hecht called Sherwood Anderson a genius every other Wednesday. On the alternate Wednesdays, Anderson worried and chewed over the great problem of whether the word "genius" was adequate to convey the full scope of Hecht's powers. Sandburg and Masters paid tribute to each other with the same relentlessness. If one member of the union said that another's book would be read a century from now, the author thus honored would come back with the opinion that the work of the first member would be acclaimed two centuries from now. Naturally, nobody expected to be paid for exercising such privileges. Except for Sell, who did very well, everyone in the book department worked for nothing, or at least for nothing more than free drinks and a lunch every Friday at Schlogel's Restaurant, then Chicago's Mermaid Tavern.

The department was consistent in another respect; it was almost always against foreign authors. Any book by a writer outside the continental United States was certain to get the bum's rush in the *News.* Hecht and John V. A. Weaver were constantly dressing down Galsworthy, d'Annunzio, Ibáñez, and all the other important figures of European literature. Cockiness, not chauvinism, was responsible for this policy, Sell explains. "We just felt that our own writers were doing such good stuff that we didn't want readers to be distracted by all those outsiders," he says. "We weren't any too friendly to Easterners, either." The *News* came close to losing its Scribner advertising when he wrote an article on Galsworthy's ears, which were pointed. Sell had gone to New York to interview the great man, but he was so taken with the ears that he devoted his whole piece to them and went into some indelicate zoological comparisons. Scribner worked off its ire by buying space in the paper and denouncing "Henry Sell and his herd of green heifers." When foreign authors visited Chicago, they got the same treatment their books did. Literary protocol once forced Sell to invite Hugh Walpole, in this country on a lecture tour, to lunch with the crowd at Schlogel's. Sell and Hecht went to the restaurant ahead of time and sawed halfway through the legs of the chair the guest was to occupy. In the middle of the soup course, a prearranged campaign of the most outrageous flattery began. Walpole was told that Chicago regarded him as the peer of Dickens, Thackeray, and Scott. He was asked how it felt to realize that his name would ring gloriously down the ages. Did he plan to be laid to rest in the Abbey or was there some little kirk of childhood memory where he wanted his remains to be deposited? Walpole drank it all in, and after a while assumed a position favored by people who are drinking in flattery. He stuck his thumbs in his armpits and tilted his chair back, "We were really frightened at first," Sell recalls. "We thought they'd have to take stitches." The story of what happened to Walpole got around England and the Continent, and lecture managers began to notice that foreign writers booked into Chicago were strangely cool to the idea. When Ibáñez passed through Chicago on his American tour, in 1919, he demanded police protection.

Sell occasionally exempted a few foreign writers from the Sell treatment. Shaw was one of them, and Sell even managed to get a free review from him. James Joyce was also well treated. It is a curious fact in literary history, and one that was probably unknown to Joyce, that while he was still trying to find a publisher for *Ulysses*, parts of it were appearing in the *News*. At least two years before Joyce had even heard of Sylvia Beach, while *Ulysses* was still a work in progress, Sell clipped fragments of it from the *Little Review*, in which sections of it were being printed, and ran them whenever he was a column or two short of book copy. The editors of the *Little Review* almost went to jail for publishing Joyce, but Sell was never bothered by the law. Sell had a catholic enthusiasm for literature. The book that seemed to move him most was Frederick O'Brien's *White Shadows in the South Seas*. He had it reviewed twenty-six times in the *News*. Sell introduced the principle of the multiple review to literary criticism. If his affection for a book was mild, he had it reviewed just once. If it was strong, he had it reviewed several times. *The Education of*

*Henry Adams* got five reviews, *Winesburg, Ohio* and Mencken's *The American Language* seven, ánd Lardner's *You Know Me, Al* four. *White Shadows* was, however, the champion. Often, Sell let writers review their own books. Willa Cather reviewed *My Antonia* in the *News,* and Conrad Aiken examined several of his own collections of poetry. There was some evidence of collusion between Sell and Burton Rascoe, who was doing a book-review column for the Chicago *Tribune.* It is possible that *Jurgen* would have gone unnoticed, like Cabell's earlier books, but for the brawl over it between Rascoe, who liked it, in the *Tribune,* and Ben Hecht, who agreed to dislike it, in the *News.* The fight was taken up by the New York reviewers, particularly Heywood Broun, who thus brought the book to the attention of John S. Sumner. Sumner took the publishers to court on a charge of obscenity and thereby brought the book to the attention of the public. He lost his case. Some of the most informal and noncommittal literary criticism ever published was written by Carl Sandburg for Sell. "I'd give Carl a book," Sell recalls, "and he'd forget all about it for three or four months. Then I'd get a letter saying, 'Dear Harry: That was an interesting book about Iowa farmers you gave me. Thanks a lot. How are things going? Yours, Carl Sandburg.' I knew I'd never get a review, so I'd just publish the letter. I figured anything he wrote was important."

Characteristically, Sell was in top form as a bookman when he resigned his literary editorship at the *News,* in 1920. Its contributors were acquiring national reputations; its advertising revenue was steadily growing. Since he had everything going so nicely, Sell felt that the time had come for him to move on. A friend, Ray Long, who had been editing a group of magazines in Chicago, was made editor in chief of a chain of Hearst magazines that included *Cosmopolitan, Hearst's International, Motor, Motor Boating, Good Housekeeping, Harper's Bazaar,* and three British publications. Long offered Sell the choice of several vacancies. Sell chose the editorship of *Harper's Bazaar,* on the ground that it was the job for which he had the fewest qualifications and the one in which he would learn the most. "I'd never read a copy of it in my life," he recalls, "but I knew it was supposed to be a kind of classy fashion magazine. I knew Grub Street pretty well, so I thought I'd have a look at Park Avenue." He turned over the *News* book page to Harry Hansen and went to New York. Hecht decided to go with him, and the two of them, thinking that the new editor of *Harper's Bazaar* and his friend ought to *look* like the new editor of *Harper's Bazaar* and his friend, went from the train into a haberdashery in Grand Central and bought two canes and two homburgs. Sell also placed an order for a shoe trunk. He had only two or three pairs of shoes, but a trunk for nothing but shoes was the most luxurious thing he could think of. Then Sell and Hecht strolled up Park Avenue, wearing their new hats, and with their new canes twirling, to look over Sell's new beat.

Not many people on Park or any other avenue were reading *Harper's Bazaar* when Sell took over. The magazine, which had been bought by Hearst seven years earlier, was in poor shape. It had been founded in 1867 by Fletcher Harper, one of the Harper brothers, as a kind of ladies' edition of *Harper's Weekly*. The space that the *Weekly* devoted to politics and other matters of masculine interest the *Bazaar* devoted to fashions, homemaking, and child raising, but the illustrations and several of the departments, such as the "Editor's Easy Chair," were picked up bodily from the older magazine. It did quite well the first few years, but Mr. Harper, whose idea it was, died in 1877, and it began to go to pot not many years after. Hearst made it a magazine of fashion and social news, putting it in competition with Condé Nast's *Vogue*. Hearst thought that his publishing genius could conquer the rich as easily as it had conquered the poor. He was badly mistaken. For one thing, the prominent families of New York, Philadelphia, and Boston had for years looked upon him as a loud-mouthed California vulgarian.

*Harper's Bazaar* faced equally serious obstacles in Paris, the natural source of its most important features. In a fashion magazine, the pictures of the new styles are the main attraction, and in 1920 staff artists of magazines had to attend the private showings of the Paris dressmakers and sketch the new designs. *Harper's*

*Bazaar* artists, unlike *Vogue* artists, were not welcome at these showings. The *Bazaar* was in as bad a position as a newspaper would be if its reporters were barred from City Hall, the ball parks, and the criminal courts. Hearst had run through three editors trying to lick this problem. Sell, the fourth, went to Paris to see what the couturiers had against *Harper's Bazaar*. Even the name of the magazine, he found, was a drawback. The French couldn't say it. *Vogue* was a French word, but when a Frenchman tried to say *"Harper's Bazaar,"* his tongue got twisted. Sell's first step was to look for friends of the couturiers. He found several, among them the Duchess de Gramont. Sell and the Duchess exchanged courtesies: Sell introduced her to Hearst, and she introduced him to Vionnet. After Vionnet, the rest fell into line. Sell also set out to get the French dressmakers and perfumers to advertise in *Harper's Bazaar*, and as an inducement cut its advertising rates by eighty percent. Up to that time, the French had not seen much point in advertising in America. Sell accomplished two things at once: he got the French into the habit of advertising here and, by allowing them to invest money in *Harper's Bazaar* ads, he got them to take an interest in helping him out editorially. He told the French advertisers that they needn't even bother to have their ads translated ino English. Sell is not only the father of French dress and perfume advertising in this country, but of the native-language advertisement. "It just occurred to me," he says, "that an ad in French ought to draw as well as one in English. I explained to them that pictures meant more than anything else, and that, besides, the name of the advertiser would be the same in French as in English. They went for it because they'd always figured it would be a nuisance to get their stuff translated. Anyway, in some mediums, it would be better to say in French that a perfume stinks than to tell how sweet it smells in English."

Sell broke down society's prejudices against *Harper's Bazaar* largely by making people think of it not as something owned by a boor named Hearst but as something edited by a charming young man named Sell. His homburg and his cane were a good investment. He ate only in restaurants patronized by the people he wanted to read the magazine. He and his shoe trunk went to Palm Beach, to Newport, to Saratoga, and to all the other social towns, where he introduced himself to the proconsuls and politely asked their cooperation in getting society notes and pictures. He was usually accompanied by Baron de Meyer, a kind of combination Cecil Beaton and Mike Romanoff of his day. Society people loved to be photographed by Baron de Meyer, who was the son of a Viennese horse breeder. Baron was one of his given names, but many people thought it was a title. He got his start in the world through his wife, who was supposed to be a natural daughter of Edward VII; on the strength of this, they had been accepted in fashionable European circles. Society's interest in the couple ended with the death of Edward, and they started life all over again as a roller-skating act in the Middle West. De Meyer soon decided, however, to take up photography, which he thought looked like a coming thing, and worked his way up until he was *Vogue*'s star. Sell hired him away by offering him three times as much money as he was getting. Sell discovered that he could convert scorn for Hearst into something like admiration by spending Hearst's money in the right places and on the right things.

The effort to take the curse of Hearst's name off *Harper's Bazaar* was the beginning of Sell's career as a host. He won readers by feasting them. It was a slow and costly but effective way of doing the job. People felt better toward Hearst after they had had one of his filets mignons. Sell discovered, too, that one of the best weapons for conquering the American aristocracy was the British aristocracy. The British didn't care much one way or the other about Hearst and considered the distinction between a California upstart and a New York upstart too slight to be bothered with. Sell proceeded to grab off visiting dukes, duchesses, and earls for feeds at Sherry's and the Ritz. Once he had them, New York society was a cinch.

Sell was an influential man in fashion magazines. There is even a small band of Sell fanatics who claim that he was the Marconi of the industry. "I didn't invent anything," Sell says. "I just applied the methods of the Chicago police reporter to the job."

Actually, it was more the press photographer's than the reporter's methods. When Sell took over, *Harper's Bazaar*, like *Vogue*, was averaging about forty or fifty percent illustrations. About half the graphic material was sketches and half was photographs of society women. Sell left the artists who were supplying the sketches pretty much alone, but he completely reorganized the photography. The society photographs had mostly been carefully posed studio studies, the idea being to come as close as possible to Gains-borough. Generally, they were pictures of great ladies in white silk dresses sitting or standing with their backs to eighteenth-century tapestries, which mainly ran to horses. These photographs, arranged three or four to a page, were often oval-shaped or arched. Sell junked all this décor. He junked nearly all the posed pictures, too. In their places, he began to print informal Baron de Meyer snapshots of the great ladies with their backs not to frowzy studio tapestries but to the sands of Palm Beach, the seascape of the Côte d'Azur, the field-stone walls and privet hedges of their own gardens, and the gaudy murals of nightclubs. In effect, he replaced the society portrait gallery with the society snapshot album. The few posed portraits he thought worth publishing were run not four to a page but one to a page, and the backgrounds were simple—a white wall or a black curtain. Devoting a whole page to a single picture was considered radical in those days. The rule had been to make pictures no larger than was absolutely necessary to show the details without causing eyestrain. In one issue, Sell, taking his cue from some of the Continental magazines, had a particularly attractive portrait printed running across all the margins and right off the edges of the page, in what printers call a "bleed." "I picked a time when Mr. Hearst was away," he recalls. "But he liked it when he saw it, and pretty soon all the magazines were doing it."

Sell introduced the readers of *Harper's Bazaar* to a new kind of celebrity. The factual material, before his regime, had consisted principally of reports on the season at Newport, the season at Saratoga, and the season at a number of other places. Sell found the articles dull and suspected that the readers did, too. He con-

densed the information they contained into captions for his pictures and devoted the space thus saved to articles about chefs,
maîtres d'hôtels, dress designers, headwaiters, entertainers, and
so on. It was a daring move, like presenting a queen with a portrait of her chambermaid, but society people found that the help
were more interesting than they were. Sell also ran a lot of fiction
in *Harper's Bazaar*, but he made no innovations in this field. His
only important service to American letters in this phase was encouraging what turned into Anita Loos's *Gentlemen Prefer
Blondes*. Miss Loos had written Ray Long about a conversation
with a pair of chorus girls who wandered into the drawing room
she and her husband were occupying on a train to the West Coast.
Long showed it to Sell, who bullied Miss Loos into doing a story
about the pair. *Gentlemen Prefer Blondes* appeared serially in
*Harper's Bazaar* in 1925 under the title *Fate Keeps on Happening*.

Hearst was impressed by Sell, who proved that he had thoroughly absorbed the publisher's philosophy of getting things done,
which Hearst once summed up as "When you want a duck egg,
get a duck." Hearst, especially admiring Sell's talent for dinner
parties, put him to work entertaining for the Hearst organization.
Even after Sell left *Harper's Bazaar,* he got an occasional call to
supervise a party for Hearst. What with Hearst's money and his
own imagination, his parties were among the most resplendent
affairs of the twenties. Tradition went by the board when Sell got
to work. He would import handsome trees from Vermont for a
party and then have them tinted pink, white, or orange. Irish
damask, considered by many the most elegant of table coverings,
was considered by Sell acceptable for a picnic in the woods, but
for a dinner party at Sherry's, the Ritz, or the Waldorf, the tables
had to be covered with a mushy layer of rose petals. He liked
to pile one sybaritic trapping on another, then suddenly break
the sequence with an earthy touch. Three or four hours after
the guests at a party at Sherry's had begun a feast involving
nightingales' breasts under glass, some curtains along a side wall
flew apart to admit a host of hot-dog carts, manned by a merry
and noisy crew of Sicilians rounded up by Sell. In the pier shed

party, Sherry's waiters stood with magnums of champagne to slake any thirst that might develop en route. Gypsy fiddlers walked alongside the chairs as far as the gangplank. The main salon of the *Ile de France* was hung with pink tarlatan, and pink and white trees were scattered about. The only illumination came from altar candles set before each guest's place at table.

There were unique Sell features about Sell parties, which, for the most part, were given simply to make friends for the Hearst organization. At some of them, every third person was the guest of honor. This meant that every one who came was either the guest of honor or seated next to him. "I'd just take a man aside," Sell says, "and tell him that though we weren't making any fuss about it, the party was really for him. I'd ask him not to mention it to anyone else. Then I'd tell the two who flanked him that I'd chosen them to sit next to the guest of honor. It worked out fine. Everybody felt happy and important." In his entertaining days, Sell was probably the country's largest purchaser of bath salts. He sprinkled them over painted trees, shook them into the folds of draperies, placed sachets of them here and there, and dissolved them in champagne buckets full of hot water placed under the dinner tables. The idea of giving a party with only one orchestra depressed him. He never had fewer than three. Having the orchestras play in rotation, however, seemed drab and uninteresting, so he rehearsed the musicians himself until one orchestra could stop playing in the middle of a phrase and another could pick up the tune without missing a beat. No matter how Sell's parties began, they almost always ended with gypsies, who, as the clock struck midnight, would rush in on the guests shouting and singing and shaking tambourines. Then they would scatter, some to tell fortunes, some to fiddle, and some to dance. At the end of the evening, Sell would bring out a bag of gold pieces and pay the gypsies off. He always paid his gypsies in gold.

In 1926, Sell resigned the editorship of *Harper's Bazaar*, which he had held since 1920. Soon afterward, the Butterick Publishing Company—*Delineator, Adventure Magazine,* and *Everybody's*

—offered Sell a job as a kind of boss editor for the chain. He took it, but he spent only about half of his time at it. The rest he devoted to the Blaker Advertising Agency. He got some of his business—he had a few public-relations, as well as advertising, accounts—through acquaintanceships he had struck up while he was on *Harper's Bazaar*. Among them were Hattie Carnegie, the International Silk Guild, Delman Shoes, the United Piece Dye Works, the Waldorf, Louis Sherry's, Elizabeth Arden, and Lucien Lelong. He also acquired the accounts of the American Radiator Company, Kewanee Boilers, the Standard Sanitary Corporation, the Standard Casket Company, and the Church Seat Company, a maker of toilet seats. Sell still owns the agency, but he gives only a fraction of his time to it, because meat keeps him so busy. He continued to do some notable things in advertising—for example, he has done a lot of work on the campaign for CARE, the European relief agency—but his reputation in this business is based mainly on past glories. The famous slogan of the Church Seat Company, "The Best Seat in the House," is his. The idea of the Du Barry Success School came out of his office. The father of vitamin advertising was also the discoverer of one of the most familiar figures in American advertising, the hooded, wraithlike girl with the saintly pallor who appears in the Elizabeth Arden ads. He saw her in a Paris couturier's one day, and he instantly realized what she could mean to mud packs and muscle oil.

Sell had a fine time during the Depression. His business went to smash and he lost most of his savings, but he downed more champagne cocktails and more lobsters between 1930 and 1934 than in any other four-year period before or since. "I was lucky," he says. "I sat it out in Peacock Alley. I rode out the storm on the *Monarch of Bermuda*." He was a fairly big stockholder in Simmons Beds, which some customers' man had led him to believe would hold up forever. Simmons Beds began to buckle early on Wednesday, October 23, 1929, six days before the following Tuesday's climax, on which day they collapsed. Sell's agency quickly felt the effects of the market break, too. One morning he went to his office and found cancellation orders on two million dollars' worth of business in the mail. "Even the casket business went to pieces," he says. "Lord knows how people got buried." Eventually, Sell had nothing to do but sit around thinking in nightclubs and restaurants. This was a pleasant mode of existence, but in 1930 and 1931 it was a lonely one. The sound of Sell calling a waiter echoed like the voice of a hunter in a canyon. Sell loves people, and he finds satisfaction in seeing them have a good time, particularly if the good time costs a lot of money. He believes that what he calls "expensive cheerfulness" is one of the foundations of Western civilization. He approves Henry Wallace's goal of a glass of milk for every child in the world, and has recently been giving liberally of his time and money to the cause of feeding the hungry in Europe, but he would like to see the goal amended to include a champagne cocktail and a lobster for every adult.

Sitting alone in the Oval Room of the Ritz one evening, Sell was seized with an idea for reviving the festive spirit. He had seen several people walk up to the entrance, survey the empty tables, lower their eyes, shake their heads in the forlorn and sor-rowing manner of a man looking upon the bier of a friend, and move on. His experience with the food and entertainment in-dustries had taught him that success begets success, that there is no more effective stimulus to enjoyment than the sight of other peo-ple enjoying themselves. A restaurant may employ a chef of genius, but people won't have confidence in it unless they see other people eating there. It occurred to Sell that if the people who slouched on after seeing the Oval Room empty had seen it half full of people having a good time, some of them would have joined in the fun. He decided that what the restaurant business needed was pump priming. He worked out a New Deal program for hotels and nightclubs at least two years before Roosevelt came along with his New Deal for the rest of the country.

From 1930 until 1934, the chief Blaker clients were places like Sherry's, the Ritz, the Waldorf, and Bermuda's Castle Har-bour. Sell also had the Furness Bermuda Line account. They gave him their money not for advertising, however, but for nonpaying stooges. For eating places, Sell supplied diners of experience and finesse. For places with dance floors, he supplied graceful and attractive young people. Perennial travellers, generally with names that would make the papers, were provided for the Furness Bermuda Line and Castle Harbour. "We filled up the Waldorf's restaurants with people who could barely afford a Bowery dinner and we had them eat themselves out of shape on crepes suzette," he says, recalling his accomplishments with satisfaction, and probably with something less than scientific accuracy. "We had beautiful kids with holes in their shoes dancing all over the Starlight Roof. The place doesn't look half as gay today as it did then, when the hotel was losing seven thousand dollars a day."

It was really something of a good-fairy role that Sell played, and, being a rather wispy, light-footed creature, he was happy playing it. Every night for two summers, except when he was off taking boatloads of good-looking deadheads to Castle Harbour, he and his wife dined on the Starlight Roof, at an inconspicuous corner table from which he could survey the whole room while surreptitiously giving signals to the waiters and stage directions to his Cinderellas. "I had to keep my dancers dancing and my eaters eating," he recalls. "I had to see to it that none of them welshed on me and ordered pork chops. They were supposed to order only the most spectacular dishes. The idea was to have everything *en flambeau*. Crepes suzette, cherries in flames, peaches in flames, flaming soups and meats and fish. Our motto was 'If it won't burn, to hell with it.' We wanted to get the customers inside, and we wanted to get them into the I'll-have-some-of-what-he's-having spirit."

Recovery, along with repeal, brought Sell's hotel and restaurant operations to an end, and with recovery the advertising business picked up. It was through advertising that Sell later got into vitamins and then into meat, but before he went into either of these he had a brief adventure with wine. He had had the advertising and public-relations accounts of a number of the large French dressmakers and had done so well for them that when, after repeal, the winegrowers of the lower Rhine Valley decided that they wanted an American public-relations counsel, the French consul in New York recommended Sell. Sell liked the idea. He went to Strasbourg, by ship and plane, to meet his prospective clients. He was met by a delegation of vintners. He found them charming people. "A lusty crew," he says. "An obese, earthy, warmhearted, affectionate bunch." Sell got right to work. By chance, he says, he ran into a couple of pretty girls he had known in Chicago and New York, and, with his publicity instincts operating efficiently, he immediately brought the girls and the vintners together. He had pictures of the winegrowers and the young ladies taken for the American press. It was a great start for the campaign, but it cost him his job. The vintners sacked him. Actually, it was not the winegrowers who had turned against him, but their wives. When the wives saw the pictures, they took the position that their husbands' wines ought to sell themselves on their own merits. They held a meeting and passed a resolution to this effect. The husbands were informed of the consensus among the wives, and another delegation, a rather mournful one, went to Sell to tell him they had decided he wasn't quite the man for the job.

Sell has always regretted that his association with the vintners was so brief. Historically, though, it was probably a good thing that the wives felt as they did, for if they had not, alcohol might have triumphed over vitamins and meat. One of the new accounts he was offered in 1936 was a pharmaceutical house that was putting out a capsule containing several vitamins. The company asked him to prepare its advertising copy for drug and medical journals. This account completely changed the direction of Sell's life. But for it, Sell's Liver Pâté would never have been born. As soon as Sell got the account, he felt a stirring inside him, a bristling of nerve ends, a quickening of the senses. He knew nothing about vitamins, but now that they had come to his attention he was for them. The physical-culturist side of his character had been developing for a long time. Except for vitamins, which he had somehow overlooked, he had tried almost every touted method of the twenties for keeping up body tone. He was God's gift to Swedish masseurs. In 1925, he hired Philadelphia Jack O'Brien to give him lessons in shadowboxing and punching the bag. He was a confirmed deep breather. When glands came in, he twitched his endocrines daily in a series of prescribed exercises.

The capsule Sell was about to advertise was one of the first that contained all the known vitamins. Before that time, vitamin capsules had generally been taken only on doctors' orders, to make up for diet deficiencies. Authorities agreed that the feeding of vitamins might help make a sick person healthy, but they doubted that taking large quantities of all the vitamins would make a healthy person still healthier. As a matter of fact, the issue is still being hotly disputed. Today, the vitamin situation appears to be one in which the medical profession is lined up against the research men in the laboratories. Deserters on both sides have gone over to the enemy, but, by and large, it is a matter of doctors against laboratory experts. Most doctors claim that in general they have got poor results from feeding vitamins to people; vitamins, they say, don't do anybody any harm, but they don't seem to do anybody any good, either. The research men say that rats have responded magnificently to dosing, and that human beings should do the same; they say that the doctors must be giving their patients vitamins in doses that aren't large enough. The doctors say the research men can't be pinned down on how much enough is. The research men hint that maybe doctors don't want healthy patients. The doctors hint that maybe the research men are tools of vested interests. And so it goes. Sell, who got in on the ground floor of this argument, allied himself with the research men. Instinctively he is on the side of any new gimmick. He ordered a report on the latest and best research opinion on all vitamins, the benefits to be derived from them, and the quality of the particular product he was to handle. The report was mostly encouraging. It confirmed the conclusions Sell had jumped to. Vitamins could do as much for men as for rats, and maybe more. As for this brand of capsule, it stated that the vitamins were high-grade but that there weren't enough of them. Sell confronted the maker with this intelligence and laid down two conditions on which he would accept the account: first, the vitamin content of the capsules must be jacked up; second, the manufacturer must embark on an advertising campaign to take the case for vitamins directly to the people. Since there were glad tidings to be spread, Sell wanted to spread them everywhere. Vitamins, he argued, are merely concentrated nourishment, and if anyone wanted to absorb more, he shouldn't need a doctor's order to do so. Restaurants serve second helpings of apple pie on request; Americans can walk into a grocery store and buy whatever they want to eat. Why shouldn't this new superfood be obtainable everywhere? The manufacturer balked at Sell's conditions, so Sell, with financial backing from a number of his friends, became a vitamin manufacturer himself.

Sell didn't try to work out a formula for his product all by himself; he got some university biochemists to lay down general principles, on which he based his recipe. Then he had the capsules made up for him by a firm in Detroit. It was Sell's genius at advertising and selling that put over not only his own vitamins but, according to trade historians, the entire craze for multiple-vitamin capsules. One of his most inspired moves had to do with naming his product. Sell, considering the problem of advertising and marketing his capsules, couldn't help feeling that there was something colorless and uninteresting about the word "vitamins." It seemed chilly and forbidding. It was an unfortunate neologism, because it brought no image to mind. Few people had ever seen a vitamin. Sell felt that no one would be apt to glow with the conviction that something called vitamins could make his life richer and healthier. He decided that some substance people knew about ought to be added to the vitamins in his capsules, but he couldn't think what. He asked his biochemists for ideas, but most of their suggestions ran to eight-syllable chemical compounds that would only make his selling problem worse. Finally, Sell himself came up with the notion of adding liver and iron extract. The proposal was received glumly by the scientists, who would say no more than that liver and iron wouldn't hurt anyone, but Sell knew that he had what he had been looking for. The average American has a fixed idea that liver and iron are substances he ought to be getting more of. They have enormous prestige as muscle builders, chest expanders, and hair growers. "We stuck in the liver and iron," Sell says, "and after that finding a name was easy. I mumbled it over to myself a few times—vitamins with liver and iron added, vitamins plus liver and iron, vitamins plus, Vitamins Plus. Eureka!" The "plus" was one of the great concepts of American advertising. When people spend their money, they like to think that they are getting a little bit more than they are paying for, no matter what that little bit is.

For the next five years, Sell lived for vitamins. He made war on public apathy, fought the Federal Trade Commission to a standstill over his advertising claims, and took on several state boards of pharmacy in the courts, hammering away until they reluctantly agreed to give their blessings to multiple-vitamin capsules and set up standards for them. He got vitamins into department stores and on drugstore counters. Often, he was his own drummer. He started with the New York department stores. His first conquests were Saks Fifth Avenue and Lord & Taylor. "Until I came along, you couldn't get so much as an aspirin tablet in Saks or Lord & Taylor's," he says. The department stores in the cities in the Middle West and West were covered by a young woman named Janet Leckie, who began with Sell as a research worker and is now vice-president of Sell's Specialties. Miss Leckie drove across the continent a half-dozen times, sowing vitamins everywhere. Twice she was arrested for speeding. Once she got off by giving a box of Vitamin A, the anti-night-blindness stuff, to a state trooper who confessed that glaring headlights hurt his eyes. The other time, she convinced the judge that the importance of bringing buoyant health to the citizens of America was so great that no rate of speed she indulged in could be considered excessive.

The department stores sold Vitamins Plus over their cosmetics counters. The celebrated question, "Have you been taking your vitamins?" made its first appearance in a manual Sell prepared for the clerks. The pamphlet also instructed them to sell the pills to women who were having trouble making polish adhere to their nails, and to talk them up to purchasers of hair tonics and brushes by announcing that vitamins would "help to improve the sheen and texture of the hair from within while she exercises it and polishes it from without with her new brush." This scheme was usually successful. "Life begins with Vitamins Plus" was one of Sell's slogans. He didn't quite believe what it said, but he felt no compunction about saying it, because he believed that he was saying it for the public's own good. He has never relaxed his almost maternal compulsion to cram nutrition into people in whatever guise they can be persuaded to take it.

Vitamins Plus frequently got into the courts, but the firm itself was seldom a defendant. Sell was in trouble only once, when the Federal Trade Commission had him on the carpet for thirty-nine advertising claims that it asserted were false. Only ten of the charges stuck. One, for example, was that the pills would make hair curl. The ten false boasts had been made not by Sell but by an overenthusiastic department store. Sell, however, took the rap. Most of the court actions involved department stores and drugstores that were charged, generally on the complaint of a state board of pharmacy, with selling pharmaceuticals without a pharmacist's license. Sell, though no party to the actions, always handled the defense and paid the expenses. He won every case, and without any aid from the bar. His chief counsel was usually Dr. Bernard L. Oser, who was, and still is, director of the Food Research Laboratories, Inc. Dr. Oser prepared his briefs in whatever grocery stores were handy to the courthouse. He would appear in court with a bundle of groceries. Then, in the course of testimony, he would tell the judge it was his understanding that the board of pharmacy had complained that a store was illegally selling substances listed either in the *United States Pharmacopoeia* or the *National Formulary*, which are the rosters of drugs and medicines recognized by the law. He would then open up his bag and spread out his purchases on the bench—sugar, bicarbonate of soda, olive oil, yeast, salt, starch, and sulphur, all of them listed either in the *Pharmacopoeia* or the *Formulary*. In almost every instance, the judge threw the case out of court. Dr. Oser's work was a service to the language as well as to vitamins, since it helped blot out what is no doubt a false distinction between drugs and food. As it stands now, a number of foods are drugs when the doctor prescribes them, and a number of drugs are foods if someone just happens to eat them because he is hungry.

By 1940, vitamins were firmly on their feet. Vitamins Plus and a half-dozen other multiple-vitamin pills and capsules could be bought almost anywhere. Sell spent most of that year helping the Department of Agriculture out on some special administrative and public-relations problems. The Department had been sympathetic to his cause, and he had made a lot of friends in it, among them Henry A. Wallace, when he was Secretary, and Milo Perkins. While Sell was working in Washington, he attended a dinner party in the home of Secretary of Agriculture Claude Wickard at which Dr. Robert S. Harris, a leading American nutritionist, fired his imagination by outlining the specifications for what turned out to be Sell's Liver Pâté. Once the pâté was in production, Sell bought up all the shares of the Vitamins Plus stockholders and then sold out to the Vick Chemical Company. He closed his books with a true Sell touch. The principal ex-stockholders were invited to a superb luncheon at the Waldorf. At dessert time, the waiters brought in elegant silver platters bearing something under glass. What this turned out to be was handsome alligator and pigskin wallets, from which protruded brand-new currency, mostly hundred-dollar bills, to the amount of each stockholder's interest. "It seemed a little more gala than sending out checks," Sell says.

Sell has been in meat for almost eight years now. It is the longest time he has ever been in anything except advertising. When friends prophesy that another year or so will find him in hormones or television, he answers that meat, unlike vitamins or fashion magazines or any of the other lines he has worked at, is not one career but several. He is always finding out something new about meat. Meat is a permanent frontier country, he feels. For the long pull, he is working on his Project X, a food, with a meat base, that he believes may lengthen the human life span. Moreover, he expects to go on adding to his line of Sell's Specialties. This last

year, he has been working with particular zeal on his Chicken &
Rice, which is about to appear on the market in limited quantities.
Canning a combination of chicken and rice is, Sell says, one of
the toughest jobs the industry has ever tackled. There has been
for years a huge demand for it, but no one has been able to
pack it satisfactorily. The trouble is the rice, which becomes a
soggy, tasteless mush as it soaks up the meat juices. During the
war, a "converted" rice was developed for the armed forces, and
though it was not put to the ultimate test of being exposed for a
long time to chicken juices, it stood up pretty well in most liquids.
It is now on the general market, under various trade names, and
Sell thinks that it will enable him to put a permanent end to the
chicken-and-rice problem. He and Janet Leckie frequently visit
the kitchen in his Brooklyn packing house to taste samples of the
new product and order revisions in the recipe.

Even canning plain chicken has its headaches. The worst of
these is boning the bird. The price of canned fowl could be considerably lowered if the meat could be separated from the bone
rapidly and without waste. A lot of high-priced hand labor goes
into the finicky job of picking shreds of meat off the small, slippery bones of chickens and then picking bone splinters out of the
shreds. Sell ran up against this difficulty when he was concocting
his Minced Chicken. He inquired around among his meat-packing
friends and learned of a man named William A. Denissen who
had made a study of chicken stripping and had trained himself
to deflesh an average-size chicken in thirty seconds. He combines
a restless, inventive intellect with fingers as supple as a violinist's.
Denissen, a highly paid meat buyer for the Howard Johnson
organization, had discovered that the flesh of a chicken is joined
to the chassis at only six points. When these six connections are
severed, the bird peels like a banana. Sell prevailed upon Denissen
to give lessons to the chicken strippers of Sell's Specialties in his
spare time. None of Sell's employees came anywhere near match-
ing the Master's dexterity, but a substantial speedup was effected.

According to Sell, the relations between a meat packer and
the people who eat his meat are close and based on trust. He

learned this through an experience in naming his products. When he started as a packer, he called his company Sell's Planned Foods, Inc., and his products Rose Mill foods. It was Rose Mill Pâté at first, not Sell's Liver Pâté. Rose Mill is the name of a farm in Connecticut owned by Earle McHugh, a Hearst executive. On the farm is a gristmill that grinds the flour for Pepperidge Farm Bread. McHugh, along with several other friends, invested in Sell's new enterprise, and some of the ingredients Sell used came from McHugh's place. Rose Mill seemed a good enough name to Sell, who considered it far more dignified than, say, such names as Donald Duck Brand, My-T-Fine, Superba, Sweet-Um, Hav-A-Kan, and so on. Rose Mill Pâté's first few months on the market were disappointing. Sell was advised by a chain-store grocery official of wide experience that the trouble lay in the name. "It's a terrible name," he told Sell. "Might do for carrots and peas or canned peaches, but it's all wrong for meat. Meat has to have an author. The people want to know whose work it is. Look at all the successful packers—Swift, Armour, Wilson, Hormel, Stahl-Meyer, Campbell, Heinz. Every one of those names tells the public that a man, not a duck, stands behind what they're getting. Meat is supposed to have style, and the people want to know whose style it is." Sell changed the name and sales improved immediately.

Meat will probably turn out to be Sell's permanent calling, but it is possible that from time to time he will branch out into related fields. When he changed his brand name, he also changed his firm name, from Sell's Planned Foods to Sell's Specialties, Inc., which, he feels, leaves him free to go into anything that strikes his fancy. He has already made a brief excursion into, and a wise retreat from, the soap business, which is, of course, intimately related to the meat business. Two or three years ago, some of his scientist friends got him all stirred up about soap. They told him that the stuff the manufacturers were palming off on the public was a travesty on what a cleansing agent ought to be. Even the best of it was too harsh, too weak, too smelly, too slow, and too greasy. Cleansing technology had leaped ahead several centuries, but the soap kings, whose coffers could hardly hold the money that poured in, hadn't made a move to put the new knowledge to use. They were selling seventeenth-century soap by using twentieth-century advertising. Intelligence of this sort invariably inflames Sell's social conscience. He decided to put the skids under the soap kings. He told the scientific men to go back to their laboratories and make him up the best detergent science could produce. What they came up with was a liquid that undoubtedly was one of the most powerful cleansing agents ever known. Dirt fled from the gentlest application of it, yet it made a bathroom smell like an apple orchard in May. It could be used on a schoolgirl's complexion or a grease monkey's overalls with equal effectiveness and safety. Sell called it Soft-n-White. He sent samples to the *Ladies' Home Journal, Good Housekeeping, Parents' Magazine,* and the Herald Tribune Home Institute, all of which favored it with superlatives. Everything looked fine until Sell sat down to figure out what he ought to charge for the wonder soap. His arithmetic showed that, simply to break even, he would have to charge a dollar a quart, three or four times what people were paying for seventeenth-century soap. The economic facts of life were against Soft-n-White. Sell reasoned that the public, in its ignorant and somewhat soiled state of development, wasn't ready to pay that much for soap. He did not court bankruptcy by putting Soft-n-White on the market, but he keeps making it up in small quantities—the recipe is based on a formula patented as Sell's Formula 501, the Detergent Plus—and giving it to grateful friends, meanwhile looking forward to the day when people will come to their senses and realize that there is no sense in going around half dirty.

Sell also tried, without much luck, to move in on cereals. He set up a cereal factory in the Blaker Advertising Agency's art department and eventually produced Extendo, which, like Soft-n-White, grew out of his indignation over the low quality of most commercial products. "It's revolting," he says. "The cereals you buy are nothing but boxed air. The boxes themselves are half full of air, and the stuff in the other half is mostly air, too. And it's probably just as well the boxes aren't full. You would get as much nourishment from eating the boxes as you would from the contents." Extendo was a combination of whole-grain cereals packed so tightly that the boxes didn't contain so much as a cubic inch of air. It wasn't golden brown, and it wasn't especially crunchy or crispy or crackly, but it was—or so Sell felt—good, wholesome eating, the kind of cereal that men used to fill themselves on before setting out to conquer the wilderness. The public didn't take to Extendo when it was marketed, apparently having debauched itself too long on cereals that pop, snap, sing, and whistle, that are shredded and flaked and toasted and nutted. People reared back from an honest cereal like a rumpot face to face with a glass of milk. "We were able to sell Extendo to farmers for their hogs or their chickens," Sell says, "but we didn't want that. We were interested in human beings." He returned the art department to its rightful occupants and went back to meat.

From time to time, Sell has operated on a small scale in something far less tangible than soap or cereal. He has dabbled in politics. A rabid liberal, he did a lot of work for the Roosevelt campaigns. In between, he tried to help the New Dealers in their legislative battles. A few years back, he prevented, practically by himself, a penny-pinching Congress from killing the Department of Agriculture's school-lunch program. Sell was sitting by his radio one night when Dorothy Thompson attacked the House for defeating, by a vote of 136–52, an amendment to a bill providing for school lunches. It was considered a sure thing that the amendment would be killed by a similarly overwhelming vote in the Senate. Before Miss Thompson had time to get her hat on and leave the studio, Sell was on the phone asking if she would make a recording of the speech. She did it, on the spot, and within a couple of hours Sell had found a factory that was willing to give over the next few days to making 15,000 transcriptions. As they came out of the machines, he had one mailed to every governor, mayor, bishop, cardinal, columnist, editor, college president, radio announcer, school principal, and Rotary and Kiwanis official whose name he could get hold of, as well as to all members of Congress. To everyone on the list who wasn't a member of

Congress, Sell also sent a wire asking him to play Miss Thompson's speech on his phonograph and then put the heat on his Senators to vote for the program. Within forty-eight hours after Sell heard Miss Thompson's broadcast, irate telegrams from important people began flowing into Washington. Sell sent out first, second, and third followups to the people on his list who were slow about replying. One politician finally wired back what must be one of the most unequivocal commitments in the history of his temporizing profession: "I am for the school lunch. I am for the school lunch. I am for the school lunch." The Senate passed the amendment by an overwhelming voice vote. It went back to the House, which passed it by a vote of 133–23.

Sell may shed careers, but he never sheds the infatuations that got him into any of them. It is like living simultaneously in the present and several pasts. He still has, for example, a lively interest in fashion magazines and in fashions. Hattie Carnegie, Sophie Gimbel, Valentina, and Mainbocher invite him to their fashion shows, and he always attends, decked out as splendidly as he was when Vionnet first consented to allow him inside her Paris atelier, twenty-eight years ago. It is many years since he has been a professional litterateur, but he fits a heavy reading schedule into his crowded life, and he never lets himself go very long without enjoying the company of writers. Interior decoration is another abandoned career, but he keeps up with developments in the field, and he is always fussing with the things in his apartment, on East Fifty-seventh Street, which he has had ever since he came to New York in 1920. His taste runs to the elegantly modern. In 1929, he bought all the furnishings of the Gold Medal Room, a prize-winning office at the Paris Decorative Arts Exposition, had them shipped over here, and set them up inside a glass-walled room he had built in his offices. He worked in it for several years and then sold the furniture. He now does his desk work standing before a draftsman's board. He thinks that he gets more work done that way, mainly because seeing him standing up seems to persuade visitors to cut their calls short.

A life as varied and active as Sell's takes a certain amount of planning, and he finds that working out a weekly schedule for himself is the solution. Every Saturday, after he has swallowed his morning quota of vitamin pills, yeast cakes, and wheat-germ oil, and done his fifteen minutes of folding himself into layers on his inclining board, he charts his course for the next seven days by writing a program down in a black leather book. The business hours of his working days, Monday through Friday, are devoted, of course, principally to meat, and he makes no rigid plans for them. The life of a meat packer is full of crises and of opportunities that knock but once, if they bother to knock at all. Sell has to be prepared to act quickly if a carload of desirable pig liver is dumped on the market. Again, some laboratory genius may discover a new amino acid that should be added to the formula for the Liver Pâté, or else discover that some old amino acid already in the pâté doesn't do anybody any good. Recently there has been a distressing tendency among scientists to announce that a lot of the amino acids formerly considered vital to our well-being are useless. To take care of such exigencies, Sell surrounds each business engagement with ample cushions of time. He also leaves one day a week entirely unassigned. "The flight plan always includes one day of blind flying," he explains. For spiritual nourishment, he attends, in season, a concert and an opera a week. He reads for an hour or so every night before going to sleep. Usually he reads whatever happens to be lying around the house, but his schedule calls for one book of American history a month. History is one of the "fire escapes" in his life—one of the ways he has devised for running away from gloom. "I just read it to get a line on the betting odds," he says. "It gives me the feeling that we've come through so many times before that we're bound to do it again." He also takes a swim, a massage, and a dancing lesson every week. On Saturday he resets the pedometer he always wears and pledges himself to walk at least twenty miles in the coming week. He likewise allocates a certain amount of time to the trapezes and flying rings he has in his apartment. The French circuses he saw while he was abroad for *Harper's Bazaar* aroused his interest in acrobatics. Until the Three Flying Codonas' act broke up, a few years ago, Sell always invited the Codonas, old friends of his, to drop into the apartment when the circus was in town. They liked to inspect his work. "Alfredo Codona used to tell me I was the best acrobat in town at my income," Sell says.

# XI

## Lewis A/K/A Louis Halworth Rovere, Circa 1887-1975

My father died on July 27, 1975, and it was not until a week later that I began to learn who he really was and who, in a sense, I am. I got the story, or part of it, from an uncle, my father's half-brother, of whose existence I had never, in sixty years, been told.

### I. THE FATHER I KNEW

In his prime, he stood, erect as a drill sergeant, an inch or so under six feet, was heavily built, and had the dark, leathery complexion and black, curly hair of a Mediterranean peasant or fisherman, which is perhaps what his and some of my ancestors were. The most conspicuous thing about him was a scar on his left cheek—an almost perfect crescent of smooth, reddish flesh, perhaps a half-inch wide at the center, that ran from just below the temple almost to the jawbone; it was all the more striking because it was a hairless island in the heavily-bearded face of an uncommonly hirsute man. Though most of his work was sedentary —he was an electrical engineer with the Western Union Telegraph Company—he was physically vigorous and rugged. In spikes and holding belt, he could climb a utility pole with the ease of a veteran lineman. (This was in the days when those who worked on high-tension wires reached them under their own power rather than being lifted on the hydraulic devices known as "cherry pickers.") Into his sixties, he would walk the Brooklyn Bridge on the coldest, windiest days to his office in lower Manhattan. He had a deep, rather gruff voice and, though his English was always correct, spoke with a slight but distinct French accent, the result, I assumed, of his having spent part of his childhood and youth in Switzerland. He was a reserved, phlegmatic, undemonstrative man and sometimes affected the spurious heartiness that is intended to mask the discomfort of one who is ill at ease in large gatherings or in the company of strangers. But by and large, he seemed a rather typical product of his time, his class, and the city, New York, in which he lived and worked most of his life. He was an organization man, a technician who valued efficiency above most things and thought that much good would come to the country when his fellow engineer, Herbert Hoover, became President. He had little interest in ideas as such. He told me that as a young man he had been a practicing Unitarian, but while I was growing up, he attended no church and made no effort to have me attend one. He voted a straight Republican ticket into the late 1930s, when he came to admire Franklin D. Roosevelt.* Though he was not above certain forms of bigotry that flourished in the corporate world of which he was a part, he was by temperament, I think, liberal and humane, but he was largely indifferent to matters that were beyond his professional concern, and he was always conservative and conventional in expression. Apart from technical journals, he read little but the daily newspapers and *The Saturday Evening Post*.

Until I was six or seven, he was, like so many middle-class American fathers, a rather dim and transient figure in our household of three. He worked six, sometimes seven days a week and made frequent trips on Western Union business. He was also a

---

* I believe he voted Democratic the rest of his life, and I know he was much pleased when he learned that I had made Richard Nixon's "enemies list."

free-lance designer of electrical equipment—much of it patented in his name, though the rights were assigned to the companies that had paid him for his time. (His job classification was "protection engineer," and his specialty was the protection of power and communications lines and other exposed equipment from such hazards of nature as lightning, ice, high winds, and the like.) In my earliest memories of him at home, he is seated at a large oak desk, smoking a pipe, and on the desk or near it on the floor are spools of wire, drafting tools, batteries, bulbs, condensers, relays, rheostats, and all manner of dials, meters, and gauges. And blueprints. Wherever we lived, mostly in Manhattan on the Upper West Side and here and there in Brooklyn, the house was full of blueprints, and he would pore over them for hours at a time, now and then giving one he no longer had use for to my mother, who would bleach it and put the linen to some domestic use. Also, he was seldom without a slide rule, and even at meals would use it to make calculations of some sort. But there were occasional walks in the park, Sundays at the beach, train rides, and such. I am sure that he gave me as much time as he felt he could spare from establishing himself and providing for my mother and me. I do not recall ever having had any sense of deprivation or neglect. To me, in those days, it was part of the natural order of things that fathers worked at paying jobs outside the home, while mothers looked after the children. I loved him very much and never thought of him as anything but a good and dutiful father.

Later, when he became more secure and I became more sociable, we spent much time together. He gave me chemistry sets, miniature steam generators, toy electric trains—things he regarded as educational—and instructed me in their use. He now and then took my mother and me on business trips, and when we acquired a Model-T Ford, we would go on weekend excursions, often camping in the Catskills or along the New Jersey shore. He bought me a Cape Cod skiff and taught me to sail and look after it. He was an amateur astronomer—it was as close as he came to having a hobby—and from him I learned the little I was able to absorb of that science. He tried with varying degrees of success to instill in me those values he set most store by, which were, in addition to efficiency, truthfulness, responsibility, work, thrift, and that orderly, show-me way of thinking that is the hallmark of a good technician. He took more of an interest in my schooling than I did; when I did badly, which was much of the time, he did not scold me but only urged me to try harder, which I generally did—just about as all was to be lost. He was the family disciplinarian, but he did not believe in corporal punishment and sought to keep me in line by example, precept, and the occasional withholding of my weekly allowance. When I was about twenty and told him I planned to join the Communist Party, he did not reproach me or try to talk me out of it but merely said that I was of an age to make my own decisions. I would not say that our relationship was a particularly good or close one. We had few interests in common and often had little to say to each other. But it was, at least as I remember it, an agreeable and relatively untroubled relationship. Perhaps there were times of tension, hostility, jealousy, even hate; the Freudians tell us that these are always present in one degree or another between fathers and sons. That I write of him as I now do may indicate merely that I have successfully suppressed the feelings of conflict I once had; if so, it would seem to me that they could not have been of much magnitude, and I know that in the years after childhood and adolescence, I continued to think of him as a good father and later as a good grandfather to my three children.

For a man who showed so little interest in anything but facts, objects, machines, and the way things worked, he sometimes adhered rigidly to what he regarded as high moral principles. For example, he thought divorce immoral, a kind of crime against nature. In 1938, he and my mother separated. It had long been clear to me and to them that they were incompatible temperamentally if in no other way and that they would each be better off leading separate lives. They parted without rancor, and neither blamed the other for what had gone wrong. He wanted to remarry and eventually did so. But he waited seven years before he sought a divorce. Though he had no religious scruples in the matter, he could hardly bring himself to consider one. My mother would not have contested any suit he brought, and I spent many long evenings trying to persuade him that divorce would harm no one and that he was only punishing himself and the woman he wanted to marry by not getting one. Still, he let year after miserable year go by before he could bring himself to legalize the end of a marriage that had long since ceased to have meaning. And a quarter century later, when he had an advanced case of leukemia and needed blood transfusions to stay alive, he had to be persuaded by my stepmother and my wife and children and me to accept the transfusions. "I'm very old," he would say. "I don't want to take the blood away from younger people who are working and have families." We kept saying that he wouldn't be "taking blood away" from anyone who needed it, and we told him that if he insisted on viewing the matter as he did, we in his family could provide the hospital with more plasma than he would need. But each transfusion was preceded by this kind of argument, and, once, a few weeks before the end, he implored his wife to bring him his pistol so that he could shoot himself right in his hospital bed. She put him off by saying she couldn't find it anywhere.

But there were always certain mysteries about him, things he would not explain, or, if he did, left me in a state of at least partial disbelief. That scar, for example. How and when had he got it? It was the result, he said, of a household accident when he was a boy, once telling me that it had been caused by boiling water, once by a flame. But I was quite certain it wasn't a burn, and so was a doctor friend who had had much experience with such accidents. A burn scar is blotchy, shapeless; his was clearly outlined, almost symmetrical. Though it could have been the result of some accident other than a burn, it had the look of a knife wound, of a long, deep slash. As for the pistol, it was a Colt .25 that he had bought almost fifty years ago when we had a summer cottage deep in a Connecticut woods and far from other houses. He got it, he said, because he thought my mother might need it for her protection and mine while he was at work in New York, but he never taught her to use it, and I supposed that it had rusted away or somehow disappeared when we sold that house. But thirty years later, my son came upon it while poking around in his garage. It had been kept in good working order. Why? So far as I know, he had no reason to fear violence; he was living in a well-to-do, well-policed suburb, and that was at a time before violent crime had reached beyond New York's city limits. Perhaps he kept it because he foresaw a time when he would find life insupportable and would need it for suicide. I have no doubt that if he had been able to lay hands on it during those last unhappy days, he would have used it without hesitation. Though it was supported by nothing I ever heard him say, there were indications of a kind of preoccupation with violence. When I was nine or ten, he enrolled me in a boxing class at the Crescent Athletic Club in Brooklyn. It was taught by a retired and badly battered middleweight known as Harlem Tommy Murphy, and every Saturday morning for about two years, I along with a few other boys of about my age would, under Murphy's instruction, knock each other around the club gymnasium for an hour or more. I don't suppose I then asked myself why he thought this important; though I had no talent for boxing, I rather enjoyed those lessons, and I didn't get hurt. But later I asked why he had wanted me to take them. Why boxing lessons rather than tennis lessons or swimming or riding lessons? He said he wanted me to be able to defend myself. But against what or whom? I never got into anything more serious than an occasional friendly scuffle in school or on the vacant lots we used to play in, and if I had, I doubt if I could have applied anything the old pug had tried to teach me. I can only assume that there was something in his experience that made him think I would be better off if I knew how to repel assailants with my fists.

The deepest mysteries, though, concerned his origins and his early life. He gave my mother and me to understand that he was a native New Yorker, that he had been born in Manhattan and was the only child of Henry Rovere, an importer of chinaware, and of

Genevieve River, a Frenchwoman from New Orleans. He said that when he was a small boy, my grandmother had become very ill and had gone to Switzerland for some kind of cure, taking him with her and placing him in a boarding school in or near Geneva. He said that she had died when he was nine or ten and that his father had died in the San Francisco earthquake of 1906. After his mother's death, he had been sent to Culver Military Academy in Culver, Indiana, and had gone from there to Columbia University's School of Mines and Engineering, where he had been a member of the class of 1909. Of his time at Columbia, he had vivid and detailed memories and mementoes—a set of fencing foils, a clay piperack with the college seal, several photographs— and he attended class reunions until a year before he died. But aside from the few names, dates, and places he gave, he had, he insisted, no memories of the years before college. What sort of people, I would ask, were Henry and Genevieve? What did they look like? Had they been good parents? He would say that he hardly knew them, that he had seen so little of them that he really couldn't answer such questions. Where in New York had the Roveres lived? At several places in Manhattan, but he couldn't recall specific streets or sections—though once, when he was being driven around the city by my wife a few years before he died, he volunteered that he and Henry had lived for a time in the Bristol Hotel, which used to stand on the northwest corner of Fifth Avenue and Forty-second Street and was, early in the century, well-known for its theatrical clientele. Had he known any of his grandparents or uncles, aunts, cousins? No, there had been only Henry and Genevieve. What sort of things did he do as a boy? What games had he played? What did he study in Switzerland and at Culver? What was the name of that school near Geneva? Was it a good school? Had he made any friends there? He said he supposed that he did what most boys do and that he had had school friends, but he couldn't remember any names, including that of the school. It was clear that such questions made him very uncomfortable, and in time I stopped asking them, though I never stopped asking myself how it could be that a man with a memory that could store considerable amounts of technical data could recall so little of almost two decades of his life.

There were mysteries even about his name and his age. On his death certificate, the name is "Lewis A/K/A [also known as] Louis Halworth Rovere." He had used both the British and French spellings of his given name and in his later years—to avoid confusion, I assumed—took to signing himself "L.H.," the term of address used by my stepmother and by many of his friends, or "L. Halworth Rovere." Asked about the proper spelling of his first name, he would say that he supposed he could find out by checking his birth certificate but that he didn't have the time and that anyway it seemed unimportant to him. How did we come by the name Rovere? He said it had originally been Rover, but since Rover had once been a common name for a dog some British ancestor had added the terminal "e" to avoid being whistled at. Except as a child, I never took that seriously. My friends the Rover Boys, after all, had no such problem. Also, how could a man who knew so little about his own parents know what some remote forebear had done? And how could he know that the name was British? It did not take me long to learn that Rovere is a not uncommon Italian name*: it means "of the oak" and was borne by two popes, one being Julius II, who commissioned Michelangelo's frescoes in the Sistine Chapel. As for Halworth, which is also my middle name, I have no idea where it came from or what, if anything, it signifies. I have never found it as a surname in any of the many telephone directories I have checked. The closest thing to it in spelling is Haworth, the English village in which the Brontë sisters grew up. I long ago concluded that it was an invention of my father's.

When I was young, he told me that he was two years older than

---

* Not many Italian Roveres seem to have migrated to this country, but, oddly, my wife and I once sold a house we had owned in Hyde Park, New York, to a Carlo Rovere.

my mother, who was born on July 28, 1888, but I noted that on driver's licenses and other documents, the last being the death certificate, the birth date was given as October 18, 1888, which would have made him three months younger. Once when I pointed out this discrepancy, he replied as he had about the spelling of his name—that he could check his birth certificate but he didn't consider the matter important enough to bother about.

Gradually, it became clear to me that he was concealing something. I first thought either that his childhood had been so painful that he did not want to discuss it with anyone or that there was something about his origins that he considered too shameful to reveal. But, I reasoned, people whose childhoods have been wretched are less likely to bury their grievances than to nourish and trade on them (even write books about them) and, as it were, wear their hurts on their sleeves. And what could it be that he was concealing? Illegitimate birth? Neither my mother, in whose family of British colonials illegitimacy was common, almost rampant, nor I would have been troubled by any such knowledge, but perhaps he thought we would. Yet why would this lead him to deny having specific memories of his school days? Was he perhaps trying to conceal the truth about his and my racial origins? Was he in fact Italian? When I was a boy in Brooklyn, Italians were held in low esteem in the Anglo-Saxon-Protestant world to which I assumed I belonged. Some thought they constituted a criminal class, and we know from the White House tapes that a President of the United States considered them an inferior breed. Or could it have been Jewishness he was hiding? In earlier years, he was, as I assume most of his Western Union colleagues were, outspokenly anti-Semitic.* I knew that members of despised minorities often seek to dissociate themselves by adopting the stereotypes of those who

---

* I first accepted anti-Semitism as a received truth, but it was a kind of truth I found it hard to apply when about half my friends were Jewish. When I found it repellent, I told my father so. He heard me out and after a while said he thought I was right. I do not believe he ever made a racist remark after that.

despise them. But, again, what would denying Jewishness have to do with claiming no memory of where he had lived in New York or forgetting the name of the Swiss school he had attended?

I wanted to know more about my father's past, which was, after all, part of my own, but I could see that I would never learn anything from him. I could, of course, have done some geneological research, but—apart from once determining that there was no Henry Rovere in the City Directories in the years he was supposed to be importing chinaware—I did none. Perhaps I had some feeling that if I discovered what hurt him, it would hurt me also.

He died in the infirmary of a retirement home in Bradenton, Florida, a small city on the Gulf of Mexico to which he and his wife had moved in 1974. About twenty-four hours earlier, my stepmother had phoned to ask how I felt about stopping the transfusions; the doctors, she said, told her that nothing further could be accomplished by them except to allow him to vegetate for a few days, perhaps a few weeks. She felt there was no use going on, and so did I, so the transfusions were stopped—passive euthanasia, I suppose. The next morning he was dead. Eleanor and I flew to Bradenton to be of what help we could. He was cremated and his ashes dropped from a plane into the Gulf—no funeral, no memorial service. In the few days we stayed in Bradenton, the three of us talked much of him and of the questions we assumed would never be answered. We went through some of his papers, but could find none that shed any light on his early life. There were photographs of him and others at the Columbia class reunions he had attended so faithfully. There were his license to practice engineering in New York State, some copies of patents, and some tearsheets from technical journals for which he had written. I was surprised at how lucid and vigorous his prose was; in my early days as an editor, I had to beat into shape many articles by professional writers whose English syntax was crude compared to his. I was surprised that he had clung to so many letters and documents, among them my elementary- and secondary-school diplomas—certificates he must once have feared I would never earn. But there was nothing that dealt with anything before 1905, when he entered Columbia. I left Bradenton with no more information than I had taken there and with the feeling that I would die without learning any of the truth.

## 2. THE FATHER I DISCOVERED

Back in New York, I found it impossible to get the mysteries off my mind. Who was he? What had he been trying to hide? Why? It came to me that, twenty years earlier, I had been told that there was in San Francisco one Ernest Rovere, who was on the staff of the *Call-Bulletin* and the author of several books on contract bridge, and who had told someone that he thought he and I were related. I considered this unlikely for I had believed my father when he said he was an only child and knew of no other living relations. But the fact that Ernest lived in San Francisco, the site of my grandfather's death nearly seventy years ago, interested me, and when next I was there I tried to reach him; he was out of town, and I did not call again until 1975, when I felt I might as well follow up any lead I could find. Expecting nothing to come of it, I called and reached him right away. I told him my name, and he said, "I think we're related." I said that that was why I was calling, and I asked him what he thought the connection was. "Tell me," he said, "did your father have a scar on his left cheek?" Astonished, I said that he did indeed have such a scar. "Then it was Louie," Ernest said. "He was my half-brother. I'm your uncle." And immediately I knew that he was talking about my father. That scar was what everyone noticed about him—even in his old age when it was no longer so livid and vivid as it had been earlier. And I had clinching evidence when, a week or so later, Ernest sent me a photograph of himself. Though he was only a half-brother, the Rovere genes were dominant. Ernest had my father's features and his build, and the likeness to a Mediterranean fisherman was enhanced by the fact that in the picture he was wearing a beret and a fisherman's sweater.

In this and subsequent talks and letters, he dispelled some, though by no means all, of the mysteries: my grandfather's name was not Henry but Leo. His origins were not British but French. He was not an importer but a real-estate dealer. He died not in San Francisco in 1906, nine years before I was born, but in New York in 1930, when I was fifteen.

My father may or may not have been illegitimate. Ernest did not know my grandmother's name. He explained that Leo, too, was a most secretive man and that everything he, Ernest, was telling me had been told him by his mother, the former Rae Bloomfield, a New York schoolteacher, whom Leo had married in 1904. (Ernest was born the following year.) Leo had not told anyone my grandmother's name. It could have been Genevieve.

My father had not been born in New York but in France— probably Paris, Ernest thought. Sometime around 1900, Leo had come to New York with my father. From Rae, Ernest got the impression that he had left with the gendarmes in pursuit; perhaps he had been accused of kidnapping his son.

My father had not gone to school in Switzerland and had not attended Culver. He had probably gone to a French school, and in New York he attended St. Ann's Academy, a Roman Catholic institution that once stood on Seventy-seventh Street between Lexington and Third Avenues. As it had never occurred to me that he was not telling the truth about there being no relations, I had never questioned his assertions about the Swiss school and Culver. He did have a French accent and his bearing was military.

Ernest confirmed what my father had said about living in the Bristol Hotel. That had been his and Leo's first home in New York. When Leo married Rae, they moved to an apartment on St. Nicholas Avenue.

So far as Ernest knows, the name is French. Leo spelled it with an acute accent over the first "e." (Since I have never heard of a Rovere who was not Italian, I am inclined to think that Leo's ancestors were from Nice or one of those towns on the Mediterranean near the French-Italian border, places that have often changed hands over the centuries.) As for Halworth, Ernest had never heard of it and thought it unlikely that Leo would have given a son a name with such an Anglo-Saxon sound.

I asked Ernest if he had any explanation for my father's behavior. He had none, but he recalled a family scene in, he thought, 1909. Louis, he said, had wanted to marry a girl who lived in the same building on St. Nicholas Avenue. Leo disapproved; he assembled the girl, her parents, and my father and said that if the marriage went through, someone else could pay my father's tuition at Columbia. My father walked out and the two never saw each other again. Nor did Ernest, who was then four, ever see him again.

That was about all the information Ernest had that related directly to my father. He wrote me a bit about my grandfather, who seems to have been a most disagreeable man and also a dishonest one. When Ernest was ready for college, Leo said he would pay his way provided he agreed to become a lawyer; Ernest did not wish to become a lawyer and therefore had to work his way through college. (He too was a technician and for many years was a lighting engineer in Hollywood.) Ernest did not know much about Leo's real-estate business but he recalled that one of his associates went to Sing Sing for embezzlement. Leo was a member of the New York Athletic Club and two or three other private associations; though he never lived outside Manhattan, he falsified addresses to qualify for the dues of a nonresident member. When he said he would marry Rae, her family suspected that some fraud might be involved and, according to Ernest, went to considerable lengths to check on the bona fides of whoever married them and to make sure that the bridegroom was not a bigamist. When Ernest was a boy, he was frequently embarrassed by Leo's falsifying of his age in order to get reduced rates on railroads, at theatres, and the like.

I was at once gratified and saddened to have the information Ernest gave me. I at last felt myself part of a flesh-and-blood family rather than the descendent of the faceless, characterless Henry and Genevieve. At the same time, I wished that my father had not had to live with his lies. They diminished him, I think,

and perhaps me as well. There must have been something altogether anguishing that led him to do what he did. One's past is
part of oneself, and to deny it or disown it is rather like denying
oneself the use of a sense or a faculty. And the facts that Ernest
gave me raised larger and more disturbing questions than they
answered. While I accept his story of the occasion for the estrange-
ment between Leo and Louis, I cannot believe that it accounts for
my father's behavior. Opposition to an offspring's intended marriage, coupled with threats of disinheritance, are fairly commonplace affairs. They may explain alienation but not the obliteration
of almost the entire past and the substitution for it of a fictitious
one. I was still without a clue as to why he had established a false
identity. He was not a pathological liar and, far from being given
to fantasy, was a very literal-minded man who seemed almost de-
void of imagination. He was diligent in trying to have me respect
the truth—or the "facts," as he would have put it—and as far
as I know he never told me or anyone else any lies but those about
his origins and background. There are several categories of people—spies, fugitives from justice, husbands and wives who abandon their families—who adopt a new identity. But the first thing
they do is to change their surnames. My father had kept Rovere
while altering the spelling of his first name and, I assumed, in-
venting a middle one. Had anyone pursued him, he could easily
have been found and unmasked. And this was another question:
why, in almost two decades after they parted, had not his father
sought to keep track of him? It is a strange man who brings up a
child, sees to his education, and then loses any interest in knowing
what became of him. Ernest, who was three or four when he last
saw my father, had often asked what had become of his older
brother and had gotten no answer.

Armed with the knowledge Ernest had given me, I set out in
search of more. The City Directories did list a Leo Rovere in the
real-estate business between 1912 and 1925. They also listed a
Leon Rovere in the same business, although Ernest, when I told
him this, said he had never heard of Leon. But since the addresses
on St. Nicholas Avenue given me by Ernest are the same as those

for Leon, they must have been one and the same man. In the thirteen years that Leo/Leon was listed as a broker, the business address was changed seven times.

I next tried to determine when my father and grandfather had entered this country and when they had been naturalized. From the Archives Branch of the General Services Administration, which stores such data in the Military Ocean Terminal in Bayonne, New Jersey, I learned that there was no record of either having ever been naturalized. From the City Clerk's office, I learned that between 1800 and 1906 not only, as I suspected, was there no record of my father's birth but that there was no record of a naturalization proceeding for *any* Rovere in any of the courts of New York County. Knowing from Ernest that Leo/Leon arrived with my father no later than 1903—and I suspect it was two or three or more years before that—either they entered at some other port or were illegal aliens. I think the latter more likely, but the question can never be answered, for all immigration records before 1906 were destroyed in a fire that year. Ernest has the impression that my grandfather never voted, but my father always did, and I suppose that at some point he had to offer proof of citizenship. But I have learned that what sometimes constitutes "proof" to the government would not be acceptable to any newspaper reporter. Some time after I had returned from Florida, my stepmother found some papers we had not gone over while there, and among them was a photostat of a most curious letter to my father from the Passport Division of the State Department. In 1940, evidently, it had become important to him to prove that he had been born in New York City; it seems that the Federal Communications Commission wanted to make sure of this, possibly for security reasons. To establish New York as his birthplace, he must have written the State Department saying that the evidence could be found in, of all places, an application made by my mother for a passport. The Passport Division checked the files and wrote him as follows:

In her passport application, Mrs. Rovere claimed to have acquired American citizenship through her marriage to you on September 5, 1913. With the application on which the passport was issued to her on

March 29, 1917, she submitted evidence which satisfactorily corroborated her statement that you were born at New York City.

Corroborated, indeed! Satisfactorily, indeed! My mother, who had arrived in this country several years after he did, could have had no knowledge of where he was born except what he had told her. One would think that the passport people would be suspicious of a man who could offer no better evidence about himself than what his wife had written on an application twenty-three years earlier. One would think that if it mattered very much to the F.C.C., it would have requested a copy of a birth certificate, in which case it would have learned, as I did, that there was no birth certificate. But Washington was satisfied with this hearsay evidence. On the back of the photostat my father had written, "Original sent via W.U. [Western Union] to F.C.C. as part of questionnaire. L.H.R. 10/8/40." And—I suppose in case the matter ever came up again—he had the photostat notarized the following day.

From the City Clerk's office, I got a copy of the 1913 marriage certificate. On it, his place of birth was given as New York, his parents as the nonexistent Henry Rovere and Genevieve River, and his age as twenty-seven, which would have made him eighty-eight when he died rather than the eighty-six on his death certificate. And on the back of the marriage certificate, I read that, according to Section 14 A of the New York Domestic Relations Act, the "evidence" on the face of the certificate "shall constitute prima facie evidence in any judicial proceeding." He could as well have sent a copy of this to the F.C.C.

I next sought to learn what I could from his school and college records. There was no St. Ann's Academy in the Manhattan Telephone Directory, so I called the Archdiocese and asked what had become of it. I was told that it had ceased operations on Lexington Avenue in 1957 and had merged with Archbishop Molloy High School in Jamaica, Queens. I called the principal there—one Brother Terence Jones—and told him I understood my father had attended St. Ann's, probably graduating in 1905. Brother Terence, a most genial and accommodating sort who said he was himself a graduate of St. Ann's, called me back shortly to confirm that Louis Rovere had been a member of the class of 1905 and to say that he would send me what records were available. Meanwhile, he told me a bit about the school. It had been established in 1892 by the Marist Brothers; the student body was largely French or French-Canadian. There was no French colony in Manhattan in those days, but there was, I have learned, a small French-Canadian enclave just below Yorkville, and the people were served not only by St. Ann's but by the Church of St. Jean-Baptiste, a lovely Romanesque structure on Seventy-sixth Street, just across from the former site of St. Ann's and one in which, until 1966, the Mass was given in French. St. Ann's moved to Queens in 1957 after, Brother Terence told me, "part of the roof fell into the street without hurting anybody." The school was soon torn down and on its site are the Queen Anne Apartments.

When the records came, they showed that my father had attended the academy for the two years before he graduated, in 1903–1904 as a day student and the following year as a boarder. He may have been there earlier; pre-1903 records were unavailable. He appears to have ranked second in his class in his last year, being listed one from the top under the heading "General Excellence" in the 1905 commencement program, and under the heading "Regents' Certificate," I found:

Master Louis Rovere passed in

| | |
|---|---|
| English Language (3rd year) | Advanced Algebra |
| Chemistry | German (1st year) |
| Solid Geometry | U.S. History |
| Plane Trigonometry | Geography |
| Spherical Trigonometry | |

It struck me as a rather heavy and demanding curriculum, especially for a boy whose first language was French. And among the prizes he won were firsts in English composition and literature, trigonometry, and chemistry, with a second in algebra and a third in German. St. Ann's was not a military academy in the sense that Culver was, but it had a military program, and in its cadet corps Louis had the rank of major.

Brother Terence sent along some material from school cata-
logues that were probably issued about the time my father attended.* There was a picture of two of the buildings taken from
Seventy-seventh Street, down the middle of which was a lone
horse and buggy. The larger of the two was a six-story structure
with a mansard roof. Between the third and fourth floors were
block letters reading ST. ANN'S BOARDING SCHOOL FOR BOYS, and,
apparently attached to it, a smaller building, probably a renovated
brownstone, with the legend ST. ANN'S COMMERCIAL ACADEMY.
In the catalogue drawing, the place has a serene and pleasant look.
There are trees and lawns, and, except for those in the horse and
buggy, there are only four people—a couple walking along Seventy-
seventh Street and another crossing Lexington Avenue. I would
suppose that, having done so well there, my father must have held
the scene in some affection, and in the late 1920s and early 1930s,
he and my mother and I must have passed it hundreds of times,
for we always drove north along Lexington on our way to our
summer cottage in Connecticut. But in those days, as before and
later, he always insisted that he had attended Culver, the school
about which he could remember nothing.

In a letter to me accompanying the printed material he sent,
Brother Terence wrote: "I went through some of the old ledgers
and found many references to your father and his achievements.
He must have been quite a person if early hints [of] abilities and
character are any indication [of] the nature of the man. . . . After
graduation, he was accepted into Columbia University, and as far

---

* In a section headed "Physical Care," parents of prospective students
are advised that "The health of the Pupils is the object of constant care.
Food of the best quality is prepared after the French style . . . so that the
children experience none of the little hardships incidental to a separation
from the family board. Pupils recreate after each meal in the playground."
Under the heading "St. Ann's Cadets," a description of the military program
begins with this assertion: "The American people, although looked upon
as a commercial race, are essentially at heart a martial nation. A cursory
glance at their uncheckered [sic] history will amply bear witness to this."
However, "dress and drill are prescribed not to develop any undue attention . . . by show and parades, but . . . to promote a high *sense of honor
and dignity.*" In 1905, board and tuition were twenty-five dollars a month.

as I can make out he successfully completed his studies there. . . . Presently, Molloy is an excellent school, but much of this excellence . . . had its roots in traditions that were set by men of the stature of your father." Columbia was slower than St. Ann's in providing the information I wanted, and while awaiting it, I assumed that it would show that he had fulfilled some of the promise he had shown at St. Ann's. But the Columbia transcript showed that—after passing entrance examinations in twelve subjects, among them English, French, German, American history, chemistry, physics, and several in advanced mathematics—he had *failed* everything but chemistry in his freshman year and had been dropped in 1906. At the bottom of the transcript was an unsigned, pencilled note, which read "1/23/07. Application to complete his studies as he desired—denied."

So the boy from France who helped set standards of excellence at St. Ann's spent only a year at Columbia, which would not accept his application for readmission. Something must have happened to make this intelligent, industrious man an academic failure, but I cannot find any clue as to what it might have been, nor can I understand why he so treasured the memory of the one place in which he failed. (Among his papers were acknowledgments of small but regular gifts to the university, which was, I think, just about his only philanthropy.) Sometime in the nine years before 1915, when I was born and he went to work for Western Union, he must have mastered the body of knowledge that qualified him for the work he was to do and that persuaded the University of the State of New York—not a functioning university but the highest educational authority in the state—to certify him as an engineer. Though I am hardly in a position to judge his abilities, I have talked with several men who worked for him—he always had five or six assistants—and whom he worked for, and they have assured me that he was amply qualified. He was not regarded as a brilliant man, but he was generally held to be a highly competent one. He was also a teacher of engineers: I remember that every summer for several years, my mother and I would accompany him to Red Bank, New Jersey, where, each summer, Western Union,

A.T.&T., General Electric, and perhaps one or two other companies in the same field ran an orientation school, of which he was a kind of dean, for the young men they had just hired from Columbia and other universities.

If the information from Columbia raised some new questions, it also settled, or appeared to settle, some old ones. His birthplace was given as Lyons, France, his address as 28 West 128th Street, and his year of birth as 1887. So there was 1886 on his marriage certificate, 1887 on his Columbia transcript, and 1888 on his death certificate. And a file card from the Columbia Library, which maintains alumni records, cleared up the confusion about his name. It was given there, as on the transcript, as "Louis Rovere"—no Halworth, no middle initial. But the "Louis" was crossed out, and above it, in what I am fairly sure was his hand, was written "Lewis Halworth." And this must have been done in 1915 or thereafter, for the business address given was Western Union, 195 Broadway. So, since he was "Louis" on his marriage certificate, Lewis Halworth Rovere must have emerged sometime in the two years before I was born and given my absurd middle name. Between 1913 and 1915, the Frenchman became an Anglo-Saxon and decided that the family name had originally been Rover.

Had I learned all this, as well I might have, when he and I were younger, I suppose I would have had some emotional reaction. I would have been hurt to learn that he had lied to me—not only about himself but about me, for I was part of whatever he was. It would probably have led me to question his truthfulness in all matters, to distrust anything he said. But I feel no anger now and on reflection am rather glad that I did not learn the truth—or the small part of it I can now claim to know—until after his death. For it cannot be anything but painful to feel compelled to unmask a person one loves, and I simply cannot imagine what his reaction would have been if Leo/Leon had suddenly surfaced or if I had reached Ernest the first time I tried to. Knowing that I had at least some parts of the truth, it is possible that he would have told me the rest and what it was he was trying to hide. If confession is really good for the soul, this might have eased the pain he felt, but I doubt it. I have never been persuaded of the therapeutic value of confession, and I think that to have been confronted with the truth in his late sixties would simply have doubled the anguish. The past would remain what it had been, and he would have been living in a present in which the integrity he seemed to value so much would be undermined. Better, I think, that I did not undertake my search until after he had died.

As for me, I feel about him more or less as I always did. Despite the clues I have, the mystery remains, and I spend part of each day searching for explanations I am reasonably sure I will never find. I do not know much more about myself than I did before except that I am the son of a man who chose to disown and deny his past. I know that I am half French or French-Italian. There is a certain irony in this, for France is a country in which I always have rather an uncomfortable feeling. This is no doubt in part because, in spite of being required to study French for several years and of now and then having to converse in it, I have been unable to attain any degree of fluency in it, and the French, or at least Parisians, are more impatient than any people I know with foreigners who speak their tongue as haltingly as I do. (Things might have been different if I had known it was my father's first language: he could have made me bilingual as a child, but he didn't.) But ethnicity has never meant much to me. I know that on my mother's side I am English, Scotch, Welsh, Swedish, and Negro, but I have never observed in myself anything that I can identify as part of a racial heritage.

The main effect has been on me as a writer rather than as a son. I have many times written about quite bizarre forms of human behavior, and I have always managed to find motivations that were at least plausible, that made sense hypothetically if in no other way. Now I find myself utterly frustrated in my search for an explanation of what my father did. I have sought and failed to find any precedent or parallel in life or in literature. Many people, of course, have deceived the world about themselves and their pasts, and some, it would seem, have even succeeded in deceiving themselves. André Malraux, the French novelist, never fought with the revolutionaries in China in the 1920s, but, according to a recent biographer, he persuaded himself that he did and wrote a compelling account of the experience. But Malraux is an artist and a romantic, a man with a profound imagination. My father was none of these, and part of the sadness I feel about him is that, having given himself a false identity, he did not flesh it out, did not make Henry and Genevieve something more than mere names. Had he enriched his story with details of his early life, had he invented as Malraux did, I might never have suspected deception. But the very thinness of his story provided a clue to its falsity. I have asked psychiatrist friends if there is anything in their experience or their theory that suggests a motivation, and they have come up with nothing. In Freudian psychology, there is a phenomenon known as the "Romance Family," in which a child who finds his parents unkind or unworthy endows himself with imaginary ones nobler and more deserving of love. But this is what *a child* does, not a grown man, and Henry and Genevieve were not made lovable; they were ciphers, people who had names and little else. The only explanation that comes close to making sense is that he loved his French mother very much and resented being taken from her by Leo/Leon. This could generate great hatred, but I cannot see how it could account for all the misrepresentations—for making up a new educational record, for claiming to forget almost everything that had happened in the first two decades of his life, for saying that his mother died when he was nine or ten when, in all probability, he did not know when she had died, as he may not have known exactly when he was born. A devoted son does not obliterate memories; he cherishes them. And what could explain his claiming British rather than French ancestry and for adopting a British spelling for his given name? I have never known a Frenchman who wasn't proud of being one, and my father liked to use what I thought was his school French. In his sixties, he much enjoyed travelling in France, and he insisted that he knew that Genevieve was French. (That, her New Orleans background, and her early death in Switzerland were the only details about her that emerged from my questioning.) So I must rule out the possibility that he found something shameful in his racial background.

I have had, indeed, to rule out every possibility I have been able to think of. Some of the mysteries have been cleared away, only to leave me with the largest of them all: Why?

# Index

Abdullah, King of Trans-Jordan, 184
A.D.A. (Americans for Democratic Action), 120
Adler, Alfred, 175
Adams, Henry, 40
Adams, John, 108
Aiken, Conrad, 220
Allen, Frederick Lewis, 149, 151
Allen, Jay, 199
Allen, Robert S., 195
Alsop, Joseph, 66
Alsop, Stewart, 66
*American Hebrew, The* (periodical), 137
American Labor Party, 51
*American Language, The* (Mencken), 220
American Legion, 50
American Revolution, 41
*American Scholar, The* (periodical), 37
Anderson, Margaret, 217
Anderson, Maxwell, 140
Anderson, Sherwood, 10, 217, 218
Anthony, Robert, 131
Arden, Elizabeth, 203
*Armies of the Night, The* (Mailer), 42

Armstrong, Hamilton Fish, 199
Army-McCarthy hearings, 107–10
Arnold, Matthew, 191
Arnold, Thurman, 154n
Atlas, Charles, 170
Atomic Energy Commission, 120
Auchincloss, Louis, 13, 134

Baldwin, James, 13
Baldwin, Raymond E., 97–98, 99, 100, 101, 102
Balzac, Honoré de, 10, 13, 64
*Barrack-Room Ballads*, 39
Bay of Pigs, 118, 121
Beach, Sylvia, 219
Beaton, Cecil, 223
Beck, Edward S., 192
Becker, May Lamberton, 166
Bellow, Saul, 11, 13
Berenson, Bernard, 125–26, 133
Berlin, Irving, 4
Bernstein, Burton, 159
Billings, Warren K., 57
Black Brothers, 208
Borges, Juan Luis, 11
Boswell, James, 145
Bowman, Isaiah, 128
Brandeis, Louis D., 127–28, 137, 138

Bricker, John, 151
Broun, Heywood, 141, 220
Browder, Earl, 49, 55, 59, 60
Buchalter, Louis (Lepke), 158, 159
Buffalo Bill, 156, 212
Bundy, McGeorge, 131
Burke, Edmund, 8
Burnett, Whit, 199
Byrnes, James F., 97

Cabell, James Branch, 191, 218, 220
Cain, James M., 139–40
Calles, Plutarco Elias, 129
Canfield, Cass, 190
Carnegie, Dale, 166
Carnegie, Hattie, 227, 240
Casals, Pablo, 116–17, 119
Castro, Fidel, 111
Cather, Willa, 220
Cavanaugh, Jerome, 104, 111, 112
Celtes, Conradus, 177
Chaplin, Charlie, 209, 210
Chapman, John Jay, 11
Chasan, Esther, 153
Chaucer, Geoffrey, 79, 188
Chicago *Daily News*, 193
Cianni, Josephine, 71–81
Codona, Alfred, 242
Cohan, George M., 15
Cohn, Roy, 107, 108, 109, 119
Columbus, Christopher, 177
*Coming Struggle for Power, The* (Strachey), 57
Commager, Henry Steele, 117
*Common Sense* (periodical), 147
Communist Party, 55, 56, 57–58, 59
Coolidge, Calvin, 129

Cowles, Fleur, 124
Cowles, Gardner, 124

*Daily Worker*, 45–46, 59
D'Annunzio, Gabriele, 218
Daughters of the American Revolution, 50
*Days of Shame* (Potter), 103
*Death Be Not Proud* (Gunther), 182
Debs, Eugene V., 55
*Decline and Fall of the Roman Empire* (Gibbon), 171
de Gaulle, Charles, 143
Dell, Floyd, 217
Democratic National Convention (1968), 42
Denissen, William A., 236
De Valera, Eamon, 194
Dewey, John, 2
Dewey, Thomas E., 149, 151, 152, 153, 155, 160
Dickens, Charles, 13, 64, 185, 219
Dirksen, Everett, 108, 110
Dodge, Mabel, 134–35
Dos Passos, John, 58
Dreiser, Theodore, 63, 217
Dulles, John Foster, 130, 136, 146
Duranty, Walter, 199
Dworshak, Henry, 108

*Education of Henry Adams, The*, 220
Edward VII, King of England, 223
Einstein, Albert, 137, 145
Eisenhower, Dwight D., 104, 105, 106, 130, 136, 149, 150n, 154

Emerson, Ralph Waldo, 13, 145, 147
*Eminent Victorians* (Strachey), 163
*English Men of Letters*, 163

Fabian Society, 126
Faulkner, William, 63
Fineman, Frances, 195
Fitzgerald, F. Scott, 193
*Flair* (periodical), 124
Flanner, Janet, 78n
Flynn, Edward, 150
Fodor, M. W., 195
Ford, Gerald, 9, 55
Forster, E. M., 11
Fourteen Points, 128, 129, 131
Frank, Jerome N., 162, 199
Frankfurter, Felix, 128, 138
Franklin, Benjamin, 41, 42
Freud, Sigmund, 126, 145
Frost, Robert, 153n
Furst, Bruno, 146, 164–81

Gainsborough, Thomas, 224
Galsworthy, John, 218
Gardner, Mrs. Jack, 125
*Gentlemen Prefer Blondes* (Loos), 225
George II, King of Greece, 184
Gest, Morris, 203, 216
Gibbon, Edward, 171
Gilmour, Ian, 119
Gimbel, Sophie, 240
Goethe, Johann Wolfgang von, 169
Gold, Michael, 10
Goldberg, Dr. Sidney, 177–78
Goldwater, Barry, 122
*Gone With the Wind* (Mitchell), 185, 188

*Good Society, The* (Lippmann), 144
*Good Taste in Home Furnishing* (Sell) 202, 216–17
*Gourmet* (periodical), 207
Gramont, Duchess de, 208, 222
Graves, Oral, 166
Greenfield, Rachel, 47
*Green Mansions* (Hudson), 16
Gromyko, Andrei, 122
Gunther, Eugene McClellan, 190
Gunther, John, 146, 181–99
Gunther, Johnny (son), 181, 182

Hagerty, James C., 149
Hammond, Percy, 192
Hansen, Harry, 192, 221
Harper, Fletcher, 221
*Harper's Bazaar* (periodical), 221
*Harper's Weekly*, 221
Harris, Richard, 163
Harris, Dr. Robert S., 235
Harrison, Benjamin, 156
Hearst, William Randolph, 208, 223, 224, 225
Hearst publications, 45, 47, 220, 223, 225
Hecht, Ben, 217, 218, 219, 220, 221
Heine, Heinrich, 169
Hellman, Geoffrey, 164
Hemingway, Ernest, 193
Hersey, John, 115
Hicks, Granville, 49
*High Sat White Helen* (Gunther), 192
Hiss, Alger, 141
Hitler, Adolf, 128–29, 141, 172, 195
Hoffa, Jimmy, 119
Hogan, Frank, 155

Hoover, Herbert, 151, 200, 244
Hopper, Hedda, 124
Horthy, Leon, 194
Houdini, Harry, 159
House, Edward M., 128
Howe, William F., 155–56
*Howe and Hummel: Their True and Scandalous History* (Rovere), 156–57, 158, 160, 161
*How to Read Better and Faster* (Norman Lewis), 165
*How to Remember* (Furst), 166, 179
*How to Win Friends and Influence People* (Carnegie), 186
*Human Understanding* (Hume), 171
Hume, David, 171
Hummel, Abraham H., 155, 156
Humphrey, Hubert, 42
Hunt, Lester, 101

Ibáñez, Vicente Blasco, 218, 219
*Indianapolis Star, The*, 214
Inquiry, The, 128–29
*Inside Asia* (Gunther), 182, 184, 187
*Inside Europe* (Gunther), 182, 183, 184, 187, 188, 194, 195
*Inside Latin America* (Gunther), 182, 184, 185, 188, 189, 197
*Inside U.S.A.* (Gunther), 182, 184, 185, 186, 187, 188, 190, 197, 198, 199
Irving, Washington, 13
Isham, Mr. (Rovere instructor), 22, 32–33, 36–37

Jackson, Andrew, 169
Jackson, Henry, 108

James, Henry, 5, 10, 13
James, William, 126
Jaugey (Rovere landlady), 80, 81
Jefferson, Thomas, 41, 42
*Jews Without Money* (Michael Gold), 10
John Birch Society, 119, 120
Johnson, Lyndon B., 108, 122, 130, 138–39, 143, 146, 154
Johnson, Samuel, 145
Jones, Ernest, 126
Jones, Robert, 105, 106
Jones, Bro. Terence, 258–59, 260
Joyce, James, 219
Julius II, Pope, 250
Jung, Carl, 175
*Jurgen* (Cabell), 220

Kahn, E. J., Jr., 119, 121
Kazin, Alfred, 13
Kefauver, Estes, 101
Kempton, Murray, 119
Kennan, George, 143
Kennedy, Caroline, 118
Kennedy, John F., 113–23, 154, 155
  McCarthyism position, 113
  military arms and foreign policy position, 120–21
  Nixon and, 114
  on other presidents, 117–18
  on Presidency, 115, 120
  on right wing politics, 119–20
Kennedy, Joseph P., 130
Kennedy family, 111, 118
Keynes, John Maynard, 126
Khrushchev, Nikita, 114
Kipling, Rudyard, 39
Kirchway, Freda, 147
Knickerbocker, H. R., 196
Knopf, Alfred, 206

La Guardia, Fiorello, 148, 150, 160
Landon, Alf, 130
Lardner, Ring, 220
*Law and the Modern Mind* (Jerome Frank), 162
*Lays of Ancient Rome* (Macaulay), 39
Leckie, Janet, 233, 236
Leffingwell, Russell, 136
Lehman, Herbert, 50, 137
Leighton, George, 149
Lelong, Lucien, 208, 227
Leonard, Tom, 56
Levin, Bernard, 116
Lewis, Norman, 165–66
Lewis, Sinclair, 126, 199
*Life of Johnson* (Boswell), 145
Lincoln, Evelyn, 115, 118, 122
Lindbergh, Charles A., 39, 129–30
Lindbergh, Mrs. Charles A., 130
Lindsay, Vachel, 217
Lippmann, Walter, 66, 124–44, 146, 160, 194
  anti-Semitism, 137–38
  Brandeis Supreme Court appointment supporter, 127–28
  foreign policy troubleshooter role, 129–30, 131, 132, 143
  Lyndon B. Johnson and, 138–39
  John F. Kennedy and, 130–31
  Oral History Project, 132–33
  personality, 125, 133, 134, 139–40, 141–42
  political and journalistic influence, 126–27
  political philosophy, 135, 136, 142–43, 144
  religious interest, 126–27
  World War I service, 129

Lippmann, Mrs. Walter, 132, 134
*Lives of the Poets* (Johnson), 145
Lloyd, Harold, 22
Lloyd George, David, 194
Lobrano, Gustave, 64
Long, Ray, 220, 225
Longfellow, Henry Wadsworth, 185
Longworth, Alice, 198
Loos, Anita, 225
Lorimer, George Horace, 200
Lowell, A. Lawrence, 140
Lowell Commission, 140–41
Lucullus, 211
Lynes, Russell, 149
Lyons, Leonard, 161

MacArthur, Douglas, 153
*MacArthur Controversy, The* (Rovere and Schlesinger), 153
Macaulay, Thomas B., 39
McCarthy, Joseph, 53, 68, 97–111, 146, 150n
McCarthy, Mary, 13
McClellan, John, 108
McCracken, Henry Noble, 44
McGrath, J. Howard, 150n
McGuinness, Peter J., 150
McHugh, Earle, 237
McIntyre, O. O., 208
McIntyre, Thomas, 103–12
MacKinder, Sir Halford John, 128–29
Macmillan, Harold, 120
McPhee, John, 164
Mailer, Norman, 42, 121
Mainbocher (fashion designer), 240
Malmédy affair, 97–102
Malraux, André, 264
Mann, Thomas, 169

Mao Tse-tung, 111
Marcantonio, Vito, 148, 149
Marconi, Guglielmo Marchese, 223
Marist Brothers, 259
Markey, Gene, 217
Marx, Karl, 55, 57, 145
Masters, Edgar Lee, 217, 218
Mencken, H. L., 126, 200, 217, 220
*Men of Destiny* (Lippmann), 126
Mexico, foreign policy (1927), 129
Meyer, Baron de, 223, 224
Michelangelo, 250
Mill, John Stuart, 171
*Miscellany News, The*, 47
Mishima, Yukio, 11
Mitchell, Joseph, 14, 163–64
mnemonics, 164–65, 166–67, 168, 169, 173, 174–75, 176–77, 178–79, 180–81
Monroe, Harriet, 217
Moody, Blair, 105
Moon, Rev. Sun Myung, 11
Mooney, Thomas J., 57
Morris, Newbold, 150, 163
Morris, William, 216
Morrow, Dwight, 129
Motherwell, Hiram, 214
*Mr. Citizen* (Truman), 117
Mundt, Karl, 108
Murphy, Harlem Tommy, 248
Mussolini, Benito, 192
*My Antonia* (Cather), 220

Nasser, Gamel Abdul, 137
Nast, Condé, 221
*Nation, The* (periodical), 127–28, 147
Nelson, Ralph, 104
Nevins, Allan, 131–32, 133

New Deal, 43
Newhouse, Edward, 64
*New Masses, The* (periodical), 54
*New Republic, The* (periodical), 128
*New Yorker, The* (periodical), 13, 61, 62, 63, 64, 65, 68, 68n, 148, 163
*New York Post*, 119
New York State Legislature, allegiance bill in, 45, 47
*New York Times, The*, 127–28
Nicolson, Harold, 126
Nixon, Richard M., 43, 113, 114, 119, 139, 142, 154, 163, 244n
Nutt (mnemonist), 167–68

O'Brien, Frederick, 219
O'Brien, Philadelphia Jack, 208, 230–31
O'Dwyer, William, 62, 158
O'Dwyer, Mrs. William, 62
O'Harrow, Maud Ann, 216
Olson, Samuel, 104
Omar Khayyám, 185
Oser, Dr. Bernard L., 234–35
*Outline of History* (Wells), 196
Owens, Patrick, 111–12

Paddleford, Clementine, 207
Paris Peace Conference (1920), 129
Parker, Dorothy, 70
Pearson, Drew, 195
*Pere Goriot* (Balzac), 10
Perkins, Milo, 235
Pershing, John J., 129
Platt, June, 206
Plaza, Galo, 188, 189
Plutarch, 163

Poehlmann, Ludwig, 171–72
*Postman Always Rings Twice,
    The* (Cain), 139
Potter, Charles E., 103, 104, 105,
    106, 107, 108, 109, 110,
    111
Pound, Ezra, 153–54
Poynter, Nelson, 153
*Preface to Morals, A* (Lipp-
    mann), 136n
*Preface to Politics, A* (Lipp-
    mann), 126
*Public Opinion* (Lippmann), 143–
    44
*Public Philosophy, The* (Lipp-
    mann), 135
Puckette, Charles, 25–37, 39
Pynchon, William, 201

Rascoe, Burton, 220
Reston, James, 130
Reuther, Walter, 105
Rice, Elmer, 81
River, Genevieve, 249, 254, 255,
    257–58, 266
Rivera, Diego, 58
Romanoff, Mike, 223
Romney, George, 104
Roosevelt, Franklin D., 43, 138,
    150, 244
Roosevelt, Theodore, 126, 139
Rose, Alex, 51
Ross, Harold W., 61–70, 147,
    148, 158, 159, 163, 200
    editor, 62, 63–64
    *New Yorker* influence, 65
    politics, 67–68
    on writers, 64n
Rovere, Ann (daughter), 72, 89,
    91
Rovere, Betsy (daughter), 72, 89

Rovere, Eleanor (wife), 72, 73,
    74, 75, 76, 77, 78, 80, 86,
    87, 89, 93, 94, 118, 152
Rovere, Ernest (uncle), 253, 254–
    55, 256, 257, 262
Rovere, Leo (Henry) (grand-
    father), 248, 254, 255, 256,
    258, 262, 264
Rovere, Lewis (Louis) Halworth
    (father), 243–65
Rovere, Mark (son), 72, 73, 89,
    91
Rovere, Rae Bloomfield, 254, 255
Runyon, Damon, 11
Rusk, Dean, 131
Russell, Lillian, 156

Sabath, Adolph, 97
Sacco, Nicola, 141
Sachs, Julius, 125
Sainte-Beuve, Charles Augustin,
    191
Salinger, Pierre, 115, 116, 120
Sandburg, Carl, 154, 208, 217,
    218, 220
Santayana, George, 126
Sayre, Joel, 62
Schell, Jonathan, 163
Scherman, Harry, 185
Schine, G. David (McCarthy
    staffer), 109
Schlesinger, Arthur, Jr., 114, 115,
    117, 132, 153
Scott, Sir Walter, 219
Scottsboro boys, 57
Secret Service, 119
*See Naples and Die* (Rice), 81
Sell, Henry Blackman, 146, 199–
    242
Sell, Mary Blackman, 212
Sell, Maud Ann, 202

Sell, Rev. Henry Thorne, 211–12, 213

*Sell's Bible Study* (Rev. Henry Thorne Sell), 211, 214

*Senator Joe McCarthy* (Rovere), 103, 113

*Serve It and Sing* (Platt), 206

Settle, Elkanah, 191

Shakespeare, William, 188, 200

Shapiro, Jacob (Gurrah), 158, 159

Shaw, George Bernard, 126, 194, 219

Shawn, William, 61, 62, 66, 69, 70, 114, 148, 149–50, 163, 200

Sheean, Vincent, 199

Shelley, Percy Bysshe, 85

Shirer, William, 199

*Silas Marner* (Eliot), 31

Simonides (Greek poet), 176

Smith, Margaret Chase, 105, 106

Smith, Rev. Sydney, 188

Socialist Party, 55, 56

Somervell, D. C., 197

Stalin, Josef, 43, 59, 184

Steel, Ronald, 134, 160

Steffens, Lincoln, 40, 125

Stevenson, Adlai, 130, 154

Strachey, John, 57

Strachey, Lytton, 126, 163

Stravinsky, Igor, 119

*Study of History, A* (Toynbee), 197

Sullivan, John L., 156

Summerfield, Arthur, 105–6

Sumner, John S., 220

Sutherland, Duchess of, 208

Swift, Gustavus, 201

Swift, Jonathan, 201

Swinburne, Algernon Charles, 39

Swing, Raymond Gram, 199

Taft, William Howard, 128

Tagore, Rabindranath, 208

Taper, Bernard, 116, 121

Teller, Edward, 120

Thackeray, William Makepeace, 219

*This Side of Paradise* (Fitzgerald), 192

Thomas, Norman, 55

Thomas of Erceldoune, 191

Thompson, Dorothy, 199, 239, 240

Thoreau, Henry David, 13

Three Flying Codonas, 241–42

Thurber, James, 61, 64, 68, 159

Tolstoi, Leo, 64, 185

Torrio, Johnny, 218

Toynbee, Arnold, 197

Treaty of Versailles (1918), 129

Trotsky, Leon, 194

Truman, Harry S., 115, 117, 150n

Tunney, Gene, 208

*Ulysses* (Joyce), 219

United Automobile Workers, 105

U.S. Congress Joint Committee on Atomic Energy, 120

*Use Your Head* (Furst), 166

*U.S. Foreign Policy* (Lippmann), 142

*U.S. War Aims* (Lippmann), 142

Valentina (fashion designer), 240

Vandenberg, Arthur, 130

Vanzetti, Bartolomeo, 141

*Vassar Chronicle*, 41, 47

Vatican, 129

Veblen, Thorstein, 1

Victoria, Queen, 156

Vietnam War, 42, 43

Vionnet (fashion designer), 222, 240

Wallace, Henry Agard, 208, 228, 235
Wallace, James Garrett, 160–61, 162
Walpole, Hugh, 218–19
Washington, George, 146
*Washington Merry-Go-Round* (Pearson and Allen), 195
Wason, John, 74–75, 77, 78
Watergate, 42
Weaver, John V. A., 218
Weeks, Edward, 132
Wells, H. G., 31, 126, 196–97, 200
Welty, Eudora, 11
West, Rebecca, 126
*West Side News*, 111
Wharton, Edith, 13
Wharton, James, 13
*What Is It All About?* (Sell), 216
White, E. B., 4, 8, 159
*White Shadows in the South Seas* (O'Brien), 219, 220
Whitman, Walt, 10, 13

Wickard, Claude R., 204, 235
Wiesner, Jerry, 120
Willkie, Wendell, 146, 184
Wilson, Charles, 104
Wilson, Edmund, 135–36
Wilson, Woodrow, 127, 128, 131, 146
Winchell, Walter, 124
*Winesburg, Ohio* (Anderson), 220
Wordsworth, William, 188
Wright, Frank Lloyd, 216
Wrigley, William, 203

*Years with Ross, The* (Thurber), 64–65
Yeats, William Butler, 208
*You Know Me, Al* (Lardner), 220
Young Communist League (YCL), 44, 47, 56

Zenora, Queen, 214
Zufall, Bernard, 168